Between
Emotion and Cognition

Between Emotion and Cognition

The Generative Unconscious

Joseph Newirth, Ph.D., A.B.P.P.

OTHER

Other Press
New York

Permission to reprint excerpts from the following is gratefully acknowledged:
-Excerpt from "The Hollow Men" in *Collected Poems 1909-1962* by T.S. Eliot,
© 1936 by Harcourt, Inc., © 1964, 1963 by T.S. Eliot. Reprinted by permission
of the publisher.
-Extracts from *Envy and Gratitude and Other Works* by Melanie Klein, © 1975
by The Melanie Klein Trust. Reprinted with permission of The Free Press, a
Division of Simon & Schuster Adult Publishing Group.
-Excerpts from *Countertransference* by Harold Searles, © 1979 by International
Universities Press. Reprinted by permission of International Universities Press.
-Excerpts from *Melanie Klein Today, Volume 1: Mainly Theory*, by Elizabeth
Bott Spillius, © 1988 by Routledge. Reprinted by permission of the publisher.
-Excerpts from *The Spontaneous Gesture* and *Psycho-Analytic Explorations*,
by Donald W. Winnicott, © 1987 and 1989, respectively. Reprinted by
permission of Paterson Marsh Ltd. on behalf of The Winnicott Trust.
-Excerpt from *The Work of Hanna Segal: A Kleinian Approach to Clinical
Practice*, by Hanna Segal, © 1981 by Hanna Segal. Reprinted by permission of
Jason Aronson.

Library of Congress Cataloging-in-Publication Data

Newirth, Joseph.
    Between emotion and cognition : the generative unconscious / Joseph
Newirth.
        p. cm.
    Includes bibliographical references (p.   ) and index.
    ISBN 1-59051-040-2
        1. Psychoanalysis. 2. Subjectivity. 3. Subconsciousness. 4. Civilization,
Modern-21st century. I. Title.

RC506.N495 2003
    616.89'17—dc21

                                                            2003043866

For
Eleanor

without whose love and inspiration this book would not have been written

Contents

Acknowledgments

This book is the culmination of many, many years of doing psychotherapy and psychoanalysis, of teaching and supervising graduate students, psychoanalytic candidates, and other psychoanalysts. I wish that I could express my gratitude to all of those patients and colleagues who have contributed to the development of my ideas and have encouraged me to formalize them into this neo-Kleinian approach that focuses on the generative unconscious, integrating concepts derived from relational psychoanalysis and the work of Klein, Winnicott, Matte Blanco, and Lacan.

However, I do want to express my gratitude to those always-present colleagues and friends who have provided support, encouragement, and feedback, allowing me to persevere and grow. I want to thank Bob Mendelsohn, Richard Billow, Kathy Bacon Greenberg, and Jay Greenberg for their continued support and encouragement. It is a source of sadness that I cannot share the joy of completing this project with my good friend and colleague Steve Mitchell, who died prematurely.

If writing a book is a journey into the unknown, then my travel companions deserve special recognition. I want to express my most heartfelt thanks to Karen Lombardi, Michael Civin, Nancy Berger, and Bruce Tuchman, who accompanied me in charting this new territory and in valuing these clinical and theoretical directions as they were being developed.

There are no words to express my appreciation and gratitude to my family—Eleanor, Michael, and Karen. You have stood by me, encouraged me and sacrificed so that I could follow this course to completion. Thank you for being with me during the long difficult times and now in my excitement and happiness.

Books are more than ideas and words, they are substance. I want to express my appreciation to the staff of Other Press, especially Judith Gurewich and Stacy Hague, and to my administrative assistant at Adelphi University, Marge Burgard, who helped to transform my thoughts into a physical reality.

Introduction: Wrestling with the Demons of the Unconscious

Early in the development of psychoanalysis, Freud warned us of the dangers inherent in the clinical practice of psychoanalysis, which he analogized to "wrestling with the demons of the unconscious." Indeed, Freud cautioned in 1905, "No one who, like me, conjures up the most evil of those half-tamed demons that inhabit the human breast, and seeks to wrestle with them, can expect to come through the struggle unscathed." This imagery reflects the experience of psychoanalysis as an active, two-person, physical and kinesthetic experience—one that captures the important moments of contact between patient and analyst as the psychoanalytic relationship evolves into an intense, personal reality. In my own experience, as an analyst, as an academic, and as a clinical supervisor, Freud's words have been a comfort, the words of an experienced guide accompanying me as I face the demons and the dilemmas that are inherent in the two-person relational model of psychoanalytic treatment. This image has provided reassurance as the classical distinctions between analyst and patient inevitably become lost in the growing confusion of transference and countertransference, conscious and unconscious experience, intentional and unwitting actions, and hateful and loving desires.

In this book, I focus on those intensely personal clinical experiences in which the usual categories of psychoanalytic explanation have lost meaning in the intensity of the affect storms that accompany the experience of wrestling with the demons of the unconscious. I focus on these often frightening encounters in order to illustrate possible resolutions to the daunting interpersonal complexities of psychoanalytic and psychotherapeutic practice. Clinical examples anchor the more abstract theories that guide us as we traverse the strange agonies of the clinical process. Our theoretical maps develop a neo-Kleinian, two-person approach to psychoanalysis, emphasizing the structure of internal experience and a generative view of the unconscious within contemporary American relational psychoanalysis. This neo-Kleinian model integrates concepts developed by Klein, Winnicott, Bion, and Matte Blanco, and focuses on failures in the patient's development of the capacity for symbolic experience, failures that result from an excessive use of projective identification and a pathological level of externalization of hateful experiences of self and other. In this model, the analyst's central task is the transformation of the patient's externalized concrete experience into internal symbolic experience through mutual processes of reverie, the development of enactments, and transitional experiences.

The clinical illustrations in each chapter return to Freud's vision of the deeply emotional, interpersonal, and intrapersonal elements of the psychoanalytic relationship without succumbing to the easy or heroic vision of the psychoanalyst as the "brave knight fighting the terrible dragon." This model of therapeutic action entails the analyst's volitional acts of introjective identification and his/her courageous creation of a space in which both he/she and the patient can speak of their conscious and unconscious experience, thus thawing the pathological relational schemas and allowing change and growth. The analyst's courage and willingness to articulate his/her internal experience of the analytic relationship often involves facing his own demons, the self-critical internal objects, which are often experienced as a condemning voice, persecuting the analyst for his cruel and sadistic acts, which hurt the patient who has become his other, his reference point for his capacity to be loved.

The patient's projective identifications and acting out are viewed as the externalization of unarticulated and unsymbolized unconscious fantasies that are experienced as real events in the external world. The critical analytic task is the transformation of these concrete externalized experiences into analytic objects (Ogden 1994), symbolic experiences that the patient is able to internalize and use. Bion's (1962) concept of the analyst's or mother's use of reverie and Winnicott's (1971) concept of the parent's and analyst's development of transitional experiences refer to processes through which unconscious externalized experiences are transformed into symbolic internal experience. It is my belief that these processes operate more effectively when the analyst is eventually able to identify volitionally with the patient's externalized concrete fantasies, often becoming the bad object. This difference between an analyst's volitional identification and an *unwitting* involvement is a critical difference between the relational/interpersonal perspective and a relational/neo-Kleinian perspective on the psychoanalytic relationship.

From a similar neo-Kleinian perspective, Ogden (1995) has written about the process of the transformation of concrete experiences of the patient's projective identifications, which leave him feeling deadened, unable to think, and struggling with his own unarticulated body experience until he slowly becomes able to symbolize these experiences and understand their relevance to the transference–countertransference relationship with his patient. This intersubjective sequence of projective identification, enactment, reverie, symbolization, interpretation, and internalization allows the patient to integrate disowned aspects of the self and to become more fully alive—in contact with a generative unconscious in which personal meanings are created and symbolized. This sequence illustrates the neo-Kleinian model in which the goal of treatment is not simply an expansion of the patient's capacity for decision making and consciousness, but the symbolization and integration of previously externalized unconscious fantasies that then become a source of creativity and energy: the generative unconscious.

This focus on symbolizing unconscious fantasy is particularly important for patients who present the modern dilemma of being successful in their activities in the external world while simultaneously feeling deadened and disconnected, and that their choices are not meaningful, subjectively validating, or emotionally enriching. As a way to facilitate the symbolization and integration of the patient's externalized unconscious fantasies, this neo-Kleinian approach emphasizes listening and speaking within the structure of unconscious logic, the logic of dreams, art, and poetry. In unconscious logic, differences among time, place, and person are effaced, creating similarities through metaphor, ambiguity, irony, and playfulness. For example, a woman who experienced intense conflict around her need to be good and to disown her bad desires and greed resolved her struggle through splitting and projecting the unconscious fantasy into her friends, her husband, and her analysts. Her unconscious fantasy could be articulated as that of the "sinner who can't be saved" who is simultaneously the "savior who fails to save the sinner." This fantasy repetitively organized her relationships with the men and women in her life, each of whom she failed to save from their lives of sin. In each of her personal relationships she projected the "sinner" into the other and then tried to save him/her. I believe that these attempts failed because she was unable to symbolically internalize both dimensions of her unconscious fantasy; she could neither express nor enjoy herself as the sinner integrating her "badness," or as the savior, a parental fantasy, integrating her sense of grandiosity and power. The reverse was true in her relationships with previous therapists. There she projected the "savior" into the therapists and experienced herself as the "sinner," until either her envy of the therapist's goodness or the therapist's inevitable self-disclosure of "badness" disrupted the stability of the split between good and bad, which resulted in a precipitous termination of the treatment as she fled from her experience of hatred that she felt destroyed the therapist's role of the "savior," who was to contain or constrain her experience of herself as the "sinner."

The analytic question for a future therapist is how to avoid becoming the idealized savior, while not disclosing, or perhaps confessing, his own sins in an attempt to affirm a shared humanity. The strategy of being the idealized savior both maintains the use of splitting and continues the externalization of the patient's unconscious fantasies as a set of concrete events in the real world. The strategy of self-disclosure, in which the therapist expresses a shared humanity that attempts to differentiate the patient's childlike view of good and evil from a more mature view, avoids the attraction to and minimizes the power and pleasure of badness, which is incorporated in the fantasy of the "sinner who can't be saved." My goal would be to symbolize and integrate this fantasy, to find ways to volitionally enact the different aspects of this fantasy, symbolizing it through the development of a series of transitional experiences that would develop within the course of our work. Through these enactments the patient would experience the pleasure of desire and of sin, and the possibility of compassion, concern, and reparation in her relations with others. Rather than differentiating myself from the failed previous therapist and enjoying the grandiose pleasure of being the superior one, the true savior, I would identify with the failed savior, effacing the difference between myself, the previous therapists, herself, her husband, and her friends, possibly pointing out in a humorous way that I had "clay feet," and that, as she could see, I am rather clumsy. I would attempt to symbolize the unconscious fantasy by joining the sinner and the savior rather than act out the patient's projection of the split-off unconscious fantasy of the therapist as the savior and the patient as sinner. Over the course of the analytic relationship I would find other ways to enact the transference–countertransference fantasies and to playfully identify with and symbolize the images of savior and sinner so as to facilitate the movement of the unconscious fantasy from being projected into external objects, where they are enacted as concrete experiences, into the analytic realm of transitional experience where these unconscious fantasies can become an internal, symbolic source of creativity and energy.

This brief clinical vignette begins to illustrate the complex process of a neo-Kleinian approach to psychoanalysis and psychoanalytic psychotherapy that emphasizes the integration and symbolization of the patient's disowned, externalized, unconscious fantasies. A patient's ability to symbolize unconscious experience is a critical aspect of the development of subjectivity, the experience of being emotionally alive, of a sense of control or agency, and of the capacity to maintain intimate relationships with others. The clinical approach that I develop in this book focuses on five aspects of the analyst's participation that extend the usual two-person relational perspective. The five clinical dimensions are: the dialectic between the analyst's unwitting and volitional participation in the transference–countertransference relationship, the analyst's regression to primitive states of mind, the analyst's use of reverie in the transformation of the patient's projected and acted-out concrete unconscious fantasies, the development of enactments and transitional experience that bring into a symbolic realm the lived unconscious fantasies, and the recognition of the analyst's subjectivity as an integral part of the development of the patient's subjectivity.

Chapters 1 to 3 develop the concept of the individual as a subject that shifts the focus of psychoanalysis from that of conflict to the creation of meaning, the clinical implications of defining psychic structure in terms of the ego, the self, or the subject, and the importance of omnipotence in the development of subjectivity. Chapters 4 to 6 expand the Kleinian concept of the paranoid position, developing the concepts of projection, identification, enactment, power, and control in the psycho-analytic relationship, focusing on characteristics of concrete and symbolic thought. Chapters 7 and 8 focus on a neo-Kleinian theory of mind and its implications for technique involving the development of enactment, transitional experience, and the use of unconscious logic in interpretation. Chapters 9 and 10 focus on subjectivity as a function of the development of the generative unconscious and illustrate failures in the development of subjectivity as a function of both the pathology of consciousness and the inability to use symbolic processes.

In addition to expanding contemporary psychoanalytic approaches to clinical practice, this book provides a unique integration of theory, bringing together the American two-person relational perspectives that have dominated psychoanalytic thought and practice on this side of the Atlantic, with an emphasis on unconscious processes and fantasy, which has been associated with Kleinian theory, and a focus on the development of meaning and issues of pleasure, which have been central to Lacan and French psychoanalysis. I hope that this book begins to restore the psychoanalytic concept of the unconscious, from a view of the unconscious as a center of pathological relatedness to a view of the unconscious as a developing structure that is a source of creativity, strength, and energy. In my own work I have often thought about reversing the common view of psychoanalytic cure as making the unconscious conscious to making the conscious unconscious, through helping our patients to integrate and symbolize their terrifying and unacceptable fantasies, which would allow them to enjoy and benefit from their own experiences of "wrestling with the demons of the unconscious."

Failure in the Development of Subjectivity and the Creation of Meaning

We are the hollow men
We are the stuffed men
Leaning together
Headpiece filled with straw. Alas!
Our dried voices, when
We whisper together
Are quiet and meaningless
As wind in dry grass
Or rats' feet over broken glass
In our dry cellar.
T. S. Eliot, "The Hollow Men"

T. S. Eliot gives voice to the empty and meaningless lives of postmodern man. We are flooded with images and experiences of deadness, emotional numbing, and the ennui of mechanical lives that contemporary psychoanalysts have thought of as the core of narcissistic, schizoid, and borderline disorders. In a recent turn in psychoanalytic theory (Benjamin 1995, 1998; Stolorow et al. 1987), these symptoms have been thought of as reflecting a failure in the development of agency and subjectivity. This failure in the development of subjectivity is the implicit complaint of patients who describe themselves as confused and disoriented in a meaningless world, a thing in a world of things, living lives focused on acquiring material goods without a sense of personal uniqueness, passion, or agency.

Let me illustrate the experience of the failure in the development of subjectivity through the words of several patients. The first, a successful international businessman who was filled with the despair of T. S. Eliot's poem, described himself as an "empty suit" and was haunted by the feeling that he had not accomplished anything of significance in his life. This patient lived his life believing that he would achieve happiness and that his life would be made meaningful only when he was recognized in an obituary in the *New York Times*. This patient yearned for recognition, to be seen and deeply known by another. However, like many others, he could only conceive of recognition as occurring within the world of celebrity and public acclaim. A second patient, a woman who felt her life was dead and meaningless, corrected my misattuned attempts at empathy saying, "I don't feel like shit, because shit was once part of a living being; rather I feel like dust, something that was never alive." A third patient described himself as an automaton, no different from the many others who did similar work, totally lacking any experience of personal value and unique individuality. In the middle of his analysis, with a newfound sense of pride, he said, "I am not yet something, but I am no longer nothing." These patients illustrate failures in the development of subjectivity; they are the "hollow men," embodying the illness of our time and our culture's failure to provide values and meaning.

Patients who have failed to develop the capacity for subjective experience present many challenges for contemporary psychoanalytic theory and practice. Unlike traditional patients, they do not present ego-dystonic neurotic symptoms, inhibitions, or character pathology that they wish, often reluctantly or ambivalently, to change. Rather, like the people in T. S. Eliot's poem, they feel empty, they experience their lives as meaningless, they are unable to think and feel as if they barely exist in the arid, passionless, hopeless world of the dead.

LIFE DISPLACED ONTO THE VIDEO SCREEN

Christopher Lasch (1978) approached the problem of the emptiness of contemporary man from a cultural and historical perspective. In his classic work, *The Culture of Narcissism*, he traces the destructive effects of the evolution of our culture from one that valued competitive individuality to one of narcissism, of extreme self-centeredness, lacking historical consciousness, and indifferent to the values of the past. He contrasts the contemporary narcissist, who experiences the world as a mirror, with that of the rugged individualist of the past, who saw the world as an empty wilderness to be shaped to his own design. Lasch describes the historical and cultural evolution that contextualizes the social and psychological failure in the development of subjectivity. He describes the contemporary psychopathology in which people cannot give meaning or value to their own experience but desperately need to be seen, recognized, and acclaimed by an external other. Lasch is perplexed by the paradox that in spite of the extensive freedom that the contemporary individual can enjoy, there is a pervasive sense of insecurity, which can only be overcome "by seeing his 'grandiose self' reflected in the attentions of others, or by attaching himself to those who radiate celebrity, power and charisma" (p. 10).

One of the most interesting aspects of Lasch's analysis is his focus on the effects of the media and the development of an electronic culture, which has expanded the possibilities of being seen as an object in the external world, of being the shadow on the wall of the cave rather than a center of personal action, experience, and satisfaction. Lasch gives a frightening and prescient description of life mediated through electronic images:

> We live in a swirl of images and echoes that arrest experience and play it back in slow motion. Cameras and recording machines not only transcribe experience but alter its quality, giving to much of modern life the character of an enormous echo chamber, a hall of mirrors. Life presents itself as a succession of images, of electronic signals, of impressions recorded and reproduced by means of photography, motion pictures, television and sophisticated recording devices. Modern life is so thoroughly mediated by electronic images that we cannot help responding to others as if their action—and our own—were being recorded and simultaneously transmitted to an unseen audience or stored up for close scrutiny at some later time. [p. 47]

Lasch suggests that postmodern culture has radically changed the experience and the nature of being human. Like T. S. Eliot, Lasch focuses on a shift from an awareness of self, centered in inner psychic reality, to the audience, to how one is seen, to the performance, to being an object or a thing, an automaton without a vital coherent core. Lasch and Eliot focus our attention on this inner sense of deadness and emptiness that I describe as a failure in the development of subjectivity. This failure in the development of subjectivity involves a sense of emptiness, meaninglessness, deadness, an inability to be self-reflective, and the experience of being an object who only exists when on display, a thing pushed or driven, performing impersonal tasks and feeling little pleasure or gratification.

CHANGING PSYCHOANALYTIC PERSPECTIVES

The changes in contemporary society that Lasch and Eliot described from cultural and literary perspectives have had profound effects on psychoanalytic theory and practice. Kohut's (1977, 1979) development of self psychology and Kernberg's (1975) focus on the treatment of borderline conditions were initial attempts to understand these changes in contemporary psychopathology. Kohut and Kernberg expanded psychoanalytic theory through focusing on patients' failures in the internalization and development of cohesive internal structures, which were often manifested in labile, alternating states of vulnerability and rage. Kohut (1977) and Kernberg (1975) thought of these failures in the development of cohesive internal self and ego structures as reflecting developmental deficits, preoedipal pathology, that required modification of the parameters of the psychoanalytic treatment situation. They thought that when the developmental deficits were resolved in the analytic relationship, the patient would then have a more traditional neurotic personality structure, and that the analyst could resume a traditional interpretive mode of treatment. These early attempts at modifying psychoanalytic theory and technique reflected a "strategy of accommodation" (Greenberg and Mitchell 1983) in which the theoretical and technical parameters of classical psychoanalysis were extended to accept modifications that would not permanently alter the assumptions or techniques of traditional psychoanalytic theory.

Kohut's (1984) theoretical contributions focused on the phenomenological or experience-near aspects of patients' experience, developing the concept of the *self* as a structure that reflects a series of adaptations of the individual's unique potentials to the caregiving environment. This process of adaptation is mediated through the interaction of the individual's developmental needs and how they are received by the other, which are represented in this theory as *self self-object* organizations (transferences) through which the individual grows and affirms his or her sense of being. Kohut's emphases on the necessity for the other in both the mirroring self self-object transference and in the idealizing self self-object transference reflect important revisions in the Freudian theory of motivation. He emphasized the primary motivational importance of real relationships and interpersonal experience as contrasted to drive; he reintroduced a teleological view of meaning defined by future goals as contrasted with meaning defined as the repetitions of past events. Kohut minimized the importance of the unconscious, focusing on psychological structures as potentially conscious experience, on affect regulation, and on the capacity for being an expressive, coherent, and authentic self (Miller 1985).

Kernberg (1975) similarly focused on the importance of the other and the caregiving environment in shaping the individual's personality; however, he maintained a more traditional view of the importance of the unconscious as a source of both drives and specific content. Kernberg expanded the ego psychological model of drive and defense by introducing Kleinian concepts of projection, splitting, and projective identification. In integrating Kleinian theory with contemporary ego psychology, Kernberg introduced a more active interpretive style, one in which the analyst's countertransference became a critical element, directing interpretations at elucidating and integrating the split-off parts of the self. Kernberg's narrative strategy focused on the Kleinian themes of aggression, greed, envy, and the patient's difficulty in seeing the analyst as a good object. For Kernberg, like Kohut, the analyst's task is to help the patient develop past the structural deficits that are manifested in the symptoms of narcissistic and borderline pathology. Although Kernberg's focus was on the unconscious, he maintained an essentially ego psychological approach, emphasizing the importance of the reality principle and the analyst's traditional position of authority.

As a result of these changes in theory and clinical technique, there has been a paradigm shift in contemporary psychoanalytic theories from a one-person to a two-person model of the psychoanalytic relationship. The two-person model describes the analyst as a more active participant (Gill 1994), and moves away from a narrow focus on genetic interpretations to a focus on the here-and-now aspects of the transference–countertransference relationship. In reviewing the literature on psychoanalytic technique, Kernberg (1993) concludes that there is a developing convergence in modifications of psychoanalytic technique that involve "earlier interpretation of the transference, increased focus on transference analysis, as well as a growing attention to countertransference analysis . . . character defenses and the unconscious meaning of the here and now" (p. 670). These changes in technique reflect a consistent movement toward a two-person view of the psychoanalytic situation in which the critical mutative factors have changed from the development of rational understanding through genetic interpretation of the transference to the internalization of new affective experiences and patterns in the psychoanalytic relationship. This growing emphasis on the importance of the psychoanalytic relationship (see Mitchell and Aron 1999, Renik 1996) includes increased uses of countertransference experience, modifications in the concept of the analyst's neutrality, a focus on the mutual influences of patient and analyst, and a greater acceptance of the value of self-disclosure.

The technical innovations associated with the evolving two-person model of the psychoanalytic relationship are often presented from a phenomenological or experience-near perspective, where the analyst asserts the humanistic and pragmatic value of the new analytic experience as contrasted with the patient's destructive childhood experience. Although often moving, these clinical descriptions fail to provide a comprehensive theoretical or structural explanation for the process of change and growth. It is as if in the movement toward a two-person model focused on current transference–countertransference experience, psychoanalytic theory has become a learning theory, minimizing the importance of the unconscious and simply advocating for liberal, humanistic values. This contemporary psychoanalytic view seems to suggest that if the analyst can be a good object, he/she will provide sufficient new experience that compensates the patient for the bad experiences of childhood. In this view, maturity becomes an achievement of a conflict-free experience of authenticity, the capacity for the conscious expression of need, and the ability to rationally negotiate relationships.

There are several problems in this development of the two-person model of psychoanalysis. The concept of the unconscious as unarticulated experience and the phenomenological concept of subjectivity are a return to Freud's earlier topographic model in which conscious and un-conscious experience are defined by the presence or absence of aware-ness and are not seen as encompassing different dynamic, structural, lin-guistic, or thematic realms or functions. The unconscious is thought of as containing either pathological or infantile wishes, drives or relational patterns, and not as a developing structure of mind that makes impor-tant positive contributions to the individual's development. Because the concepts of the unconsciousness and of subjectivity are thought of as phenomenological concepts, the focus of psychoanalysis and psycho-analytic psychotherapy becomes more and more the provision (see Lindon 1994) of an affective relationship different from the pathologi-cal experiences of the patient's childhood. In this book I develop an al-ternative two-person model centered on a view of the unconscious as a developing structure that allows the individual to create personal mean-ing, which leads to a dynamic sense of subjectivity.

CREATING MEANING: THE SYMBOL
IN PSYCHOANALYTIC THEORY

The psychoanalytic and psychotherapeutic process of creating meaning and of the subject developing the capacity to create meaning is the most significant aspect of a therapeutic experience. The psychoanalytic pro-cess of creating meaning is completely entangled with the psychoana-lytic function of interpretation, which is modeled on the interpretation of dreams and dream symbols. Freud (1900a,b) described dream inter-pretation as the "royal road to the unconscious," as the process of making the unconscious conscious, revealing hidden motives, fantasies, relational patterns, and desires. The Freudian view of symbols, of the unconscious, and of the process of interpretation of symbolic content was explicated in 1916 by Ernest Jones (Rose 2000, Segal 1957) in a classic paper. Jones defined the traditional psychoanalytic view of the symbol, such as a dream image, as a representation of a repressed wish that had a relatively fixed meaning. He contrasted the symbol as an unproductive representation of an unconscious wish with sublimation, in which there is a resolution of unconscious conflict, allowing for the development of compromises and the achievement of satisfaction in the external world. In defining symbolic content as unproductive representations of unconscious wishes, interpretation became a process of translation, from the disguised and infantile content of primary-process thought to the more mature secondary-process thought of consciousness and language.

Rose (2000) discusses this traditional view of symbols as unconscious representations of repressed wishes, and contrasts it with Susanne Langer's (1942) philosophical analysis of symbols in which she describes two types of symbols: presentational symbols and discursive symbols. From her perspective, the traditional psychoanalytic view of symbols can be thought of as *discursive symbols*, representations of meaning, or packets of information, that are encoded in a different language system. In contrast to discursive symbols, Langer conceptualized *presentational symbols* as artistic productions, and suggested that they expressed a mode of symbolic activity that has a different purpose from traditional discursive, verbal symbols. Langer states:

> The purpose of presentational symbols was to present the pattern of our emotional and experiential life in an evocative and sensual way. Their purpose was not primarily to present ideas as propositions, which was the role of discursive symbols (secondary process or rational language), but to show the nature of patterns in which we live and the experiences we have. The discursive symbolism of language, on the other hand, conveyed relations and discrimination in the world of objects through an agreed set of conventional symbols that merely referred to but did not iconically or imagistically present that which it symbolized. [p. 466]

This distinction between presentational symbols that function as iconic, poetic, evocative images or actions that generate experience and meaning, and discursive symbols that represent information is critical in understanding approaches influenced by Klein, Winnicott, and Matte Blanco. Most traditional and contemporary psychoanalytic approaches view symbols primarily as discursive symbols, which suggests that the unconscious is a container of disguised, immature, and hidden meanings. Those approaches influenced by Klein, Winnicott, and Matte Blanco tend to view symbols as presentational symbols in contrast to discursive symbols, and view the unconscious as a generative organization creating meanings and evoking new experiences. Bateson and his colleagues (Etchegoyen and Ahumada 1990, Newirth 1999, Watzlawick et al. 1967) described a similar understanding of two types of linguistic processes in his study of communication and psychopathology; from this perspective, discursive symbols represent a report function of language in which information is exchanged, while presentational symbols represent a command function through which an individual organizes his/her relationships and specifies how a particular message should be experienced and received.

THE KLEINIAN VIEW OF SYMBOL FORMATION

Kleinian theory describes the development of meaning as a dialectical process between the paranoid-schizoid and the depressive positions. In the paranoid-schizoid position, objects are experienced as concrete, emotionally real events with singular meanings, actions, or demands for action. In the depressive position, objects are experienced symbolically, integrated in terms of affects and represented as fantasies, metaphors, or poetic images that generate multiple levels of meaning. For Klein, the analyst's interpretive focus is not on the development and clarification of discursive symbols, differentiating experience or developing understanding through translating from one linguistic/cognitive system to another, but on helping the patient develop from a limited and limiting concrete paranoid experience dominated by externalized unconscious fantasies experienced as real external events, to the ability to symbolically experience, articulate, and integrate those previously terrifying unconscious fantasies into potential aspects of the self.

Hanna Segal (1979) describes the infant's earliest activities as attempts to segregate good experience and feelings from bad experiences and feelings through splitting and projective identification, which she defines as the first attempts at *symbol formation*, the creation of meaning. Segal notes that these early processes of symbol formation are neither true symbols nor substitute ideas (discursive symbols) standing for a repressed or absent impulse, but are felt to be the original object itself reflecting the use of concrete, presentational symbols. She conceptualized these early attempts at organizing the world and creating meaning as *symbolic equations* in which the mental object and the external object are experienced as the same thing: concrete experiences in which the internal representations are treated as if they are real external events.

Segal (1979) illustrated the difference between true symbols and symbolic equations with a discussion of two patients' use of the symbol of a violin. The first patient, a schizophrenic, when asked why he no longer played the violin in public, violently responded, "Why? Do you expect me to masturbate in public?" This patient's rage and terror reflected his experience of the life-threatening dangers inherent in the symbolic equation of playing the violin and masturbating in public. The second patient dreamed that he was playing a violin duet with a girl and through his associations of "fiddling" and masturbating came to see the violin as representing, but not being, his penis, and the dream as representing his sexual desires. This dream suggests both a narrow and a broad view of the concept of symbolic thought inherent in the distinction between discursive and presentational symbols. The narrow view of discursive symbols conceptualizes the violin as a representation of repressed and forbidden sexual wishes that when recognized can be sublimated and brought under the control of the reality principle, becoming a part of lived experience; the man can ask the woman out on a date. The broader, Kleinian concept of symbols, like Langer's concept of presentational symbols, is that the violin creates a new meaning in the patient's experience of himself and his sexual desire, and that it also generates new experiences that can be integrated by the patient. The fantasy of playing a violin duet with a woman describes not only a disguised sexual wish, but also an extremely sensual experience of sexual possibility, including an exciting and terrifying loss of self as the music reaches a crescendo in the mutuality of climax. The fantasy of this violin duet may also represent a positive and a terrifying view of the current analytic relationship, which is experienced as both an exciting and a fearful exchange in which there is an "attunement" of being and a potential loss of boundaries.

Klein (1975) illustrates the process of interpretation as the transformation of concrete to symbolic experience and the development of the capacity to use symbolic processes in the analysis of a 5-year-old boy who was flooded with paralyzing anxiety about his aggressive oedipal feelings:

> He has brought forward a lot of material mostly through play, but he shows the tendency not to realize this. One morning he asks me to play shop and that I should be the one who sells. Now I used a technical measure that is important for the small child who is often not prepared to tell his associations. I asked him who I should be, a lady or a gentleman, as he would have to speak my name in coming into the shop. He told me I would have to be "Mr. Cooky-Caker" and that we found very soon that he meant someone who cooks cakes. I had to sell engines, which represented for him the new penis. He

called himself "Mr. Kicker," which he quickly realized as kicking somebody. I asked him where Mr. Cooky-Caker had gone. He answered, "He has gone away somewhere." He soon realized that Mr. Cooky-Caker had been killed by his kicking him. "Cooking cakes" represented for him making children in an oral and anal way. He realized after this interpretation his aggression against his father and this fantasy opened the way to others in which the person he was fighting against was always Mr. Cooky-Caker. The word (symbol) "Cooky-Caker" is the bridge to reality that the child avoids as long as he brings forth his phantasies only by playing (in action). It always means progress when the child has to acknowledge the reality of the objects through his own words. [p. 314]

In this illustration, Klein underscores the important distinction between unconscious fantasy experienced as real, concrete, external events that are experienced as action, inhibited action, or anxious play, and unconscious fantasy experienced as symbols, creating meaning, integrating experience, and affects. Early symbolic experiences, like "Mr. Cooky-Caker" and "Mr. Kicker," increase the child's capacity to explore and utilize aggressive feelings and to repair and integrate the split between the good loving object and the bad murderous object. The Kleinian concept of interpretation and of symbolic thought involves the capacity to create new meanings through the development of presentational symbols that generate new experiences, define identity through organizing self–other relationships, and are emotionally evocative experiences that function like poetic structures. Jacobus (1999) suggests that Klein's concept of symbols, like Lacan's and Kresteva's, has powerful, generative evanescent qualities associated with presentational symbols, poetic images, and metaphors in which meanings are multilayered, supersaturated experiences, constantly shifting and expanding in their ability to evoke and create meanings.

WINNICOTT'S AND BION'S VIEWS OF SYMBOL FORMATION

Winnicott (1977), like Bion (1962), developed Klein's theory into an explicitly two-person theory. Each of these theorists focused on the interpersonal context for the child's or patient's development of the capacity for symbolic thought through interpersonal processes of identification, internalization, and the imaginative elaboration of unconscious fantasies. Bion's focus was closer to Klein, developing the relationship between projective identification and processes of symbol formation. In his view the process of creating meaning begins when the individual evacuates bad thoughts, which are experienced as a concrete symbolic equations, into the other (parent or therapist), who either may react with anxiety, rejecting the projective identification in a never-ending game of "hot potato," or may identify with the projection and through processes of reverie imaginatively and affectively elaborate this symbolic equation so that it becomes "detoxified," a true symbol generating meanings that can be internalized, understood, and used by the subject rather than being experienced as a concrete fact or state of being that can only be passively endured by the subject. For Bion, the creation of meaning is a two-person process in which the capacity to think and create meaning occurs both intrapersonally and interpersonally, with the therapist or parent functioning through reverie to detoxify and imaginatively elaborate the evacuated concrete fantasies.

Winnicott describes a similar process of the creation of meaning and symbol formation in which the other, the parent or therapist, joins the child or patient through processes of identification and imaginative elaboration in the creation of transitional objects and experiences in which meaning becomes mutually created through an evolving two-person experience. For Winnicott, the creation of meaning is often contextualized as play, in which both people affectively and imaginatively elaborate one individual's frightening concrete experience, which can be understood as externalized or evacuated symbolic equations. In describing the process of the creation of meaning and the development of transitional experiences, Winnicott develops the concept of illusion (Kluzer-Uselli 1992), which he views as an important, positive experience, a third area of experience that contrasts with objective or external reality and purely internal psychic experience. This third area of experience becomes the location of cultural, artistic, religious, and subjective experiences in which meaning is not simply based on the individual's ability to describe happenings and objects in the external world or to reach a social consensus about the nature of interpersonal experience, but rather on the ability to express aspects of personal or subjective meanings such as those involving the emotional relationships of love, hate, and personal ideals. This third area of experience, the area of transitional experiences, is related to Winnicott's (1960; see also Khan 1974) differentiation of the false self and the true self, in which the false self represents the individual's incorporation of the meanings of the other while the true self represents meanings that the individual creates from his/her own experience.

Winnicott's (1977) theory of transitional experience suggests two parallel forms of meaning, the first representing external or objective reality reflecting the concept of discursive symbols, and the second representing subjective meanings incorporating the concept of presentational symbols. Winnicott views the development of the capacity for transitional experience as related to the development of the capacity for creativity and a sense of aliveness. For Winnicott, the creation of meaning is not only a two-person process but also one that emphasizes a playful and joyful process in which subjective and intersubjective meanings are seen as different from the capacity for mature thought as it reflects the world of external objects. The patients described at the beginning of this chapter who were unable to feel alive and that their lives were personally meaningful can be thought of as having failed to develop the capacity for transitional experience and symbolic thought.

MATTE BLANCO AND THE CREATION OF MEANING

Matte Blanco (1975, 1988), a Chilean analyst who studied with Klein, developed a theory of conscious and unconscious mental processes as parallel modes of organizing experience based on different systems of logic rather than on the Freudian biological, hierarchical concept of the unconscious. Matte Blanco describes consciousness as organized through Aristotelian or asymmetrical logic (our usual concept of logic), which functions to differentiate experience within the dimensions of person, place, time, and causality, and can be thought of as primarily involving discursive symbols. Unconscious experience is organized through symmetrical logic, which creates similarities and effaces differences within the dimensions of person, place, time, and causality, and can be thought of as primarily involving presentational symbols. Asymmetrical and symmetrical logic can be exemplified through comparing newspaper articles, which emphasize the distinctions of who, what, when, and where, with poetry or dreams, in which these distinctions are effaced through condensation, where one person or a particular event can stand for many individuals in many places at many different times.

Matte Blanco's differentiation of symmetrical and asymmetrical organizations of experience, along with the Kleinian dialectic of concrete and symbolic thought, has allowed us to conceptualize the creation of meaning as the central event in a neo-Kleinian approach to psychoanalysis. In developing a neo-Kleinian approach to psychoanalysis, integrating and extending the works of Klein, Winnicott, Matte Blanco, and their followers, the linked concepts of the unconscious, interpretation, and symbolism have become a central focus comparing a repressed or relational model of the unconscious with a generative concept of the unconscious. In Kleinian and neo-Kleinian theories, the unconscious is conceptualized as a structure in which the use of presentational symbols and the symbolic function is an ongoing, progressive process of creating meaning as contrasted to the traditional archaeological model of the unconscious, which utilizes discursive symbols and the uncovering of meaning embedded in past experience, or the relational unconscious, which focuses on the articulation of repetitive childhood relationships in new contemporary forms. Interpretation has traditionally been thought of as a process of making the unconscious conscious, of linking language with the repressed impulse and freeing the patient from a cycle of repeating past relationships and pathological wishes. From a neo-Kleinian perspective, interpretation involves both processes of symmetrical dedifferentiation of historical experience from current experience and the symmetrical construction of new meanings through the development of symbolic processes, presentational symbols such as metaphors, and experiences of enactment and transitional experiences.

EPISTEMOLOGICAL PERSPECTIVES

One of the underlying difficulties that many American's have in working with Kleinian and neo-Kleinian ideas is an implicit shift in the epistemological assumptions of these theories. Klein rejected the epistemological assumptions of modernism, which defined the scientific perspective of the twentieth century and reflected Freudian and most other contemporary psychoanalytic perspectives assumptions about knowledge and understanding reality. Klein and other analysts whom we have loosely brought together as representing a neo-Kleinian approach have organized their work within the epistemological assumptions of post-modernism. Understanding the epistemological assumptions of different psychoanalytic theories illuminates critical differences and enriches our understanding, particularly as it affects the clinical process of interpretation, the development of the capacity to create meaning, and the development of symbolic thought and language.

Psychoanalytic theories seem to suggest three alternative epistemological systems, each of which presents equally valid ways to generate knowledge about the nature of the world, about what constitutes knowing, and about our understanding of what it means to be a person. Each epistemological structure provides an understanding of human experience and a method of dealing with difficulties in living and the therapeutic transformation of experience defined as cure or healing. Each epistemological system provides a different picture of human nature, different ways of conceptualizing health, a theory of therapeutic transformation, a system of logic, and an understanding of time. From an individual or subjective perspective, each epistemological structure provides a different answer to these questions: "What is truth?" "What makes me feel that I am fully myself?" "What is the meaning of life?"

The three epistemological structures are the discourse of faith, love, and religion; the discourse of science, positivism, and modernism; and the discourse of literature, art, and postmodernism. The discourse of faith, love, and religion emphasizes a higher power through which knowledge is revealed to the individual in relation to his/her capacity to surrender to a transpersonal Other, which may be an idea, a lover, or a deity. The discourse of science, positivism, and modernism emphasizes the discovery and finding of knowledge in nature or society conceived of as an external world, through methods that are public, repeatable, and objective. The discourse of literature, art, and postmodernism emphasizes the development of personal knowledge as a construction that is created through the development and articulation of images, symbols, or metaphors such as those in poetry, art, or theater. Each epistemological discourse presents a different concept of truth, knowledge, and reality.

In the discourse of faith, love, and religion, experience is organized through symmetrical logic, through creating or generating similarities. Time is conceptualized synchronically; life is a series of repeating events leading to concepts of forever, eternity, and the infinite. Transformation, cure, healing, or salvation is based on surrender or sacrifice to a transpersonal experience, giving over the individual self to the other, whether God, a lover, or a set of political or social values or ideals. Psychological treatment incorporates traditional religious values, such as twelve-step programs and Buddhist practices, and utilizes presentational symbols. In the discourse of science, positivism, and modernism, experience is organized through asymmetrical logic, in which information is found or generated through the development of discrimination between natural or social occurrences. Time is conceptualized diachronically, describing linear movement from past to present to future. Transformation, cure, or personal growth is based on the development of objective understanding, gathering information and the use of discursive symbols, rational choice, and the delineation of cause–effect sequences. Examples of psychological treatment are traditional approaches to psychoanalysis, cognitive behavioral treatment, and biochemical approaches to mental illness. In the discourse of literature, art, and postmodernism, experience is organized through symmetrical logic in which experience is expanded through the development of metaphors, presentational symbols, and evocative speech. Time is conceptualized synchronically, with an emphasis on the present as encompassing all time. Treatment is conceptualized as a transformational process and includes the use of enactments, transitional experience, and metaphoric interpretive structures that generate presentational symbols as in Kleinian, Winnicottian, and neo-Kleinian approaches to treatment.

Figure 1–1 illustrates these three epistemological systems.

THE NEO-KLEINIAN PERSPECTIVE: SUBJECTIVITY AND THE GENERATIVE UNCONSCIOUS

In the following chapters I develop a postmodern, neo-Kleinian psychoanalytic approach to the problems presented by contemporary narcissistic and borderline patients, the "hollow men," individuals who have failed to develop the internal structures that are the basis for subjectivity and the creation of meaning. From this neo-Kleinian perspective, sub-

EPISTEMOLOGICAL STRUCTURES AND PSYCHOANALYSIS

	FORM OF LOGIC	TIME	TRANSFORMATION	EXAMPLE OF TREATMENT
DISCOURSE OF FAITH, LOVE, and RELIGION	Symmetry presentational symbols	Synchronic; sequences of repeating events leading to forever infinity, eternity	Surrender or sacrifice to a transpersonal experience. Giving over the individual self to the other; god, a lover or an ideal	Incorporating traditional religious values, Buddhist practice, and twelve-step programs
DISCOURSE OF SCIENCE, POSITIVISM, and MODERNISM	Asymmetry discursive symbols	Dyachronic; discrete units, linear movement from past to present to future	Observable technique; objective processes, causal relationships, rational choice	Traditional psychoanalysis, insight oriented therapy, cognitive behavior therapy, biochemical approaches
DISCOURSE OF LITERATURE, ART, and POST-MODERNISM	Symmetry presentational symbols	Synchronic; sequences of repeating events leading to forever infinity, eternity	Creating meaning, evocation of affect fantasy and personal associations	Neo-Kleinian and Lacanian approaches; use of transitional experience; poetic images metaphors

Figure 1–1

jectivity is not simply a phenomenological expression of affect and experience but involves the developing capacity for symbolic thought, which is as an aspect of the depressive position. This approach integrates and extends the work of Klein, Bion, Winnicott, and Matte Blanco within the context of an American two-person relational approach to psychoanalysis. Each of these theorists was struggling with limits of the tripartite structural model and presented alternatives to the traditional linear, archaeological, drive-defense model of psychoanalysis. These theories, although often using different theoretical language, have a common underlying structural view and dynamic concept of human development and the psychoanalytic situation. The theories that form the conceptual foundation of the neo-Kleinian approach view the unconscious as both a developing structure and a source of creative experience and energy. In this model the unconscious operates through a series of dialectical relationships involving externalization and internalization, hopefulness and despair, and passionate aliveness and numbed deadness.

In the neo-Kleinian view, the unconscious is a developing organization that primarily functions to create, generate, and apprehend meaning both in pathology and health. The unconscious is a developing or evolving organizational structure that includes both the concrete, externalized, persecutory fantasies that are felt to be real and located in the external world, and more symbolic experiences of metaphors and transitional experiences. In this model the task of the analyst is to facilitate the transformation of the concrete experiences of the paranoid-schizoid mode into the symbolic experience of the depressive mode where unconscious fantasy enlivens experience and relationships.

CLINICAL ILLUSTRATION: THE DEAD HERO

This clinical illustration focuses on the difference between the discourse of science, positivism, and modernism and the discourse of literature, art, and postmodernism. Interestingly, this patient's personality often seems to reflect the discourse of faith, love, and religion. Mr. A., a man in his mid 40s, feels that his life is meaningless. He is often quite disconnected from others and his own affective experience, and he sees himself as one of the "hollow men." He has been having a great deal of difficulty at work and is concerned that he will be asked to leave. He has had consistent difficulties with authority, often feeling that he knows better than his boss, although often reluctant to challenge him directly. In a recent session in which we were continuing our conversations about his difficulties at work, he comments that he is surprised that he has not felt anxious or angry. He then reports, in what appears to be a disconnected manner, that he has felt very stiff and has had a lot of muscle aches when he gets out of bed in the morning. I interpret this and suggest that he has probably been suppressing a great deal of anger in his sleep. He immediately amplifies my intervention with the further observation that it is like people who grind their teeth in their sleep.

The beginning of this session can be thought of as an ambivalent attempt by Mr. A. to understand his recent difficulties with authority and anger while at the same time remaining quite concrete and reluctant to attribute meaning to his experience and become the active center in his subjective world. From a Kleinian perspective, this represents the passive paranoid position; he is evacuating his anger both into the environment and into his body, where it is experienced as an alien, painful force. The patient is evacuating his experience through the use of a series of metonymic displacements through which he avoids his central concerns and desires. The evacuated sequence of displacements moves from denial and his statement of not being angry, to body symptom and muscle aches, to an objective or asymmetrical description of people who grind their teeth. Mr. A. is avoiding his angry, destructive desires and his own subjectivity, being at the center of a world of vital immediate experience.

Mr. A. continues, in his usual disconnected way, saying that he had had a dream that was like many dreams that he has had before. "I was in the White House and someone was trying to kill George W. Bush. I stepped in front of him and took the bullet for him. I died." We can think of many ways to interpret this dream, to translate the symbols and to create meaning for and with the patient. The interpretation of the dream symbols will depend on the analyst's theory and the epistemological system in which that the theory is embedded. In approaching this dream from the perspective of Freudian theory, and the discourse of science, positivism, and modernism, the dream represents a series of discursive symbols reflecting the patient's oedipal conflict, his repressed wish to kill the father, his unacceptable feelings of superiority as the oedipal victor, and his grandiose compromise of being the self sacrificing son. This dream and the possible interpretation can be thought of as similar to the Rat Man (Freud 1909) in which Freud's patient was paralyzed by his need to repress his anger and his destructive oedipal wishes. In a traditional approach in which these dream images are thought of as discursive symbols, the analyst's task would be that of translating and differentiating the unacceptable and unrealistic childhood oedipal wishes within the context of the patient's current transference and life experience. For example, interpretation might focus on his unacceptable anger and contempt toward his boss/father and his need to defensively idealize and protect the analyst from his hostility.

From a Kleinian and a neo-Kleinian perspective, within the discourse of literature, art, and postmodernism, interpretation or the process of creating meaning occurs through generating and developing presentational symbols through which the patient could begin to experience, integrate, and enjoy his aggression. A neo-Kleinian interpretive strategy would involve a process of symbol formation, finding metaphors that would allow these aggressive desires to become integrated and subjectively alive, transforming his experience of himself from that of a passive and disconnected self-sacrificing son to an active and engaged phallic (powerful) father. My first comments to him involved an attempt to put his dream into a symmetrical and synchronic context, describing the content of the dream as metaphors for his experience of himself. I then focused on the necessity to deaden himself, to kill his desire, his inability to tolerate the excitement of being the president, and his reluctance to be the assassin, and finally integrating these interpretations with the metaphor that the only good hero is a dead hero. In all of these attempts to generate symbols, there is a dedifferentiation of time from a diachronic to synchronic organization and a dedifferentiation or symmetrization of the objects in the dream so that they each represented disowned aspects of himself.

Reacting to my interpretations, the patient smiled and said that this dream reminded him of the fantasy that he used to have as a child when he would imagine that he would become the hero of his school by pushing a little girl out of the way of a speeding car and being killed. His association is a symmetrical elaboration of my interpretation, incorporating and generating new meaning and adding an evocative symbol to this metaphoric structure. The subsequent series of playful exchanges led to the elaboration and development of the metaphor of the dead hero, a presentational symbol that reflected this patient's dilemma that the only way he could be a powerful man is to be a dead hero. The jointly created metaphor of the dead hero functioned as a presentational symbol. It was evocative, and it reorganized and gave voice to multiple memories and to a continuing series of associations functioning as a living poetic image. This metaphor became a transitional experience, an articulated dream image. The dead hero became a creative expression for the patient's negated desire to be triumphant, to be powerful, to have the paternal phallus, and to enjoy his aggression. In our work on this dream, the patient developed the idea that he could only accept his desire to be powerful if he was dead and was not conscious of being looked at, admired, and seen.

This brief clinical example allows us to consider different directions in the process of creating meaning in psychoanalysis. From a neo-Kleinian perspective, meaning is created through the elaboration of the evacuated, dissociated aspects of the patient's unconscious fantasies and desires into a symbolic form that emphasizes presentational rather than discursive symbolic functions. Like the development of transitional experiences (Winnicott 1977), presentational symbols are evocative, demanding, and express the patient's unconscious desire. This process of creating meaning involves successive articulation of the patient's and analyst's experience so that it moves from states of being dissociated to forms of poetry where the patient can experience himself as a subject and as the author of the narrative of his life. It is this process that facilitates the patient's development from the emotional deadness and the affective instability involved in the failure to develop subjectivity, to the capacity for symbolic experience that is the basis for the experience of subjectivity.

2

Ego, Self, and Subject: The Person in Structural Theory and Clinical Practice

Psychoanalysis as a scientific study and as a therapeutic practice has struggled with understanding and treating the patients of our time: the borderline, the schizoid, the narcissist, and the "hollow men." This struggle reflects confusion among different theoretical voices, each using similar conceptual language while describing different dynamic and technical approaches. I believe that this confusion is a result of a premature assimilation of concepts from object relations theory that have ignored important differences in underlying values, technical recommendations, and implicit definitions of mental health that are at the center of each psychoanalytic model. Although all psychoanalytic theories consider the patient's capacity to make decisions, to express authentic feelings, and to create meanings, each school of psychoanalysis defines one of these characteristics as its epistemological core and the others as secondary or derivative to the primary dimension. It is a theory's core concept and implicit values that organize an analyst's approach to patients and to the psychoanalytic situation.

In contemporary psychoanalytic theory there are three distinct concepts of the person, each defining different core issues and values, different developmental processes, different ways of organizing the psychoanalytic situation, and different concepts of analytic success and psychological health. The classical Freudian or contemporary ego psychological model understands the central structure of personhood as the development of the ego and the capacity for rational choice in resolving conflict between competing structures and wishes. The interpersonal and self psychological models view the central structure of the person as the self: a personality organization that is molded and warped by interpersonal experience and interpersonal anxiety, and that under the best of circumstances develops the capacity for authentic expression of feelings and needs. The neo-Kleinian approach, which reflects the evolution of British object relations theory and Matte Blanco's and Lacan's contributions to psychoanalysis, has led to a conceptualization of the person as a subject, a personality organization that focuses on the capacity to develop, organize, apprehend, and generate symbolic meaning.

All psychoanalytic theories have three dimensions: a structural or metapsychological dimension, a developmental dimension, and a theory of psychoanalytic technique. These dimensions may be thought of as a series of alternative formulations of the basic concepts and values of the theory as they operate within an abstract or theoretical, a historical or developmental, and a therapeutic or change-oriented system. The abstract, theoretical, or structural dimension is a set of universal propositions that describe the consistent relationship between a person's current behavior, fantasies, or symptoms and his or her biological and interpersonal history. Freud's (1923) papers on metapsychology; Rapaport and colleagues' (1951, 1967), Hartmann's (1958), and Jacobson's (1964) development of ego psychology; and Bion's (1962) attempts to formulate psychoanalytic theory as a set of mathematical relationships that he presented in a grid are all examples of the abstract or theoretical dimension and represent different sets of universal or structural propositions that define human experience.

Each school of psychoanalysis also presents a theory of human development that outlines the individual's growth and maturation from infancy to adulthood. This dimension focuses on a set of developmental crises or a series of personal achievements that provide an explanatory framework for healthy adult development and for psychopathology. From a treatment perspective, developmental theories provide a narrative that captures the drama, poetry, and passion of human experience. Freud's (1905a) choice of the tragedy of Oedipus Rex, Mahler's (1975) description of the drama of separation and individuation, and Klein's (1957) imagery of the infant's envious attacks on the mother's good breast are three of the most powerful developmental narratives in psychoanalysis. The clinical usefulness of developmental theory is not simply a function of the extent of the empirical support that it has obtained; rather, it provides the clinician with a set of personal myths or narrative structures (Spence 1982), powerful affective representations or construction of what might have been (Freud 1937), or a way of helping the patient make a coherent personal history (Schafer 1992) in which he/she may become the central character determining and being responsible for the life he/she leads.

Most relevant for this book is the theory of psychoanalytic technique presented by each theory—what the analyst does and does not do to facilitate the patient's growth and development. Each psychoanalytic theory describes a clinical technique and set of technical recommendations that are the pragmatic translations of its structural and developmental theories, a series of steps or algorithms (Levenson 1983) that describe how one goes from the beginning to the end of the treatment, from the patient's state of disease to a state of relative health, from "neurotic to normal misery." In this chapter I compare the core concepts and values developed by different psychoanalytic theories, and I argue that in order to understand and treat contemporary patients, the "hollow men," with their experience of meaningless, empty, and dead lives, we need to revise our definition of the person to one that focuses on the structures of subjectivity, on how experience and meaning are generated rather than on the structure of ego or the self. I will place these different psychoanalytic theories in their historical, sociopolitical contexts and highlight their theoretical or structural principles, their poetic and dramatic narratives, their pragmatic recommendations for treatment, and their preferred algorithms of change.

THE EVOLVING DEFINITION OF
THE PERSON IN PSYCHOANALYSIS

In *Ghandi's Truth*, Erickson (1969) points out that when an Indian patient is asked to draw a picture of a person, he draws the person embedded in a group and not, as most North Americans do, as an individual standing alone with little elaboration of background or context. Other non-Western and traditional cultures also represent the individual as embedded within a context of place or time, as part of the flow of generations, conceiving of each life as a step in a transpersonal, purposeful, historic journey. Each culture and each historical period defines what it means to be a person, specifying the desired dimensions of the psyche or soul and the failures and distortions of living that are seen as either sin or pathology. Bloom (1985) suggests that it would be impossible, in contemporary Western culture, to write about being human apart from Freud's theory, including the distinction between the conscious and the unconscious mind, the importance of sexuality and aggression as core motivational systems, repression, and the resistance to self-awareness and personal responsibility. Khan (1974) argues that a critical aspect of Freud's invention of psychoanalysis was his separating the individual from the social frame that had defined him as ill. Khan suggests that Freud's invention of the psychoanalytic situation occurred through replacing this social frame with a therapeutic frame in which the alienated person could find his/her symbolic voice in a new place and in a new relationship.

Unlike earlier philosophical and religious definitions of being human, Freud transformed our ideas of what it means to be a person through the psychoanalytic method replacing the moral or religious view of man with a scientific view. From this perspective, Freud can be thought of as extending modernism (Borgman 1992) to the study of man where he elaborated the principles developed by Bacon, Descartes, and Locke, which incorporated man's domination of nature, the primacy of method, and the sovereignty of the individual. Freud's psychoanalytic theories continued to change as he had new clinical experiences that he saw through the prism of the scientific method. In Freud's early clinical work (Breuer and Freud 1895, Freud 1894), the techniques of abreaction, hypnosis, direct suggestion, and free association became the foundation for the development of the topographic model, which defined the person in terms of consciousness and unconsciousness, and incorporated an early concept of repression involving affective and cognitive blockages. In contrast to this early psychoanalytic definition of the person that focused on conscious and unconscious experience, the development of a more complex structural theory that focused on sexual and aggressive instincts, the id, the ego, and superego, and the concept of man as "guilty" (Kohut 1977) reflected Freud's (1914b) developing understanding of the importance of transference as repetition in contrast to his simpler view of transference as resistance. The view of transference as repetition and the associated technical recommendations of neutrality became the methodological core of classical psychoanalytic technique and of the tripartite structural model of id, ego, and superego.

THE PERSON AS EGO

Freudian theory has evolved from the structural model to the model of ego psychology (A. Freud 1937, Hartmann 1958, Jacobson 1964, Rapaport 1951) and most recently to contemporary conflict theory (Arlow and Brenner 1964, Beres 1965, Richards and Lynch 1998). Although there has been considerable evolution in contemporary Freudian thought, including jettisoning many aspects of Freud's metapsychological theory (see Schafer 1976, for a discussion of this issue), it has maintained the metapsychological importance of the ego as a mediating structure, which then defines the clinical goal of psychoanalytic treatment as increasing the individual's capacities for reality testing. The contemporary Freudian model, consistent with the past, identifies the person with the ego and remains committed to the values of nineteenth-century modernism, incorporating the natural science values of the search for empirical truth, the adaptation of the scientific method, a fundamental belief in positivism, rational thought, and the importance of external reality, interpreting Freud's statement of "where id was there ego shall be" as the subordination of the irrational to the rational.

Richards and Lynch (1998) describe contemporary conflict theory as the heir to ego psychology and classical psychoanalysis, and point out that it is based on the core belief that "mental life and all psychic phenomena (are) the expression of intrapsychic forces in conflict and the resulting compromises" (p. 14). Jacob Arlow (1985), who has made many significant contributions to the development of contemporary conflict theory, describes the analyst's activity as aiding patients in reconstructing or renegotiating the compromises inherent in their symptoms and the underlying unconscious fantasies. The revisions in contemporary conflict theory are attempts to move away from the anthropomorphic elements of structural theory in which the ego, id, and superego are described as willful, independent actors struggling with each other, and to emphasize the core values of developing rational control over irrational elements in the personality. The emphasis on rational control expresses many of the values that had been associated with the mature ego. For example, Arlow (1985) describes the patient's inner conflict and the analyst's task in the following way:

> Because of the interplay of the effect of opposing forces in the mind, what finally appears in consciousness represents a compromise formation. Towards this compromise formation each of the various agencies of the mind—the ego, the super-ego and the id—has made a specific contribution. From our clinical work we learn to appreciate that what appears in consciousness is a derivative of unconscious conflict. . . . At a certain level, the ego's attempt to resolve fundamental, recurrent intrapsychic conflicts is organized in the form of an unconscious fantasy. Essentially, the interpretive work during psychoanalysis consists of *reconstructing the nature of the unconscious fantasy* from the derivatives which it produces in consciousness, and analyzing and resolving the consequences of the specific component contributions of the forces in conflict. [p. 25, italics added]

The focus on the functional qualities of the ego and "reconstructing the nature of the unconscious fantasy" is a contemporary version of Freud's concept of the ego replacing the id and of secondary process thought superseding primary process thought. This focus on rational thought replacing irrational thought forecloses an independent constructive function for unconscious fantasy and suggests that the analyst operate as an agent of the reality principle, standing against the patient's irrational desires. This interpretive position maintains a positivist, asymmetrical relationship between analyst and patient, where the analyst defines the meaning of the patient's experience and reality.

This issue of whether the analyst knows and can or should define reality for the patient has been an important and controversial problem in contemporary psychoanalytic theory. This controversy has been addressed as a set of dichotomies that contrast the constructionist or hermeneutic perspective with the positivist or realist perspectives. The constructionist or hermeneutic view is that reality is a construction developed jointly by the analyst and patient, and that neither participant has a privileged position in knowing or defining reality. In the constructionist view, reality may be thought of as either an aesthetic experience or as the expression of internal or psychic reality. The positivist or realist view is that reality is not a construction; it is not an aesthetic or affective experience, but is knowable through particular methods and is part of an external material world.

The contemporary Freudian analyst maintains a positivist view of reality, which is a major determinant organizing the analytic relationship and the analyst's interpretive strategy. For example, Rangell (1996), a contemporary Freudian analyst and theoretician, emphasizes these values in describing the psychoanalytic relationship as striving to achieve a "scientific vantage point of observation, as close as one can aspire to in a human, social science" (p. 146). In keeping with the positivist view of reality, Rangell asserts that the analytic relationship is not a symmetrical relationship and it is not a dialogue: "Only one person free associates; the other does something entirely different. As Fenichel (1945) has stated, psychoanalytic treatment is (proceeds) through the rational ego" (p. 149).

The core concepts and values that organize the clinical work of the contemporary Freudian analyst have remained centered on the ego and the executive function of reworking the pathological or infantile compromise formations that are represented as symptoms and unconscious fantasies. The nature of unconscious fantasy, which is a critical issue for all psychoanalytic theories, is subordinated to external reality in contemporary Freudian theory. For example, Grossman (1996), a contemporary Freudian analyst, takes a strong positivist position on the nature of unconscious fantasy, arguing against the constructionist view of unconscious fantasy as an independent "psychic reality" that exists in parallel to an objective or "material reality." He suggests that "if the concept of 'psychic reality' elevates fantasy to the status of an alternative 'reality' in the mind of the analyst, the outcome may be collusion with the patient's pathological blurring of the distinction between fantasy and reality" (p. 510). He believes that a critical aspect of the analyst's role is to strongly demonstrate how and why the patient confuses, disavows, and denies reality while favoring untested and cherished fantasies. He illustrates his position with a personal anecdote that illustrates his strong positivist views, emphasizing the importance of reality testing:

One morning, at a time I was on a strict diet, I awoke with a feeling of shame and irritation with myself, for having succumbed to the temptation to eat some forbidden food. I felt annoyed with myself all day, until someone happened to ask me how the diet was going. When I thought about it, I realized that I had not gone off the diet; I had dreamed the lapse, and by refraining from asking myself any questions about the reality of the event—i.e., by not "testing reality"— I had preserved the illicit satisfaction of the dream snack. [p. 510]

This example, perhaps meant to be an everyday experience of psychopathology, seems naive; the author does not consider that his "shame," "irritation," and "annoyance" might reflect some other unconscious meanings embedded in the dream that he did not remember and that it did not simply refer to the manifest content of his diet. In this interpretation he affirms that it is the actuality of his experience, material reality, not having strayed from his diet, that is important, as contrasted to his experience of fantasy and psychic reality. He believes that the essence of psychic reality is that it is unquestioned and untested by the rule of congruence with external or objective experience, and that it is imperative that the analyst represent material reality and the development of the ego function of reality testing. Although this example might seem somewhat stilted, it represents an enduring aspect of the contemporary Freudian position, emphasizing the importance of expanding the province of the patient's ego and developing the capacity for rational choice through a positivist interpretive strategy, conceptualizing unconscious fantasy or psychic reality as something that needs to be tested and re-shaped into a rational view of the individual in the world.

THE PERSON AS SELF

The second psychoanalytic model, the person as self, views the individual from the perspective of social rather than natural science, focusing on issues of interpersonal communication, empathy, and the development of mutual or consensual influence and understanding. This model incorporates the twentieth-century social science and humanistic values of perspectivism or constructionism, views pathology as the individual's adaptations to disturbed environments, and endorses the democratic ideals of equality and each individual's right to happiness and to fulfill one's potential. If the Freudian theories reflect a scientific, dispassionate, and pessimistic view of the universe, the theories of the person as self reflect humanistic, liberal, and optimistic social values.

The major theories of the person as self are interpersonal psychoanalysis, developed by Harry Stack Sullivan (1953), and self psychology, developed by Heinz Kohut (1977, 1984). Interpersonal psychoanalysis and self psychology developed within different theoretical traditions and use different theoretical language; however, they share similar critiques of the classical model of the person as ego, and developed similar structural, developmental, and therapeutic approaches. In focusing on the underlying values and assumptions of self psychology and interpersonal psychoanalysis, I highlight their humanistic, cultural, dynamic, and technical similarities rather than their historical and linguistic differences.

The focus in both interpersonal psychoanalysis and self psychology is on the patient's experiences and adaptations to the demands and anxieties of important people in the environment, theoretically described as either the interpersonal field or the intersubjective field. The focus on interpersonal or intersubjective experience is a critical difference between theories of the self and traditional views of the person as ego, where the focus is on the individual's internal world as it develops a series of compromise formations between the irrational and infantile demands and the rational necessity to accept the limits of the reality principle. By contrast, the theories of the self assume that it is the environmental demands and threats that cause the individual to become less than he or she might have been in an ideal family situation. Sullivan's (1953) statement that we all become a caricature of who we might have been is a reflection of this humanistic perspective on the conflict between the innocent child and the corrupting social environment. From this perspective, psychopathology (Feiner and Levenson 1968) has been thought of as a compassionate sacrifice in which the child becomes the identified patient in order to rescue and distract the other family members from the necessity of becoming aware of their own difficulties and hypocritical communications.

Theories of the self conceptualize psychopathology as a form of arrested development, reflecting the individual's adaptations to a pathological environment in order to maintain security and a minimal experience of recognition or mirroring. Anxiety in interpersonal theory and in self psychology is conceptualized as a fear of social disapproval, rejection, neglect, or abandonment. The theories of the self view psychopathology and the transference relationship as new additions of earlier pathological relationships that are thought of as either interpersonal schemas (Hirsch and Roth 1995) or model scenes (Lachmann and Lichtenberg 1992). The psychoanalytic relationship is conceptualized as a process of facilitating growth and development rather than conflict resolution, and is conceived of as an empathic, warm, active engagement that values both the analyst's and the patient's capacity to freely express feelings, be spontaneous, emotionally expressive, self assertive, authentic, and genuine. This model views healthy development as involving the capacity to choose and develop relationships in which the person is able to freely express feelings, to verbalize wants and desires, and to develop an authentic version of the self in terms of one's inherent abilities and current goals and ideals.

Sullivan's development of interpersonal psychoanalysis (Greenberg and Mitchell 1983, Perry 1999) reflected a paradigm shift from conceptualizing the individual as embedded in biology and the physical world to seeing the human being as understandable through the social sciences, linguistics, anthropology, and Dewey's pragmatic philosophy. The development of interpersonal psychoanalysis reflected Sullivan's sense of being an outsider in America as well as the experiences of the émigré European analysts of the "cultural schools" (Munroe 1955) of psychoanalysis, Horney, Fromm, Fromm-Reichmann, and Rank, whose theories were in part a reaction against the positivist, authoritarian, and biological assumptions of classical psychoanalysis. They developed theories based on sociopolitical and romantic perspectives, conceptualizing psychopathology as a function of the exploitation of the weak by the powerful and the psychoanalytic relationship as a two-person situation in which the analyst contributed to the patient's growth through experiential as well as interpretive means. The development of contemporary relational theory is an outgrowth of this interpersonal perspective and the idea of the analytic relationship as involving new experiences, including mutual influence (Aron 1996) and mutual help (Singer 1971), which becomes a counter to the patient's repeated expectations and distortions of current experience based on early paradigms of connection and anxiety avoidance.

Levenson (1985) described the central difference between the Freudian and interpersonal approaches as the difference between "*the search for the truth behind appearances* versus *the search for truth inherent in appearances*. For the Freudian, the key question is, What does it truly mean? For the interpersonalist, the question is, What's going on around here?" (p. 53). For the interpersonal psychoanalyst, the focus is always on what can be observed in the patient's interactions with others and with the therapist. The analytic method is one of "participant observation" (Hirsch 1985), in which the analyst uses his own affective and cognitive experiences in understanding and confronting the patient's experience of self. Interpersonal psychoanalytic treatment involves the development of undistorted and authentic communication about how each member of the analytic pair affects the other. The analytic goal for Sullivan, as well as for contemporary interpersonal psychoanalysts, is to facilitate patients' *consensual* understanding of their experiences as children and as adults and to be able to function successfully in having their current needs met. Sullivan's concept of consensual thinking is similar to the Freudian idea of secondary process thought, although it is based on the development of a social or interpersonal consensus about the nature of external as well as internal reality. The emphasis on consensual reality reflects a positivist value based on a normative rather than an objective approach to reality. Gill (1983) describes the therapist's level of activity and the focus on interpersonal dynamics both in the here and now and in the patient's development as the critical factors that differentiate the interpersonal from Freudian approaches.

According to Levenson (1985), aspects of experience are typically thought of as reflecting unconscious processes: "Dreams, fantasies, free associations, slips are in no sense disregarded, but are seen as efforts the patient is making, through imagery and imagination, to grapple with and comprehend affectively distorted experience. However distorted or caricatured it might appear to be, fantasy is considered more the reflection of poorly comprehended real-life interpersonal experience than the emergence from the depths of solipsistic, primitive impulses" (p. 49). The goal of treatment is facilitating the patient's and analyst's capacity to articulate in rational, normative, and consensual language the unformulated (Stern 1996, Wolstein 1975) unconscious experience that organizes the patient's interpersonal experience. From the interpersonal perspective, a major aspect of the analyst's work is the demystification of the patient's emotional distortions in the transference and in real relationships.

Stern (1996) addresses the contradiction that arises in interpersonal and relational psychoanalysis as a result of defining the analytic situation as a two-person relationship in which the analyst is no longer in the privileged position of authority.

> While analysts are still experts in the room, it is no longer because they know exactly how to relate or exactly what to look for in the patient's experience—or in their own. Rather, they know how to look. They know to expect to be entangled and to expect to have trouble seeing the tangle and digging out of it. They are often unsuccessful, or rather they may be unsuccessful for long periods. But when they are successful, disembodying themselves helps their patients do the same. Experience that had never been formulated enters the realm of language and can finally be reflected upon by both participants. . . . Once the analyst finds his way to kicking over the traces, the same old *unwitting* kind of relatedness becomes impractical and unnatural, even unpleasant, for the patient as well. [p. 283, italics added]

Stern describes the interpersonal treatment as beginning with an inevitable, albeit unconscious, enmeshment in the transference–countertransference relationship, a repetitive experience that is modeled on the patient's childhood experience. Both analyst and patient feel entangled in a relationship that feels problematic and that is difficult to formulate into language that is rational and understandable. The analyst's work and the therapeutic process involve formulating, understanding, and verbalizing in consensual or secondary-process language the previously unformulated experience, which then leads to growth and change.

One difference between the interpersonal and the self psychology view of this process of change involves questions of the analyst's consciousness and choice. In the interpersonal literature the focus tends to be on the analyst's inevitable but unwitting involvement in the evolving transference–countertransference enactment and his or her subsequent attempts to clearly formulate and communicate the answer to Levenson's question, "What's going on here?" In the self psychology literature, the analyst becomes intentionally engaged in meeting the patient's developmental needs, which leads to the development of the transference–countertransference (self self-object) relationship and attempts to provide new self-object experiences that disconfirm (similar to Weiss et al. 1986) the patient's historical expectations as well as providing the patient with new developmental experiences that facilitate growth from archaic to mature self-object relationships. In self psychology an important distinction that parallels Stern's views of the importance of formulating unformulated experience is the difference between archaic and mature self-object relations, which involves the patient's ability to use language as opposed to action in expressing needs, organizing relationships, and registering and experiencing self-objects.

Self psychology has developed a theory of *self-object transferences* that defines patterns of relationships as either mirroring or idealizing self-object transferences. Self-object transferences are relationships that provide the individual with important psychological input: relationships that maintain a sense of self-cohesiveness and connectedness and when absent lead to an intense experience of fragmentation anxiety. Motivation in self psychology and in interpersonal psychoanalysis focuses on the need for self-cohesion, the development of goals and ideals, and the need for human attachments, whether healthy or pathological. This view of motivation, which emphasizes the critical importance of relationships that maintain and affirm the self, is similar to Fairbairn's (1954) idea that libido is object seeking and not pleasure seeking and Erickson's (1959) concept of identity.

Kohut (1984) presents an interesting example of a conscious choice in the provision of a new experience of a self self-object and the use of the psychoanalytic relationship to facilitate growth and provide new experiences for the healthy progressive development of the self, emphasizing self-expression and the anticipation and satisfaction of needs. The following example illustrates important aspects of the underlying value structure of theories of the self and suggests Kohut's implicit critique of the Freudian emphasis on the importance of external reality, the analytic frame (money), acting out, and the analyst's function of representing the prohibitions and restrictions of the reality principle. Kohut describes the following situation, which I believe suggests a provocative stance toward the traditional psychoanalytic establishment.

> One of my analysands, a forty-year-old university professor, began his analysis with me—a previous analysis, ten years earlier, had relieved him of some circumscribed inhibitions but had left him dissatisfied about a persistent restrictedness of his personality and lifestyle—by saying that he would like to postpone the payment of my fees for several months because he wanted to make a down payment

on some property in a Colorado resort, a favorable opportunity, to which he had committed himself at this point. Would I be willing to wait for the payments? My reply—not without misgivings at that time—was that, yes, as far as my finances were concerned, I could wait. But I added that, although I appreciated the realistic issue that had prompted him to make the request, I did not know what else might be involved for him. It might well be, I said, that we would later discover that his request and my compliance with it had a significance for him that went beyond what we could know at this point. . . . I ultimately became convinced that the patient, a very moral, straitlaced person, had neither embroiled me in a delinquent maneuver by inducing me to accede to his request nor "acted out" a specific drive wish from childhood. He had simply begun his analysis with an act that expressed the hope that this analysis, perhaps in contrast to the previous analysis, would be for him and not for the analyst, that is, not for me. As we recognized years later, the buying of the property did in fact reinstate a situation from his early life: a situation away from home in which, for brief periods, he could give himself over to expansive, imaginative, creative play with an alter ego friend. For short periods he could be temporarily unencumbered by the stifling restrictions to his creative potentials that had been exposed at home. [p. 73]

The values expressed in Kohut's illustration are critical aspects of both interpersonal psychoanalysis and self psychology, and focus on the development of the self as capable of authentic expression, the capacity to find relationships that can satisfy the individual's needs, and the importance of joyful fulfillment. Kohut's willingness to accept and to participate in the patient's delay paying his fee in order to buy a vacation house illustrates an enactment in which the patient is able to grow from an archaic to a mature self-object relationship in which the expression of the patient's emotional needs develop from an early mode of action to the capacity to verbalize his experiences, and the therapist's parallel movement from being behaviorally responsive to verbally explaining.

Atwood and colleagues (1989), contemporary self psychological theorists, describe experiences of "entanglement" that occur between patient and analyst as aspects of either intersubjective conjunction or intersubjective disjunction. Intersubjective conjunctions occur when "the principles structuring the patient's experiences give rise to expressions that are assimilated into closely held similar central configurations in the psychological life of the therapist," while intersubjective disjunctions occur when the therapist "assimilates the material expressed by the patient into configurations that significantly alter its meaning for the patient" (p. 555). They believe that these intersubjective situations can either facilitate or obstruct the progress of treatment to the degree that the analyst or therapist has the capacity for self-reflective awareness of one's own organizing principles and patterns of self-object relationships. Stolorow and Brandshaft (1987) have focused on the critical importance of clear, authentic communication through clarifying the analyst's failures in empathy in the process of being responsive to the patient's developmental or self-object needs. In the interpersonal approach, the focus is often on the repetition of historical relationship schemas, and the ability to describe the unformulated, affectively and historically distorted aspects of the evolving clinical process. Both approaches view the ability to verbalize and explain the complicated and newly constructed relationship between patient and analyst as the key to analytic growth and change. For both theories of the self the central focus is in the movement from inchoate, unconscious (unarticulated) organizations of action and experience to rational explanations, linking the past with the present and including recognition of the analyst's participation, affects, and history in the evolving narrative structures.

THE PERSON AS SUBJECT

The third psychoanalytic model of the person is that of the person as a subject. This model differs from the previous models in that it is not identified or defined by a single contemporary school of psychoanalysis. Ogden (1992) suggests that the person as a subject is implied in Kleinian theory and in Winnicott's extension of object relations theory. The concept of the person as a subject reflects an evolving postmodern critique of traditional psychoanalysis that has been strongly influenced by concepts drawn from existentialism and deconstructionist thought in philosophy and literature (Frie and Reiss 2001). The model of the person as subject reflects a postmodern focus on language, the ambiguity of meaning, the existence of multiple realities, issues of political and personal power, and the pervasive impact of culture in defining psychic and material reality. The model of the person as a subject is an amalgam of Kleinian object relations theory, social constructionism, feminist psychoanalysis, Lacanian theory, and deconstructionist literary criticism. Although these approaches to defining the person have not developed as a single articulated theory, they incorporate several essential dimensions and values that differ from the classical model of the person as ego and the interpersonal and self psychological models of the person as a self. A critical element in the views of the person as a subject, and one that defines the postmodern perspective, is an emphasis on language as a means of creating meaning and reality and as a powerful tool influencing and controlling the other's experience of self and reality. Lacan, more than any other contemporary psychoanalyst, has focused on the relationship between language and psychoanalysis that is reflected in the frequently repeated phrase that the unconscious is organized as a language (Dor 1998). Lacan (1977) believed that all experience is mediated through language (culture), and his theory focuses on the relationship between signifiers (words) and the signified (objects).

Lacan (1977) introduced the concept of the subject in psychoanalysis in an attempt to move beyond the mechanical, biological perspective of drive theory and ego psychology's emphasis on conscious choice and adaptation to external reality. Lacan contrasts the idea of the ego as an organization that adapts to the world of social roles, parental images, wishes and desires with a concept of the subject as an alienated center of desire that comes into being through the development of language and the separation of being into conscious and unconscious realms. Lacan's approach involves a rereading of Freud from the perspective of structuralism and linguistic theory, which focuses on relationships between signifiers and the signified and between signifiers and other signifiers that create networks of meanings. For Lacan, the analyst's task is to evoke the individual's capacity to speak his/her unconscious meaning and desire as different from that of the other through mapping the network of signifiers or meanings.

Lacan (1978) thought of subjectivity as an expression of unconscious meanings and as located in the unconscious:

> I am not saying that Freud introduces the concept of the subject into the world—the subject as distinct from psychical functions, which is a myth, a confused nebulosity—since it was Descartes who did this. But I am saying that Freud addresses the subject in order to say to

him the following, which is new—*Here, in the field of the dream, you are at home. Wo es war, soll Ich warden.* This does not mean as some execrable translation would have it, *Le moi doit deloger la ca* (the ego must dislodge the id). See how Freud—and in a formula worthy in resonance of the pre-Socratics— is translated in French. It is not a question of the ego in this *soll Ich warden*; the fact is that throughout Freud's work—one must recognize its proper place—the *Ich* is the complete, total locus of the network of signifiers, that is to say, the subject, *where it was*, where it has always been, the dream. . . . *Where it was*, the *Ich*—the subject, not psychology—the subject must come into existence. And there is only one method of knowing that one is there, namely to map the network. [p. 44]

In an interesting review of the literature, Leary (1994) suggests that the development of concepts of the person as a subject is intertwined with the contemporary transformation of psychoanalysis, from a positivist discipline that focuses on the cause-and-effect relationship to a hermeneutic discipline that focuses on how meaning is created. This postmodern interest in language and the creation of meaning is reflected in the idea of narrative (Schafer 1992), social construction (Hoffman 1991), the analyst's implicit referential activity (Jacobs 1993), and the development of the capacity to use symbols (Ogden 1994, Segal 1957, Winnicott 1971). An important difference in how language is conceptualized exists between many American analysts, who see language as a one-dimensional, rational system of representation and communication, and many European and Latin-American analysts, who have been influenced by Klein and view language in terms of levels of symbolization, whether it is experienced as concrete, reflecting a paranoid-schizoid organization of experience, or as symbolic, reflecting a depressive organization of experience. In contrast to the American representational view of language, those analysts influenced by Kleinian theory have consistently emphasized the capacity to move between the concrete language of the paranoid position, in which the symbol and the symbolized are experienced as identical, and the capacity to use symbols, which is a function of the depressive position. The capacity to use symbols, which is different from the capacity for abstract thought, is a critical element in the development of subjectivity, focusing on the creative as contrasted to the representational aspects of language. This distinction in how language is conceptualized has important implications for the process of analysis and the development of patients' subjectivity.

The postmodern view of a patient's experience of alienation and deadness differs from that described by interpersonal and self psychological analysts where the experience of alienation is primarily thought of as a disconnection between the individual and his/her environment and the social or familial failure in responding to the developing individual's needs. Theories that focus on the person as a subject see the experience of alienation as an inevitable aspect of being human, a dialectic between two psychic states: being an object and being a subject (Winnicott 1971); a slave and a master (Benjamin 1998); subject to and subject of (Kennedy 1997); the paranoid-schizoid and depressive positions (Klein 1946a), and symmetrical and asymmetrical organizations of experience (Matte Blanco 1975, 1988). Theories of the person as a subject define psychic structure as a dialectic between two potentially parallel, cohesive, separate organizations of experience that bring into the center of the psychoanalytic stage a fundamental and inevitable dichotomy of being an object, a thing, in an alienated, deadened state or as a subject, feeling alive and present. This concept of the person suggests that any event is experienced differently as a subject and as an object. For example, motivational states experienced as an object are felt to be impersonal forces but when experienced as a subject are felt to be personal experiences of desire and agency. The dilemma of being a subject and being an object is at the heart of contemporary life as it is represented in contemporary poetry, art, film, and literature.

Ogden (1995) focused on the affective state of being an object as an experience of deadness, which encompasses the transference–countertransference relationship and may be seen as a failure in the development of subjectivity. Ogden (1992), Rucker and Lombardi (1998), and Kennedy (1997) suggest that Klein's and Winnicott's theories provide the cornerstone of a dialectical theory of being both an object and a subject. Kennedy, in commenting on Klein's contribution to this concept of the person as subject, points to the development of multiple modes of experience in which language is not simply a representation or a distortion of external reality but that "the subject that does the experiencing goes in and out of different structural positions . . . movement away from and toward the possibility of some sort of integrating organization" (p. 561), which is based on the apprehension of experience in either the paranoid-schizoid or the depressive positions. The Kleinian approach does not focus on the discovery and clarification of past or present experience, but rather on the development of symbolic experience that leads to the development of a new psychological entity, the person as a subject. Ogden (1992) captures this important element in the Kleinian view of the psychoanalytic process when he says that "analysis is not simply a method of uncovering the hidden; it is more importantly a process of creating an analytic subject who had not previously existed" (p. 619). It would appear that for Ogden the coming into being of the person as a subject is an aspect of a dialectical relationship in which the person is both an object and a subject.

Winnicott (1971) developed Kleinian theory into an explicit, two-person theory, where the person potentially organizes and experiences the world as both a subject and an object. In his important paper "The Use of an Object," Winnicott (1969) describes the individual's complex multiple experiences of being both a subject and an object and the experience of the other as either a subject or an object, which results in four possible relational organizations. Winnicott defines one possible relational configuration as the experience of the other as a *subjective object*, which is a function of projective and introjective identification and reflects an experience in which the analyst is the container for the patient's projections. He also describes a state of being an *objective subject*, in which the individual is able to be aware of the other's internal experience of subjectivity; of having his/her own internal experience, of personal feelings, of a unique history and a particular relationship. The experience of the other as an objective subject is an achievement and involves both the capacity to be fully alive and to recognize the other in terms of gratitude for having suffered through the experience of being an object during the hateful and destructive rages of the paranoid position. From this perspective, the experience of deadness can be thought of as that of being an object, of an absence of subjective experience.

Masud Khan (1974) illustrates the dialectical relationship between the experience of being a subject and being an object and the development of the patient's experience of subjectivity through the analyst's use of his own internal (subjective, symbolic) experience in facilitating the patient's growth. Khan (1974) describes the case of a young woman who is promiscuous and spends much of her time in analysis describing her sexual relationships with men, which she experiences as emotionally dead. The patient's history involves many traumatic events that she also described in a deadened way, suggesting that she has not been affected by these traumatic experiences. The traumatic events included both parents having died while she was still quite young and her stepfather seducing her and maintaining a sexual relationship with her from early adolescence through her young-adult years, which encompassed the beginning of treatment.

I want to focus on Khan's (1974) interpretation, which was in response to an evolving transference in which the patient asked him whether he was a Pathan chieftain after having read that older Pathan chieftains adopt a young boy as a protégé with whom they may have a sexual relationship. The patient's interest in this aspect of Khan's background can be understood as a derivative of her incestuous oedipal relationship and an expression of her own desires to be sexually special to a father surrogate. Khan's interpretation suggests a refusal to replay the relationship that existed between her and her stepfather while simultaneously appreciating its positive potential. In response to her question whether the information about the special relationship between the elder chieftain and the young boy was true, Khan said, "It was, though not everyone could indulge this very *specialized* and *responsible* luxury. She laughed" (p. 239, italics added). He followed this direct comment with a long interpretation that explained his view of the patient's dissociated experience of her subjectivity and provides an illustration of the model of the person as both a subject and an object:

> I started by saying that I had been wondering all these months what made her come to these interviews, and today for the first time I could see that the bond between her and me was like between the young boy and the elderly Pathan chieftain of the article. I now related this to the paradox in my subjective impression of her physical presence in the sessions and what she had been telling me about orificial exploitation of her female body by others. That she had always struck me as a handsome person, with very little sexual tantalization to her way of being a body. That now it was possible for me to say to her that she was two distinct persons in her body presence: a girl and a boy. That she presented herself as an *object* to herself and others as a *girl*, but as a *subject* she was a *boy*, and this no one had recognized so far, not even she herself. That she had been coming to me to try and help me see this duality in her experience of her body and recognize it, and state it. [p. 239]

It is interesting that the locus of this interpretation is primarily within the analyst's internal, subjective experience, and its focus is the recognition of an unconscious aspect of the patient's subjectivity rather than a clarification of history, transference, or a focus on the reality principle. In this example Khan merges the patient's unarticulated experience of a special oedipal relationship, the image of the elder Pathan chieftain and his young protégé, and the analytic relationship between Khan and the patient illustrating the dialectic between the patient's experience of herself as an object and as a subject and of the analyst's focus on elaborating this dialectic in the development of subjectivity.

A COMPARISON OF MODELS: WHO SPIT IN MY SOUP?

Levenson (1983) contrasts hypothetical Freudian, interpersonal, and Kleinian psychoanalysts' responses to a patient's dream that someone spit in his soup. I want to use this hypothetical example to illustrate the clinical differences between these three models of the person as ego, self, or subject. For the Freudian, the manifest dream would be a path into the exploration of a set of underlying motives, causes, and structures through which the patient gets satisfaction for his desires though maintaining his masochistic relational patterns. The Freudian interpretive strategy would focus on the patient's repetition of childhood wishes and anxieties that caused the patient to perceive and distort his experiences in the analytic relationship as devalued, castrated, and feminine. In this view, the content of the dream, the manifest experience, would be seen as a defensive structure covering the actual underlying structures and wishes. The analytic goal would be for the patient to develop a more realistic perception of the analytic relationship, and become more autonomous and separate from the incestuous objects of the past, which are incorporated in the dream.

The interpersonal analyst would also see the dream as a distortion; however, from this perspective it would be a distorted and encoded commentary on the current relationship between analyst and patient. Here the analytic goal would be to understand what happened between the analyst and patient that the patient needed to represent as the analyst spitting in the soup. From the interpersonal perspective, the focus is on the patient's purposeful distortion and deformation of his experience and self so as to be unable to perceive, comment on, and present his view of the analytic relationship in a more authentic and free way. The masochism of the Freudian position is the low self-esteem, self-denigration, anxious attachment, and need for security reflected in the repetition of archaic relationship patterns for the interpersonal analysis.

The hypothetical Kleinian analyst can be thought of as representing the view of the person as a subject. The Kleinian, like the interpersonal psychoanalyst, would see the dream as an expression of the patient's experience of the analytic relationship. However, it would not be seen as a distortion of the patient's experience of the analyst, but rather as a dissociated, concrete, paranoid expression of the reality of the patient's experience in analysis; for the patient the dream would probably be a shameful reality. The focus of the dream would be on the transformation of the patient's envious experience of the analyst's words from a warm, nurturing flow of milk to disgusting, poisonous excrements that are to be evacuated rather than taken in. Through projective and introjective identification, both analyst and patient would alternately be experienced as poisoning the other, as forcing destructive substances into the other's body openings. The analyst's words and the patient's words would be experienced concretely as spit, feces, or semen, suggesting that the patient experiences the world in the paranoid mode and is unable to symbolize experience. The focus of the analytic discourse would be on transforming the dream from a concrete expression of the unconscious paranoid fantasy in which the world, the analyst, and the patient are experienced as a persecutory, poisoned breast into a symbolic expression that recognizes the inevitable destructiveness of human relationships.

One difference between the Kleinian position and the ego psychological and interpersonal positions is that rather than viewing the dream as either a historical or current transference distortion, the Kleinian analyst would see it as an expression of the patient's dissociated, concrete externalized experience of aggression, which through the analyst's processes of reverie (Bion 1962) and the imaginative elaboration of the patient's unconscious fantasy, the patient's concrete and externalized experience of persecution can be transformed into a symbolic, internal experience of the patient's aggression. In this model the analytic transformation is not from a distorted, albeit understandable, experience, to a more realistic or consensual understanding of the transference—countertransference situation, but from a concrete to a symbolic experience of the aggression in the transference–countertransference relationship. In the Kleinian model the analyst identifies with the patient's projection, and through reverie the analyst's symbolic and affective elaboration of the patient's concrete projective identifications facilitates the patient's internalization of these aggressive feelings, which allows for the development of a sense of aliveness and of subjectivity.

CLINICAL ILLUSTRATION: THE PHANTOM PENIS

This case illustrates the analyst's use of reverie in resolving an impasse in the treatment of a patient who experienced herself as subjectively dead, while able to successfully function in the external world as an object. There is a pathological split between the patient's experience of being an object and of being a subject. In this illustration, the analyst, through reverie and identification with the patient's experience of being an object, was able to develop in a concrete, proto-symbolic language within the paranoid position, a transitional experience that facilitated the development of the patient's experience of being a subject. It is important to note the shift in the form of the analyst's participation from the objective, denotatively specific language of the external world into the dense, surrealistic, or poetic language of the subjective world. This shift involves the dedifferentiation of the analyst's and patient's experience of self and other and a movement from a dialogue that focused on the objective or consensual description of experience to one that focuses on internal, personal experience in which the life or death issues of aggression and destructiveness moved into the center of the analytic relationship. This process is a step toward the development of the patient's subjectivity, and it involves a shift from a positivist to a constructivist perspective and includes a loss of the sense of objective, consensual reality and the elaboration of multiple, shifting realities.

The patient, a woman in her early 30s, had been in psychoanalytic psychotherapy for many years. At the beginning of treatment she was a very troubled person who was addicted to drugs. The patient is now drug free, deeply involved in work and in a stable love relationship. She is a lesbian and says that she feels and thinks about herself as a boy and that this has been the case as long as she can remember. She describes herself as a having been a tomboy and believes that she had probably been sexually abused. In high school she was promiscuous with men and be-lieves that she was always high when she would have sex, and then sub-sequently would feel abused, used, and exploited. Her mother had a severely disordered body image with frequent hypochondriacal concerns that resulted in many unnecessary medical procedures. The patient was very close to her father, who was a successful, aggressive businessman and made many overtly sexual comments about the patient and her friends.

The analyst, a man, felt that there was an impasse in the treatment that focused on his difficulty in understanding what the patient meant when she said that she "wished" that she was a boy. He interpreted this as a failure in her identification with her mother, as a metaphor for being powerful and autonomous, or a wish to be like father rather than like mother. These interpretive efforts did not seem to affect the patient's experience in the analytic relationship or in her life. The patient also refused to talk about her sexual relationships, because she felt that the therapist "represented an authority figure like my parents or teachers."

Although the patient felt that she had made a great deal of progress, she resented the analysis as part of a process of socialization that has made her feel alienated and despairing about her life, which she experiences as repetitive, dull, and affectively dead. She describes each day as the same joyless pursuit: getting up, going to work, coming home. She feels as if she has lost her former self and is very unhappy about her inability to even fantasize about acting out, as she had been able to do before analysis. The patient feels hopeless and beaten down, and wants to know when she will feel alive again. The patient sees herself as successful, al-though she feels like an object, pushed along in life, with an absence of a sense of agency, desire, and pleasure. With great despair, after describ-ing the lethargy and pain of having to get dressed and choosing her cloth-ing for the coming day, she asked the analyst how he managed to face each day, to get dressed, and to go to work. At this point the analyst withdrew into his own thought process, thinking about his difficulty facing the day, choosing his clothes and getting dressed in spite of know-ing that he felt good and deeply satisfied at work. In a seemingly spon-taneous expression of both empathy and mutuality, he described some of his morning struggles to the patient. After being told of the analyst's difficult moments in getting dressed for work, the patient again asked how he got over it. The analyst surprised himself in his response, which was personal, strange, and concrete. "Socks," he said, "there are socks that I love—not that I like, but that I love. I put them on and then I feel good." The patient immediately began to cry and reported feeling better as she left the session.

The next session the patient came in with a great deal of energy and said that she wanted to talk about two dreams. The first dream was about a woman in her office who had a really big dick. I'm playing with it so she won't fuck me. The second dream is about a male star on a soap opera who wanted me to fuck him with a "strap-on." He is a real goody, goody—Brenda's twin. The therapist asks if they are identical twins. The patient laughs and says what a stupid question, how can they be identical twins. The therapist did not understand this, until the patient said how could a boy and a girl be identical twins. The therapist then asked what a strap-on is, and the patient contemptuously replied that it is a strap-on dick. In response to the analyst's questions, she described it in detail and for the first time comfortably described her sexual activities including her experience of pleasure in her "penis," which reminded the analyst of the phantom limb phenomenon. This session was the first in a series in which the patient's experience of being subjectively a sexual man was contrasted with her experience of being an object as a woman. As with many patients the confounding of subjectivity, gender, sexuality, and a resulting failure in the development of subjectivity were critical issues in this patient's treatment (Khan 1974, McDougall 1989, Winnicott 1971).

I want to focus on the transition from the deadened experience of the patient as an object who needed to put on a disguise each morning to enter the world, to the enlivened experience in which deeply dissociated aspects of the patient's experience of her sexuality and gender, her aggression, and her experience of herself as a subject became available in the analytic discourse. This transition occurred in conjunction with the analyst's identification with the patient's experience of being an object in the world and his seemingly spontaneous, deeply subjective, proto-symbolic, and poetic comment about loving his socks. Rather than thinking about this intervention as spontaneous, unwitting, or impulsive, it reflects the analyst's values and theoretical beliefs in the importance of his own reverie as a way of joining the patient in a dialogue of inchoate meanings that parallels Winnicott's use of the squiggle game, another form of complex unconscious communication. The analyst's comment about his socks represented a switch from the experience of analyst and patient as objects to the experience of analyst and patient as subjects. The analyst's countertransference identification involved his parallel feelings of deadness and a lack of vitality. He identified with the patient's experience and recognized his own daily experience of entering the world of objects where he must also be an object. To survive his daily routine, like the Phoenix rising from the ashes, or Sisyphus pushing the boulder up the hill, he is reborn each day through putting on his socks. This concrete proto-symbol becomes a metaphor that both patient and analyst can recognize (Benjamin 1990) and identify with, and through which the patient can experience the analyst's subjectivity—that he also suffers the loss of subjectivity in his daily life. The patient's developing experience of becoming a subject involves an integration of the split-off experiences of sexuality and gender, which were initially expressed through concrete experiences of dress and which became proto-symbolic and metaphoric aspects of subjectivity.

Ogden (1994) describes the use of reverie in the development of "the analytic third," a mutually created subjective experience that is separate from but includes aspects of the patient's and the analyst's unconscious, symbolized, subjective experience. The concept of the analytic third extends Klein's view of symbolization and Winnicott's concept of transitional experiences in the development of the capacity for symbolic thought and for subjectivity (Segal 1981). In this example, as in many others (Newirth 1996), this shift into the realm of transitional or subjective experience is a result of the analyst initiation of the transitional experience through a dedifferentiation of objective and subjective experiences in the analytic dialogue. This treatment approach, which focuses on the development of subjectivity, shifts the analytic algorithm from one that focuses on the acceptance of reality or on the failures in communication and the patient's ability to articulate authentic self-experience to one that involves the movement from the externalized concrete experiences of the paranoid mode to the capacity for symbolic poetry-like moments in the depressive mode of experience.

3

Psychic Reality, Omnipotence, and the Development of Subjectivity

We experience ourselves as both victims and heroes; as acted upon by the forces of history and as having made the decisions that direct our lives; as either filled with guilt or as finding ourselves the protagonist in a cosmic tragedy. From a scientific perspective we live in a world of causality where our actions, our lives, can be understood through elaborating the social, historical, and biological factors that have converged to define a particular life, a person. From moral, philosophical, romantic, or religious perspectives we live in a world of choice, of free will, of personal responsibility. Erich Fromm (1964) suggests that one of Freud's important contributions was his ability to integrate the scientific perspective of determinism with the romantic and philosophical perspectives of free will, uniting these two incompatible trends as the architectural elements of psychoanalytic theory. It is within the context of the integration of these two central trends in Western thought that we can understand Freud's (Breuer and Freud 1895) struggle with Breuer to move beyond a simple causal theory of hysteria in which the patient's symptoms reflect the isolation of unacceptable affects that, when discharged, cleaned out like a gangrenous infection, would return the patient to a state of health. It was Freud's early rejection of the simple explanations of hypnoid states and the seduction theory as the cause of hysteria that allowed for the development of this more complex integration of the scientific with the philosophical, romantic, and religious perspectives of individual choice and responsibility.

Freud's (1905a) rejection of the seduction theory and his recognition of the dynamic importance of the patient's fantasies and wishes led to the development of the structural model, which incorporated both the scientific and romantic perspectives through defining two spheres of the individual's experience of reality, psychic reality,[1] and material reality. While material reality reflected the domain of scientific causality and universal laws, psychic reality reflected the domain of the phenomenological, individual, romantic, and superstitious elements of human experience. Unlike other dualities in Freud's thought (Bloom 1985) (primary and secondary process thought, pleasure and pain, male and female), the concepts of psychic and material reality were structured in a dialectical rather than a hierarchical relationship. This dialectical conceptualization of material and psychic reality maintained a tension between the scientific and the moral or romantic viewpoints, freeing psychoanalysis from the constraints of a simple learning theory, and focusing attention on the complex relationship between an inner psychic organization and the individual's actions and experiences in the external world.

The concepts of material and psychic reality are the precursors to contemporary interest in subjectivity and intersubjectivity. However, the dialectical relationship between psychic and material reality provides an important contrast to contemporary theories of subjectivity and intersubjectivity, which are largely phenomenological. Implicit in the dialectical concept of psychic and material reality are three dimensions that are critical for theories of subjectivity and intersubjectivity and that focus on issues of agency and personal responsibility, of dual or multiple modes of experience or information processing, and of omnipotence and grandiosity in pathological healthy development.

---

1. The question of the current status of the concept of psychic reality was the theme of the 1995 conference of the International Psychoanalytic Association; some of the ideas presented at that conference are cited in this chapter.

PSYCHIC REALITY, PERSONAL RESPONSIBILITY, AND AGENCY

Psychoanalytic experience and the psychoanalytic situation is centered in the paradox of personal responsibility—that we are not responsible for our personal actions, which are caused by universal drives and early experience, and that we are responsible for our personal actions, which reflect our wishes. Friedman (1995) maintains that the concept of psychic reality was at the heart of Freud's argument that symptoms were caused by children's wishes rather than by the events that had been inflicted on them, establishing the conceptual ground for concepts of personal responsibility or agency within the context of a scientific theory of causal relations. Friedman captures a critical aspect of the psychoanalytic paradox of personal responsibility and agency, which he describes as the integration of the experience of "inflicted fact," that which has happened to the individual in childhood, and the "purposeful editing," which represents the individual's memory, the process of construction of his or her life. Friedman seems to be critical of self psychologists, intersubjective theorists, and others who minimize the experience of personal responsibility and present a purely phenomenological approach to psychic reality through an emphasis on the elaboration of inflicted fact. Friedman believes that these theorists choose to give up the dialectical notion of psychic and material reality "so that they will be free to enjoy the purely intelligible world of narrative and are content to describe treatment as the multiplication of viewpoints" (p. 27).

The concepts of personal responsibility and agency are the critical, albeit unspoken, subtext in most theories of psychoanalytic treatment and reflect a capacity to personally assimilate and understand the dialectic of psychic and material reality: the purposefulness that exists both in and out of awareness and the organized processes of editing through which we construct the narrative of our life experience. Schafer (1978) presents an interesting conceptualization of the structural model in which he reinterprets the biomechanical concepts of repression and drive derivative as involving processes of disowned action, which he believes inhibits the individual's capacity to create a life history, a personal narrative in which individuals become the protagonist, an agent, at the center of their life history. Schafer describes this process of constructing a narrative, a life history, as a development of the rule of free association, which he sees as a providing the analyst with a license to ask the patient contextual questions such as, "What made you think of that just now?" or "What made you say that in this context?" He suggests that rather than allowing for the expression of impulses, of drive derivatives, the rule of free association brings into the foreground the underlying purposefulness and meaning in the patient's symptoms, speech, and thoughts, which allows for the development of a life historical narrative in which the patient is both author and agent.

This view of psychoanalysis as a hermeneutic or narrative process is a complex idea that suggests two problems in relation to the analyst's authority. First, it transforms the analyst's authority from the one who knows, a representative of the reality principle, to a Socratic listener, an editor, an active participant in the creative process. Second, it raises the question of truth, of who is to define truth, and what are the criteria for a successful analysis and a successful narrative.

Faimberg (1995), a French psychoanalyst, addresses the joint issues of authority and interpretation and is critical of simple phenomenological approaches, which through excluding the dialectic between psychic and material reality "fall prey to a certain solipsism (i.e., that the subject is the only knowable or existent thing)" (p. 10). For Faimberg, the problem of multiple phenomenological perspectives is the solipsism inherent in one-person constuctivist approaches. She describes how this problem arises in the transference when there is a discrepancy between what the analyst says and what the patient hears, which she thinks of as the patient's experiencing her interpretations as being spoken by a historical figure. Faimberg presents an interesting approach that centers on her becoming an active participant struggling with her patients' projections, and she asks the question, "Why does B (a patient) listen to the interpretation as though it could *only* mean that she is 'someone of no value' and that she *only* comes up with foul smelling projects?" (p. 12). Faimberg suggests that this transference dilemma is resolved through the analyst's helping the patient develop a decentered way of listening, which she describes as learning "to listen to how I listen to her and thus to become able to listen to herself. I am trying to *create* an intersubjective and an intrasubjective link: two subjects listening in a decentered way" (p. 11, italics added). Faimberg's concept of the development of decentered listening as an important element in the development of a narrative constructed by two people is similar to Ogden's (1994) concepts of the development of the analytic third. Ogden believes that the process of analysis involves the development of a new set of experiences, a new way of organizing or creating the facts of a person's life that includes a shift from concrete or fixed modes of experiencing to symbolic modes of experiencing that are mutually created by analyst and analysand and lead to the development of a new analytic subject, a new and more complex level of consciousness. Both Ogden and Faimberg present approaches to the experience of psychic reality and agency that focus on the analyst's transformation of the patient's experiences of life as a set of fixed "historical facts" to an understanding of the many possible psychic realities that exist simultaneously through the development of a decentered mode of listening. This view of the evolution of psychic reality focuses on the analyst's capacity to transform the patient's literal or concrete experience of historical or inflicted fact into an experience of alternative views of reality through developing a mode of listening to one's self with possibility and compassion, which becomes internalized as aspects of agency, authorship, and subjectivity. This leads to the development of the capacity to experience compassion for the tragic aspects of life, to have fully developed characters in the evolving narrative and not simply the heroes and demons of melodrama.

PSYCHIC REALITY AND MULTIPLE MODES OF GENERATING EXPERIENCE

Kleinian theory maintains a focus on the individual's developing capacity to think, to organize, and to generate experience within both the paranoid-schizoid and the depressive positions. Kleinian theory has focused on the cognitive dimensions of how an individual comes to know the world and to experience it, including Klein's (1975) early interest in inhibitions in learning, fantasy as an organizing process (Isaacs 1948), differences between concrete and symbolic thinking (Segal 1979), and the process of transformation of passively experienced raw experience into actively organized personal experience (Bion 1962).

Britton (1995) focuses on an aspect of this cognitive dimension of the individual's modes of organizing and generating experience in the evolution of psychic reality from simple, literal, or concrete melodramatic narratives of good and bad, victim and hero, to ones that include the tragic complexity of life and the capacity to utilize more complex symbolic modes of thought. He sees a critical aspect of the analytic process as facilitating the process of transforming the patient's concrete experiences of psychic reality as an imposed or external certainty in the paranoid-schizoid position into the psychic reality of the depressive position, which involves an internal experience of possibility, of symbolic content, and of personal agency. Britton describes psychic reality as encompassing conscious and unconscious beliefs, counterbeliefs, and the annihilation of beliefs, which he distinguishes from the process of knowing which involve reality testing and external confirmation. For Britton, equating belief and knowledge is characteristic of the concreteness of the paranoid-schizoid position while "emancipation from the equation of belief with knowledge is an aspect of working through in the depressive position" (p. 22). He describes the analytic process as one that brings the patient's unconscious beliefs into an alive conscious transference–countertransference enactment that results in the patient's relinquishing the absolute certainty or the concrete quality of his/her unconscious beliefs. Although essentially agreeing with the dialectical relationship between psychic and material reality, the Kleinian approach to the development of the experience of agency differs from Friedman's and Faimberg's interpretative approaches. The most significant difference in Britton's clinical approach is that the analytic process utilizes the concrete or paranoid mode of experience; he does not question the patient's beliefs but rather identifies with the patient's unconscious experience, dedifferentiating the transference–countertransference experience and articulating the patient's projections rather than focusing on the discrepancy between the patient's and analyst's differing experience.

Britton presents the following clinical vignette to illustrate the process of working through the patient's experience of his unconscious concrete belief system and how these beliefs are the underlying organizations (fantasies) of his ongoing experience of psychic reality. It is interesting to note how Britton accepts the patient's attributions, and instead of focusing on reality testing he focuses on the dilemma that the patient's unconscious beliefs create in the current analytic relationship. The patient is a man who obscures and denies his persecutory, paranoid beliefs, substituting manic, idealized, generous counterbeliefs for more complex knowledge, and becomes intellectually self-critical and attacking.

I [Britton] said: "Here also you invest everything in me; that is, you credit me with more than you have in the way of a good opinion of me. When you idealize me like that, you yourself feel favoured and welcome. This relieves you of your apprehensions about our relationship and me. When you lose the idea that I am good and you well off, fortunate, and favoured, I think you are exposed to a sudden sharp discomfort, a fleeting painful doubt about me."

The patient was then thoughtful and then said he was thinking of the story of the students who died in their flat because of the landlord's negligence. The gas fire due to his disregard of its defects poisoned them. (I have a gas fire in my room.)

I commented that when he puts himself in my hands, that aspect of him that should protect his vulnerable self and take seriously his misgivings about his treatment prefers to dismiss danger in order to get on well with me on a basis of mutual esteem. So he allows himself to be, in effect, poisoned or buggered.

There was an intense silence, after which he said, "I thought last week when I spoke to you about my colleague's anal fissure and you said that it was an example of a condition that gets worse before it gets better. (I had linked this with analysis.) I understood what you meant about dilation as treatment but I thought you said it with (searching for a word) . . . relish. I thought it showed you're . . . um . . . can't think of the word . . ."

"Sadism?" I suggested. "You mean my sadism?" "That's right," he said. "I thought you were sadistic." [p. 21]

Britton views the unconscious and psychic reality as organized by processes of splitting and projective identification, through which unwanted unconscious wishes and impulses are evacuated or externalized so that the sadistic impulse is experienced in the analyst, and the generous, good impulse is experienced in the patient. Briton does not attempt to correct the patient's perception or fantasy but seems to enter into it, accepting the patient's psychic reality and attempting to articulate it. Britton explains this example as an attempt to "make the point that until a patient discovers that he really believes an idea, its correspondence, or lack of it, with external reality is irrelevant. His belief remains suspended, unconscious, unmodified, and universified, in parallel with a contrary belief" (p. 21). Britton seems to identify with the patient's disowned sadism, and rather than asserting a different view, attempts to articulate the patient's experience. This approach is based on the Kleinian theory of dual modes of organizing and generating experience involving the dimensions of paranoid-schizoid concrete and depressive symbolic experience within the domains of psychic and material reality. This brief dialogue illustrates Britton's attempt to articulate, to make more alive, the unconscious paranoid fantasy rather than to transform it through reality testing into a "consensual experience" of the transference–countertransference relationship. The emphasis here is on parallel modes of representing, organizing, and generating experience in the world, which Bion (1959) represented in the reversible equation $Pa{\leftrightarrow}D$ in order to emphasize the independent, constructive, and destructive potential in the dialectic between the paranoid-schizoid and the depressive modes of experience.

In a series of papers, Fonagy (1995, 1996, Target and Fonagy 1996) focuses on the development of the individual's cognitive abilities in defining psychic reality. Target and Fonagy (1996) describe two parallel forms of information processing that structure the individual's experience of material reality and psychic reality. They describe two modes of generating experience: the psychic equivalence mode and the pretend mode. The *psychic equivalence mode* is described as follows: "In a serious frame of mind, the child expects the internal world in himself and others to correspond to external reality, and subjective experience will often be distorted to match information coming from outside." The *pretend mode* is described as follows: "While involved in play, the child knows that internal experience may not reflect external reality. . . . In normal development the child integrates these two modes to arrive at the stage of *mentalization,* or the *reflective mode,* in which mental states can be experienced as representations. Inner and outer reality can then be seen as linked, yet are accepted as differing in important ways, and no longer have to be either equated or split off from each other" (p. 459).

In describing this developmental process, Target and Fonagy turn the more traditional relationship between psychic and material reality on its head, suggesting that the young child initially experiences the self as an extension of the other, of the external world, as an object, and that it is only through the development of play in the pretend mode that the child can begin to experience the self as a subject. They state that the young child in the mode of psychic equivalence is more inclined to fit "mind to the world" than "world to the mind" (p. 470), and that the child or adult in the mode of psychic equivalence is operating like a wind vane, molding experience to conform to one's perception of external reality.[2] The young child or adult who is unable to integrate the pretend mode with the mode of psychic equivalence will treat beliefs like knowledge, and will be unable to locate his or her experience within a reflective psychic reality made up of representations or possibilities rather than the facts of material reality. Target and Fonagy view the development of the capacity to use reflective processes and to focuses on minds, the other's inner world, as a critical aspect of the dialectic of psychic reality and material reality, including the awareness of the other as a separate locus of psychic experience. They believe that the development of self-reflective thinking, the capacity to mentalize or to know the other's internal experience, reflects the child's integration of the mode of psychic equivalence with the pretend mode, which is itself dependent on healthy two-person relationships with caregivers or others who are able to enter into the pretend mode of experience and to use reflective processes that focus on the child's mind, viewing the child as a feeling and thinking being. Fonagy's (1995) work extends Winnicott's theory of transitional experience into an empirical realm, providing support as well as developing a clinical application for work with small children.

PSYCHIC REALITY, GRANDIOSITY, AND OMNIPOTENCE

Failures in the development of a dialectical relationship between psychic and material reality are reflected in the clinical disturbances seen in alternating states of grandiosity and despair, which we have come to understand as narcissistic, schizoid, and borderline pathology. These experiences of affective and cognitive liability fluctuate between a manic, godlike grandiosity and the sense of worthlessness, being a thing pushed and pulled by the impersonal forces of the material world. At one moment grandiose patients present themselves as triumphant, having great pride, extraordinary self-confidence, and feeling superior, while at the

---

2. This concept is similar to Lacan's (1977) concept of the mirror stage and the register of the imaginary, in that both concepts suggest that the individual initially organizes experience as an extension of the other, or, in terms of the current chapter, as material reality.

next moment they feel despairing, empty, unreal, and cynical about the meaninglessness of life. A patient began a session talking in his usual elated spirit, joking about previous sessions, arrogant and angry about some delays in a current project; however, by the end of the session he was in a state of despair that was untouched by his earlier manic state as he poignantly described himself (in part-object terms) as an empty suit, a haircut. This patient appears to others as an extraordinarily competent, albeit grandiose, critical, and arrogant, person. However, he experiences himself as empty, despairing, powerless, and friendless, with no personal meaning or significance in the world. This patient's experience alternates between states of manic grandiosity and deadened meaningless experiences of merely being a cog in a machine that he does not control. His experience reflects what has been referred to either as grandiosity or omnipotence.

The concepts of grandiosity and omnipotence have been presented in the literature as interchangeable concepts with few attempts to differentiate their constructive or healthy qualities from their destructive, defensive, and affective qualities. The traditional psychoanalytic view has emphasized the negative aspects of grandiosity and omnipotence, seeing them in terms of the gratification of infantile and regressive wishes. From this perspective, grandiose states are seen as manic defenses, magical denials of anxiety and aggression, and as an avoidance of reality. Self psychologists and some object relations theorists have presented a more positive view of grandiosity. Kohut (1977) suggests that if the child does not find an admiring other for his early grandiose and exhibitionistic performances, then he/she will develop an extremely fragile self structure focused on action that attempts to maintain cohesiveness though archaic self-object relations. Balint (1968), Klein (1975b), Kohut (1984), Winnicott (1971), and others view grandiose, omnipotent, and magical behavior as crucial aspects in the development of positive and hopeful aspects of psychic reality, without which intimate relationships and the development of subjectivity would be impossible. Balint's (1968) often-cited example of asking his fearful, lethargic female patient to risk doing a somersault in the session can be understood as his encouraging her to enact her previously disowned exhibitionistic and omnipotent experience while she was being seen and recognized by a supportive and admiring other, so that she would be able to experience her own inner omnipotence. Similarly, Winnicott believes that the development of omnipotence, which grows out of the child being joined in illusory, magical, and surreal transitional experiences, is the precursor to the development of the true or subjective self and the capacity for creativity and for artistic, religious, and intimate experiences. In differentiating the concepts of grandiosity from omnipotence, I will focus on the dimensions of action (external activity) and thought (internal activity): reality and illusion, defense and adaptation, and health and pathology.

Freud (1914a) first addressed the issue of grandiosity in his paper "On Narcissism," which was written with several theoretical and political purposes in mind. Its most immediate purpose was to further explain paranoid dynamics and the failure of the reality principle, which he felt he had not completely explained in the Schreber case. It was also written in response to Jung's argument for a concept of nonsexual libido and as an attempt to include Ferenczi's (Greenberg 1990) concept of a stage of omnipotence in early development. Freud presented a rich description of the phenomenology of narcissism, a revision of drive theory to account for the movement away from reality and the gratification of the object world, and a moral critique of grandiose and omnipotent behavior and thought. Freud's highly critical view of grandiosity is clear in the following comment:

> This extension of the libido theory—in my opinion a legitimate one—receives reinforcement from a third quarter, namely, from our observations and views on the mental life of children and primitive peoples. In the latter we find characteristics which if they occurred singly, might be put down to megalomania: an overestimation of the power of their wishes and mental acts, "the omnipotence of thoughts," a belief in the thaumaturgic (that is, the miraculous) force of words, and a technique for dealing with the external world—magic—which appears to be a logical application of these grandiose premises. [p. 75]

From Freud's psychoanalytic perspective, my patient's grandiose state and his subsequent sense of despair would be seen as the inevitable failure of his grandiose defense, of his primitive, childlike belief in the omnipotence of his thoughts and words with which he tries to avoid awareness of his limitations as well as the importance of the reality principle. His intense feelings of despair, emptiness, and deadness would not be seen as an independent psychological event, but rather as the result of the failure of his grandiose defenses and the emergence of recognition that he cannot be the oedipal victor. His experience of himself as an empty suit, a haircut, would represent his difficulty in feeling that he can fill an adult role as well as intense castration anxiety in relation to social authority

Daniel Greenberg (1990) traces Freud's (1914a) struggle maintaining the libido theory, which had become weakened in his revision of drive theory in "Beyond the Pleasure Principle" (Freud 1920). Greenberg focuses on Freud's incorporation of Ferenczi's original concept of *primary narcissism*, which is described as a state

> of pleasure and the absence of desire in which the subject and object are merged. This pleasurable unity is split apart when the infant discovers the external object and begins to experience painful separation. In response to separation and discovery of the external object, the infant attempts to re-establish its earlier state of unity (nirvana principle). This attempt to re-establish unity would necessarily take on a two-fold, contradictory form. On the one hand, the infant could attempt to unite with external objects that would represent the life instincts and sexuality. On the other hand, the infant could attempt to eliminate objects altogether representing the death instinct and aggression. . . . In either case the result would be the same: *a psychological state of existence devoid of external objects*, a state which the unconscious equates with absolute pleasure, primary narcissism. [p. 278, italics added]

Greenberg describes Freud's difficulty in considering the idea of merger (between the self and other), which was central to Ferenczi's theory of narcissism and to experiences of omnipotence. Freud's antipathy to concepts of merger between self and other, between subject and object, arises from his view that merger represents a regressive, maternal, or religious organization of experience in contrast to a scientific perspective that demands a separation of subject and object. Freud's view of the dangers of merger as infantile, maternal, primitive behavior and his narrow concept of the scientific necessity of the separation of subject and object set the stage for the rejection of concepts of omnipotence and a literal interpretation of the death instinct as a wish to return to the inorganic. The *death instinct* was seen as motivation, a wish to return to the inorganic, rather than as a thought, a metaphor, or a symbolic statement describing an experience of identity or affect such as, "I feel dead" or "I am dead."

The difference between what we desire and who we are is an important distinction and underlies the difference between action and thought, between acting in the external world and elaborating internal experience. This distinction between action and thought, between internal and external, is critical for understanding the difference between grandiosity and omnipotence as alternative ways of reestablishing the pleasurable unity of subject and object that Ferenzci was attempting to describe. Grandiosity is finding unity through action, through eliminating all other objects in the world that leave the individual in a meaningless, empty, barren, and dead universe. Omnipotence, on the other hand, involves unity through merger with the object in which the self feels boundless, powerful, excited, and joyful. Religious rituals of merger, experiences of passionate love, and experiences of group identifications make use of this form of merger and develop experiences of omnipotence. Kluzer-Usuelli (1992) thinks of the death instinct within the context of issues of identity and connection rather than as a drive, and views Thanatos as "inassimilable otherness, as irreducible not-me." The death instinct can be thought of as reflecting the internal awareness, the thought and not the drive toward isolation, disconnection, meaninglessness, feelings of being inhuman, insignificant, one among many. Freud did not differentiate concepts of motivation from those that reflect an internal experience of identity, self-reflection, and metaphor.

An interesting clinical discussion of grandiosity as action reflects the patient's need to eliminate and destroy all objects in the world (Symington 1985) as part of an early survival function. Symington develops Bick's (1968) hypothesis that if the infant does not experience a secure parental holding environment, he has to hold himself together:

> He is driven to *act* in order to survive. His catastrophic fear is of a state of unintegration and spilling out into space and of never being found and held again. . . . The baby holds himself together in a variety of ways. He may focus his attention on a sensory stimulus—

visual, auditory, tactile, or olfactory. . . . He may engage in constant bodily movements which then feel like a continuous holding skin; if the movement stops, this may feel like a gap, a hole in the skin through which the self may spill out. . . . A third method consists of muscular tightening, a clinching together of particular muscle groups, and maintaining them in this rigid position. This is an attempt physically to hold everything so tightly together that there can be no gap through which spilling can occur. [p. 481, italics added]

These actions, which reflect the patient's needs to hold him-/herself together, are often experienced by the analyst as rejection by a grandiose individual who must act as if there is no other person in the world in order to maintain a sense of safety from feelings of unintegration and of the inhuman, inorganic experience of death and nonbeing.

Esther Bick describes the experience and necessity of grandiose action and the destruction of the awareness of the other in a session with a 6-year-old boy (Symington 1985). The boy had just crashed a metal car into a clay car that he had made and that represented himself.

Bick said the following: "He has to master everything so that he will not collapse, because he feels that there is no one, no mother to pick him up if he does collapse. He has to rely on himself and not depend on anyone. He has to be invincible, so that he says the plasticine car is not damaged when dropped, just as he wants to deny any damage or hurt he receives. James Bond is invincible. He is assailed by so many and such terrible things and he must deal with it all by himself, and see that he is cleverer than the enemy. This boy has to be James Bond. He can't rely on anybody; nobody is there to help him, so he must do it himself. It is not the aspect of James Bond which says, "I am the greatest, the best." That is not the issue. The issue here is: "I must be so clever, I must think and think in order to protect myself." [Symington 1985, p. 484]

In the transference, Bick was the mother whom the child felt to be unavailable. The child could not risk trusting her until he felt held, but he couldn't feel held through his armor of "I must do it myself." This statement, "I must do it myself," captures a fundamental problem in working with a grandiose patient: the patient's need to deny the analyst's existence. We may think about grandiosity as an attempt to maintain an experience of being an individual while struggling against the over-whelming tide of nonbeing, of spilling out into the world of "not-me." This is Freud's death instinct. Analytic work with these patients involves the development of omnipotence, the capacity to reach a state of plea-surable unity through internal processes of symbolic and metaphorical merger of self and other in place of the destruction of the world of ob-ject and the experience of death and emptiness.

Winnicott emphasized the importance of omnipotence in the individual's earliest experiences, as it allows for the development of being a subject rather than simply an object, a part of the external world. For Winnicott (1971), omnipotence is a development of the individual's experience of merger with the other and leads to the important and powerful illusory experiences, such as having created the breast and ul-timately having created the world. His emphasis on the importance of illusion, which develops from the merger of self and other, infant and mother, patient and analyst, stands in sharp contrast to Freud's empha-sis on the separation of subject and object and the importance of the distinction between the illusory and magical thought of the infant and the objective reality-based thought of the mature adult. Winnicott gave the term *illusion* an important connotation and elevated it to the rank of a fundamental concept in psychoanalytic theory and practice (Kluzer-Usuelli 1992). Subject and object are born in the illusion of the mother-child dyad by progressive differentiation from the initial psychological merger and the fantasy of the mutual creation of the breast. The expe-rience and capacity for omnipotence develops through processes of mutual identification (Winnicott 1971) and the creation of a series of transitional experiences located in an intermediate area between mother and child, between what will become "me" and "not-me," between the internal and external world, and between subject and object. Transitional objects and transitional experience are constructed as bridges between the "me" and the "not-me" and as derivatives of the primal unity. They retain the sheen of primitive omnipotence.

My grandiose patient's despair, his poignant comment that he was an "empty suit, a haircut," reflects a failure in the development of illu-sion and the lack of experiences of merger between himself and others. His grandiose behavior reflects his attempts to hold himself together, his statement "I must do it myself," and his need to destroy external objects, which results in his experience of himself as empty, a cog in a mechanical dead world. The absence of the experience of merger between self and other can be understood as a core difficulty; he described an absence of excitement, intimacy, and friendship. He described feelings that life is meaningless, and occasional preoccupations with vague thoughts of suicide, which he minimizes in a hypomanic, joking style. The antecedents of his grandiosity and despair are reflected in his childhood, in the failure of merger in his early experience. His parents were immigrants who had made him and his success in the New World their life work. Although they invested a great deal of time and resources in their project, he was always thought of as different from them, as the American success (the other), and they were therefore unable to identify with him either as a child or as an adult. His memories of his relationship with them typically feel hollow and sad. However, understanding and acknowledging these early experiences, although helpful, does not seem to affect the fundamental issues of his grandiosity and despair. Failure of traditional analytic interpretation with this patient is a result of the nature of the pathology, which can be characterized (Kluzer-Usuelli 1992) "as an insufficiency of illusion, a gap in the transitional space exposing the subject to the impossibility of making (living) sense of his experience" (p. 181). In addition to more traditional interpretations, with this type of patient the analyst's task involves the development of the capacity for merger between self and other, which leads to the development of omnipotence, the capacity to sustain illusion, and the experience of having a meaningful place in the world.

Kohut (1984) in his discussion of sexual symptoms introduced the concept of *disintegration products* of what might have become integrated sexual and affectionate striving. In a similar way we may think of grandiosity and despair as a disintegration product of omnipotence and merger, which the individual has needed to adopt in order to survive by doing everything by himself. It is a psychological tragedy that in adopting this grandiose strategy it becomes necessary to kill off, to destroy, the other, the external objects, simultaneously destroying the possibilities of becoming a subject and being trapped as an object without hope, immersed in an experience of psychological death. The recognition of the distinction between grandiosity and omnipotence is an important aspect of the concept of subjectivity, describing the capacity for merger and the imaginative and playful organization of experience.

The following case illustrates issues of merger as it relates to the development of omnipotence in the treatment of another patient.

The patient was a cynical, depressed man who largely disowned any sense of grandiosity or omnipotence, experiencing himself as an object, no different from other people. The patient presented the following dream, which can be understood as representing his anxiety around his grandiosity and destructiveness in his attempt to rid himself of all external objects. The session moves toward a symbolic merger between patient and analyst and the development of a shared experience of omnipotence.

The patient reported that he had a dream about the analyst and was uncomfortable telling the dream because it presented the analyst in a bad light. The underlying anxiety seems to involve the patient's desire to destroy the analyst, who had become the container for the patient's disowned manic greed, a partial solution to the experience of need. The patient related the dream: "I came here for a session. You were very excited because you were expecting a very rich patient, a millionaire, and you were telling me about it. I felt repelled by your interest in this patient because he was a millionaire. The scene changes and I am at a place where there is dancing, I am not sure whether it is you or me who is dancing. The person is in a white suit and is dancing and kissing an attractive woman, a colleague. I have no feelings."

In this second part of the dream there is a defended-against experience of merger with the analyst, possibly representing the patient's disowned grandiosity, exhibitionism, and desire. The patient's initial reluctance to tell the dream involved his need to destroy me as the representative of his limitless need and his fear of retaliation, because of both his destructiveness and his view of my greed and exhibitionism. It was clear that he felt very uncomfortable in attacking me, and at the same time wanted to dismiss me. Perhaps because of the patient's denial that this was the way he saw me, I felt embarrassed and angry, both wanting to deny the accusation and wondering whether it was true. For a moment, I wanted to physically and psychologically destroy the patient, to make him disappear and interpret away the dream. I then had two thoughts. The first reflected the themes of our recent work and my understanding of projective identification. I said that in the dream I contained his disowned greed and exhibitionism, which he was afraid of, and that if he owned it I would retaliate against him. The second was a very pleasant association to the figure in the white suit who reminded me of the movie *Saturday Night Fever*, in which the protagonist struggles to move out of his dreary working-class life into the bright lights, excitement, and joy of the big city. I thought that this dream reflected the difficulty that the patient and all people have in giving up the successful aspects of schizoid adaptation in the separateness and independence to become one with others, to leave the past and to enter into new life experiences. In describing my inner subjective experience, I commented on how in the movie the image of the Brooklyn Bridge was used sensitively to express the transition from one life to the next, and how the movie seemed to speak on many levels to the threatening issues of connection and merger.

In telling the patient this association it was clear that I felt that this metaphor of dancing, and moving from one life to another, represented each of our individual struggles as well as our joined experience. My association, this metaphoric experience of merger, allowed both of us to identify with the greedy, desirous, and exhibitionistic analyst in the dream; it also allowed the patient to identify with and feel compassion for his own barren childhood and his sense of disowned desire, and the absence of illusion and merger in his early experience. My associations to the dream image presented us with an opportunity for merger; we were able to enter into the world of the dream, the magic of the dance, the acceptance of greed, and an appreciation of the self-affirming omnipotence that is involved in merger between self and other.

CLINICAL ILLUSTRATION: THE HIDDEN ASSASSINS

Another case illustrates how failures in the integration of the dual and dialectically linked experiences of psychic and material reality lead to failures in the development of subjectivity. The patient has an inability to feel alive and to understand his own experiences and others' inner desires, feelings, intentions, and significance. Failures in developing the dual structures of being both a subject and an object can be thought of in terms of the three dimensions of psychic reality: the paradox of agency and personal responsibility, the development of dual or multiple modes of organizing and generating experience, and the central importance of omnipotence. A central dimension of the neo-Kleinian approach to treatment is the analyst's use of his countertransference experiences and fantasies in the development of transitional experiences that become a mode of analytic discourse. Unlike interpretations that organize experience in a functional, usually linear, sequence of causal relationships and use countertransference as a source of information that facilitates the differentiation of current from past life experiences, transitional experiences describe the world within a paranoid-schizoid mode of experience, in which ideas are expressed from the surrealistic and often omnipotent perspectives of magic, dreams, poetry, and art. This use of countertransference facilitates a shift from an objective frame of reference to a subjective frame of reference.

In this case illustration, the analyst's use of countertransference fantasies stands in contrast to an interpretive stance that emphasizes reality testing and the importance of material reality. I will focus on the analyst's use of countertransference experiences in the development of subjectivity within the analytic relationship, to illustrate the analyst's use of the three dimensions of psychic reality, which include his focus on being an agent responsible for his thoughts and fantasies, and on the articulation of the paranoid-schizoid mode of experience and omnipotence as a way to facilitate the patient's movement from a state of deadness, of being an object, to a state of being more fully alive, a subject.

This patient's failure in development of subjectivity was presented through overwhelming concerns with the details of his daily life, negotiating the material world, which he described in a lethargic, impotent, and listlessly irritating manner. He was concerned with being paralyzed in his career and in his relationships. As the treatment proceeded, he began a relationship with a woman and started to very tentatively prepare to apply to graduate school. Although the treatment seemed to be going well, there were long periods within sessions and over the course of several sessions that the patient's repetitive descriptions of being impotent, a helpless victim, in an empty hostile world, and his lack of recognition of me as a person, resulted in my experience of a bored withdrawal, in which I would get lost in fantasies that I often could not put into words. One such time I became fascinated by the fantasy of terrorists lurking outside my office door; I could imagine several hooded and masked swarthy young men crouching with automatic weapons. In a slightly removed way I wondered about what they were doing there, who they were after. I momentarily thought of some recent newspaper articles that I immediately dismissed, being more interested in returning to the fantasy. Although I might have attempted to relate this countertransference fantasy to my boredom in the session, to my wish to kill the patient, to his dissociated hostility and his murderous rage, I preferred or could not do anything but to stay with the fantasy in the concreteness of the paranoid-schizoid mode of experience.

I commented to the patient, in a factual way, that he should be careful when he leaves the session because there were terrorists lurking in the hall and they might kill him! My comment barely disrupted his monologue, although at that point he made a dismissive gesture as if to tell me to grow up and to be serious and to stop acting childish. I would have simply noted this as another example of being dismissed, of his need to eliminate all objects, if the following sequence had not developed several weeks later.

With the approach of the summer break, he began to express a more desperate concern that without therapy he would be unable to continue to study for the GREs and then implored me to do something to save the situation. Perhaps in response to the unusual tone of this request, or perhaps because this reflected something about me at that time, I had the fantasy of his needing a magical formula from an omnipotent guru if he was not to succumb to the grinding repetitions of daily life that would destroy his ability to study. Rather than interpreting what he seemed to desire and to relate it to his disowned need for an omnipotent (m)other, I enacted my fantasy and said that I would offer him a magical phrase, a mantra, which he would have to say over and over again in order for it to help. The phrase that had suggested itself to me, and which fit in with my understanding of his dynamics and also reflected a Kleinian interpretation, was "success equals murder." Almost immediately and in resonance with my omnipotent countertransference fantasy, he reported the following fantasy, which he said he has often had. He is at his inauguration as president of the United States, and just as he is taking the oath of office, a sniper kills him. I was surprised that he had not previously mentioned this fantasy and spoke of it as if it was a dissociated experience that he had never recognized as reflecting a critical reason for his impaired functioning and his fear of success. I was also quite impressed with the similarity to my earlier fantasy about the terrorists and felt that it probably involved a process of projective identification and his lack of recognition, suggesting that he was not yet prepared to alter his grandiose need to be alone, his need to do it by himself.

Upon resuming the treatment in the fall, we frequently reentered the fantasy of his presidential inauguration; it became a part of a joined omnipotent transitional experience and became a counterpoint to the themes of his dissociated aggression. Several months later, the patient announced that his fantasy of the inauguration had changed; he now imagines that he is walking through the street to the grandstand on which he will take his oath of office. As he proceeds along, he pulls people out of the crowd to walk along with him. In the fantasy, people think that he is doing this because he is a populist; however, he knows that he is in fact using them as a human shield against the assassin's bullets. I found myself admiring this development in our transitional fantasy and his capacity both to allow others to be involved and to begin to take responsibility for his aggression, as well as his ability to survive and succeed, to begin to live with the hopefulness of omnipotence.

This transitional experience reflected an experience of symbolic merger between analyst and patient. We both participated in this transitional experience, and it became a vehicle through which the patient became able to integrate the aggression and omnipotence inherent in his fantasy of being the president and in my fantasy of being a guru. The initial element of the transitional experience involved presenting my omnipotent countertransference fantasy of being a guru who provided a magical means of overcoming his sense of powerlessness. He did not question enacting this fantasy, but rather responded with his own fantasy, which again was not questioned but became an experience of merger, of deep mutuality, a transitional experience involving success, aggression, and survival. The developmental impact of this transitional experience reflected a transformation of the paranoid position of aggression projected outside of himself into unknown persecutors, to one in which he recognized his contribution to the destructiveness, which reflected a beginning awareness of the development of the depressive position.

This use of transitional experiences reflects a choice in which the analyst becomes part of a merged experience of psychic reality, utilizing the paranoid-schizoid mode of organizing experience, and gives up the safety of being a representative of and interpreter of external objective or material reality. It is important to recognize that this is a choice between two modes of experience, one associated with the internal world of psychic reality and one associated with the external world of material reality. One of the major problems in treatment with this type of patient is bridging the pervasive feelings of concreteness and isolation in the analysis, including the analyst's concreteness and isolation, the patient's concreteness and isolation, and, most importantly, the concreteness and isolation of the spoken words that do not communicate. In many ways these patients find themselves living exclusively in the world of material reality, not having developed the capacities of functioning in the realm of psychic reality. From my perspective it is important for the analysis to facilitate the development of the three dimensions of psychic reality, those of agency and personal responsibility, the capacity to use multiple modes of organizing and generating experience, and the development of omnipotence and the capacity for merger, which are critical aspects of a neo-Kleinian concept of subjectivity.

4

Projection, Identification, and Enactment

INTRODUCTION: FROM INSTINCT TO UNCONSCIOUS FANTASY

Klein's concepts of the paranoid-schizoid position, the depressive position, and projective identification initiated a revolution in the fundamental terms and underlying systems of explanation in contemporary psychoanalytic theory and practice. Although not intentionally setting out to overthrow the Freudian patriarchal order, her work and the ensuing controversial discussions (Hayman 1994, Holland 1990) moved psychoanalysis from a one-person, biologically based, drive discharge theory toward a two-person theory focused on the sociocultural issues of identity, power, and the process of organizing, representing, and creating meaning in the world. Klein's reformulation of psychoanalysis developed within the conceptual and linguistic terms of Freudian drive theory, which provided a familiar text but was unable to accommodate her more complex understanding of human experience. The shift from a theory focused on the vicissitudes of instincts and processes of drive discharge to one focused on the vicissitudes of object relations and the creation of meaning hinged on the development of the Kleinian concept of unconscious fantasy. In this chapter I trace the conceptual and clinical evolution of the shift in psychoanalysis from a theory of instincts emphasizing an accommodation to the reality principle to one emphasizing the importance of unconscious fantasy and the struggle with countertransference anxieties associated with projective and introjective processes and the internalization of new symbolic experiences and structures.

Spillius (1988) suggests, "Klein's theory is simultaneously an instinct theory and an object relations theory. Like Freud, she thought of the individual as driven by life and death instincts, but she [Klein] never speaks of instincts in and of themselves or divorced from objects; they are inherently attached to objects" (p. 3), which are represented as unconscious fantasies and organizations of internal object relations. Klein adopted the idea of unconscious fantasy from Freud and thought of it as a psychic representation of instincts; however, unlike Freud, she proposed that unconscious fantasies are both the primary building blocks and the contents of unconscious mental processes. This reading of Freud is similar to Lacan's (1978), in that the concept of unconscious fantasy suggests a process of creating meaning, and that processes of intrapersonal and interpersonal signification define the realm of psychoanalysis.

Spillius (1988) states that Klein developed the concept of unconscious fantasy through her work with children, in which she "was impressed by the vividness and bodily concreteness of the [children's] phantasies and by the intensity of conflict that they expressed. Her emphasis on the reality of unconscious phantasy, on conflict between love and hate in the Unconscious, on anxiety as the dominant problem confronting the ego, on emotions as well as ideas as major unconscious contents, and on mechanisms of defense being expressed through specific unconscious phantasies" (p. 3) are the central elements in Klein's development of the concept of unconscious fantasy. Klein's creative leap was giving voice to her young patients' complex, nonverbal, internal representations that organized their experience in analysis and in the world. Klein believed that "through the constant operation (in phantasy) of projection, interjection, and identification, an inner world of objects and self is built up, which is used through out life *to give meaning to events in the external world*" (p. 3, italics added). For Klein, the concept of unconscious fantasy is critical and suggests a concept of subjectivity, in which the person participates from the beginning in the creation of meaning through defining identity in terms of patterns of object relations and of contrasts between "me" and "not-me," self and other.

FREUD, THE SCHREBER CASE, AND THE CONCEPT OF PROJECTION

Freud's (1911) analysis of Schreber's autobiographical account of his paranoid illness attempted to address many of the questions that are at the core of Klein's development of object relations theory. The case also reflects Freud's political concern with maintaining the cohesion of the psychoanalytic movement through attempts to accommodate both Jung and Ferenczi. Finally, he attempted to expand the clinical usefulness of psychoanalysis from a narrow focus on the transference neuroses of hysteria and obsessional disorders to include more disturbed paranoid and schizophrenic individuals.

Issues of identity, unconscious fantasy, the relationship between self-perception and self-experience, the perception of the other, and the experience of the other are at the core of Freud's (1911) discussion of paranoia and the Schreber case. In this paper, Freud struggled with what might have been a major challenge to drive theory, focusing on issues of identity and the creation of meaning rather than on explanations based on the drive theory and the dominance of the reality principle. Freud introduced two concepts that have become cornerstones for the development of contemporary two-person psychoanalytic theory and practice. He introduced the concepts of *projection* and *narcissism* as a means to understand the fluidity of Schreber's shifting experience of identity and his ability to ignore his current situation and the reality principle. Freud used the concept of narcissism to explain Schreber's withdrawal from the world of external reality, and the failure of the pleasure principle to guard against painful experiences of persecution. The case material draws our attention to differences between a system based on repression, pleasure, and cohesiveness, and one based on projection and processes of internalization, identity formation, and the relationship between fantasy and reality. However, Freud was unable to follow these directions in developing an understanding of paranoia and returned to the well-worn paths of drive theory, repression, and the oedipal complex.

Schreber's autobiography (Freud 1911) describes his second mental illness, which occurred shortly after he became the chief judge in an important regional court (Schatzman 1972). Schreber describes extreme delusional states that involve first being persecuted, sexually abused, and treated like a whore by his doctor and the hospital staff, and then being transformed into a woman. His delusions, which were initially persecutory, evolved into a grandiose religious conviction that he was chosen to be transformed into a woman in order for God to inseminate him, and that he was chosen to give birth to a new, superior race. Freud points out that this grandiose transformation is confusing because Schreber's attitude toward God is one of mixed reverence and rebellion. Freud interpreted this contradiction as reflecting his unconscious feelings toward his father, who both Dr. Flechsig, his doctor, and God represented. Freud's primary interpretation of Schreber's symptoms, and of paranoia in general, was that it was a defense against a negative Oedipus complex and the resulting unacceptable homosexual desires for father.

The most interesting part of Freud's (1911) discussion of the case is not his interpretation of paranoia as an expression of the patient's unacceptable homosexual longings and the passive feminine organization of the negative Oedipus complex, but rather his awareness of the unique role of the process of projection in the formation of symptoms:

The most striking characteristic of symptom-formation in paranoia is the process which deserves the name of *projection*. An internal perception is suppressed, and instead, its content after undergoing a certain kind of distortion, enters consciousness in the form of an external perception. In delusions of persecution the distortion consists in a transformation of affect; what should have been felt internally as love is perceived externally as hate. We should be tempted to regard this remarkable process as the most important element in paranoia and as being absolutely pathognomic for it, if we were not opportunely reminded of two things. In the first place projection does not play the same part in all forms of paranoia; and in the second place, it makes its appearance not only in paranoia but under other psychological conditions as well, and in fact it has a regular share assigned to it in our attitude towards the external world. For when we refer the causes of certain sensations to the external world, instead of looking for them (as we do in the case of others) inside ourselves, this normal proceeding, too, deserves to be called projection. Having thus been made aware that the more general psychological problems are involved in the question of the nature of projection, let us make up our mind to postpone the investigation of it (and with it the mechanisms of paranoiac symptom formation in general) until some other occasion; and let us now turn to consider what ideas we can collect on the subject of repression in paranoia. I should like to say at once, in justification of this temporary renunciation, that we shall find that the manner in which the process of repression occurs is far more intimately connected with the developmental history of the libido and with the disposition to which it gives rise than is the manner in which the symptoms are formed. [p. 66]

Freud never returned to a discussion of the process of projection, although his comments suggest that he sensed that the process of projection was an important aspect of our relationship with external reality and with processes of locating experience in either internal or external worlds. Freud's decision to postpone a discussion of projection and to focus on the libidinal dynamics and repression was a reflection of his positivist perspective, privileging material reality over psychic reality and defining the individual's task as adapting to the external world. Freud defined projection as a defense against inner impulses and emphasized distortion and defensive externalization of unacceptable impulses, needs, and desires such as in his description of unacceptable homosexual love being transformed into hatred and paranoid preoccupations.

Several authors (Niederland 1974, Schatzman 1972) have critiqued Freud's interpretative use of repression, Schreber's unacceptable homosexual longings, and the use of the negative Oedipus complex as an explanation of paranoia. They have documented the close relationship between Schreber's delusions and the reality of his childhood experiences that occurred as a result of his father's sadistic child-rearing practices. Schreber's father was a well-known physician who developed methods of training children through an elaborate series of "compulsive and rigid ritualizations that were calculated to break the will of the child and to subject him to inexorable discipline" (Meisner 1978, p. 16). Reconstruction of Schreber's childhood experiences suggests that his delusions were not the manifestations of unacceptable (libidinal) wishes but rather attempts in some way to acknowledge and understand these experiences of horror and sadistic physical abuse. These findings (Niederland 1974, Schatzman 1972) present a view of projection that is quite different from

Freud's and suggest that Schreber's delusions were attempts at enacting and externalizing these terrifying, unverbalized, intense affective experiences, in an attempt to understand, communicate, and integrate the dissociated experiences of the past through defining who he is in relation to important others. This view presents a second concept of projection, one that coincides with contemporary self and relational theory, conceiving of projection as an attempt to express through enactment as well as words the dissociated and unarticulated experiences of sexual and physical abuse. The literalness of Schreber's sexual delusions and his fluid sense of personal and sexual identity can be understood as aspects of dissociation in which there is a blurring of the boundaries of the dimensions of material reality (person, place, and time), and in which the concretization of experience is characteristic of dissociated unarticulated experience. This second view of projection, unlike the defensive getting rid of unacceptable wishes, focuses on the failure to emotionally and cognitively integrate traumatic experiences, which propel individuals into states of confusion in which traumatic experiences are repetitively acted out.[1] However, unlike Freud's concept of projection, which focuses on the internal experiences of the individual's unacceptable sexual wishes, this concept of projection within the context of trauma theory focuses on dissociation and the individual's inability to effectively and cognitively integrate experiences that occurred in the external world, particularly in relation to the abusive other, leaving the individual in a passive state of being a victim. Freud's view of projection, focusing on the patient's unacceptable wishes, creates a potentially overwhelming sense of guilt in which the analyst takes on the functions of a harsh superego. However, the perspective of projection as part of a process of dissociation has a potentially opposite effect, creating a sense of victimization and pathological entitlement in which the analyst becomes the "good" parent in contrast to the "bad" historical object.

Klein's (1946a) comments on the Schreber case illustrate a third perspective, representing a concept of projection that is different from both Freud's model, which focuses on the defensive distortion of the individual's feelings and wishes, and the model of dissociation and

1. Davies and Frawley (1994) provide an extensive discussion of the treatment of survivors of sexual abuse and the repetitive enactments of traumatic experience.

trauma, which focuses on enactment and an inability to emotionally and cognitively integrate experiences in the external world with a sadistic other. However, Klein's discussion of the concept of projection demonstrates some of the difficulty with understanding her theory; read conservatively, her concept of projective identification is a largely defensive, one-person theory of the evacuation of unacceptable libidinal and destructive impulses, whereas read from a liberal perspective it is a two-person theory emphasizing processes of intrapsychic and interpersonal exchange, which focuses on the development and integration of individual identity. Klein does not conceptualize the libido as representing a need, an expression of a wish, or a press for the discharge of energy; rather, it represents an unconscious fantasy in which the central concern is with the person's experience of identity. This difference between the defensive and the dissociative views of projection and Klein's concept of projective identification is apparent in her discussion of the Schreber case. Klein (1946a) focuses on Schreber's attempt through projective process to eternalize aspects of his identity and the ongoing struggle between his internal and his external objects:

> The conclusion suggests itself that God and Flechsig also represent parts of Schreber's self. The conflict between Schreber and Flechsig, to which Freud attributed a vital role in the world destruction delusion, found expression in the raid by God on the Flechsig souls. In my view this raid represents the annihilation by one part of the self or other parts—which as I contend, is a schizoid mechanism. The anxieties and fantasies about inner destruction and ego-disintegration bound up with this mechanism are projected on to the external world and underlie the delusions of its destruction. [p. 23]

For Klein, Schreber's delusions represent an externalization, a projection, of inner object relations into the external world. Her focus is not on unacceptable wishes or distortions of external reality but rather on the failure to integrate aspects of the self, of individual identity, through processes of splitting, externalization (projection), enactment, and introjection.

PROJECTION, INTROJECTION, AND ENACTMENT

Klein's theory developed around the concept of unconscious fantasy, internal schemata that organize and define experience of relationships with objects in the external world. Unconscious fantasies are not simply signs that describe particular events; rather, they are organizational structures, like computer programs, that are not separate from the experiences and actions in the world (see Kernberg 1976, for a similar discussion). Klein's (1946a) description of early processes of splitting, as the process that defines and organizes early experience, illustrates the relationship between unconscious fantasies and the individual's experiences and actions in the external world: "It is in phantasy that the infant splits the object and the self, but the effects of this phantasy is a very real one, because it leads to feelings and relations (and later on, thought processes) being in fact cut off from one another" (p. 6). In a footnote, Klein adds the idea that splitting also includes breaks in continuity, a splitting of time as well as space.

Klein (1946a) developed the concept of projective identification as an extension of the concept of splitting and as a defense against the death instinct and inner experiences of aggression and badness.

> Much of the hatred against parts of the self is now directed towards the mother. This leads to a particular form of identification which establishes the prototype of an aggressive object-relation. I suggest for these processes the term "projective identification." When projection is mainly derived from the infant's impulse to harm or control the mother, he feels her to be a persecutor. In psychotic disorders this identification of an object with the hated parts of the self contributes to the intensity of the hatred directed against other people. As far as the ego is concerned the excessive splitting off and expelling into the outer world of parts of the self considerably weaken it. For the aggressive component of feeling and of the personality is intimately bound up in the mind with power, potency, strength, knowledge and many other desired qualities.
>
> It is, however, not only the bad parts of the self, which are expelled and projected, but also good parts of the self. Excrements then have the significance of gifts; and parts of the ego which, together with excrements, are expelled and projected into the other person represent the good, i.e., the loving parts of the self. The identification based on this type of projection again vitally influences object relations. The projection of good feelings and good parts of the self

into the mother is essential for the infant's ability to develop good object-relations and to integrate his ego. However, if this projective process is carried out excessively, good parts of the personality are felt to be lost, and in this way the mother becomes the ego ideal; this process too results in weakening and impoverishing the ego. Very soon such processes extend to other people, and the result may be an over-strong dependence on these external representatives of one's own good parts. Another consequence is that the capacity to love is lost because the loved object is felt to be loved predominantly as a representative of the self. [p. 8]

Klein's concept of projective identification extends the concept of unconscious fantasy to include the other, the person who receives the projected fantasy and becomes engaged in a two-person dialectical process that organizes and creates relationship patterns and experience of identity. These early, paranoid relational organizations are initially based on simple complementary schemas such as, "You have everything and I have nothing" or "I am bad and you are good." From Klein's perspective, concepts of identity are dynamic intrapersonal structures, unconscious fantasies, that generate enactments, organize relationships and actions. Klein uses language as a performative rather than discursive practice, directed at evoking and generating experience and responses from the other.

Although Klein presented this concept of projective identification as an extension of Freud's concept of projection, it is quite different in two important ways. It is a break with the constraints of modernity, the positivist, Cartesian separation of thought and action, and the emphasis on the reality principle, which are at the core of Freud's model of the mind. Although Kleinian theory describes a dialect between psychic and material reality, it privileges the inner world of unconscious fantasy as the moment-to-moment determinant of external experience. Klein's (1946a, 1955) development of the concept of projective identification provides an essentially clinical and operational conceptualization of the more abstract theoretical concept of unconscious fantasy,[2] allowing her to describe the complex dialectical processes between self and other

---

2. This distinction between the theoretical concept of unconscious fantasy and the clinical operational concept of projective identification parallels Freud's theoretical concept of repression and his clinical operational concept of resistance.

through which projection, introjection, and enactment lead to the development of identity and the capacity to relate to others in aggressive, loving, and empathic ways.

Projective identification is an operational concept that describes the dialectic between projection and introjection; it is neither an intrapsychic nor an interpersonal concept, but one that bridges both realms of experience, blurring the boundaries between self and other, "me" and "not-me," feeling and sensation, thought and action. Joseph (1988) includes the following among the aims of projective identification: "Splitting off and getting rid of unwanted parts of the self that cause anxiety and pain, projecting the self or parts of the self into an object to take over its capacities and make them its own, invading in order to damage or destroy the object. Thus the infant, or adult who goes on using such mechanisms extensively, can avoid any awareness of separateness, dependence, admiration, or its concomitant sense of loss, anger, phobic panics and the like" (p. 138). Ogden (1982) defines projective identification as a "psychological process that is at once a type of defense, a mode of communication, a primitive form of object relations, and a pathway for psychological change" (p. 21). The concept of projective identification is critical to understanding analytic treatment from a Kleinian perspective, focusing the analyst's attention on the profound communication and issues of control within the transference–countertransference relationship as enactment of unconscious fantasies rather than as the exchange of historic or genetic information. Hanna Segal (1994) describes the emotional difference between the concrete literalness of the paranoid position as an "as if" experience in which the projective identification is both real and present, while the symbolic experience in the depressive position has a "what if" quality, describing possibility and imaginative elaboration of experience. However, before continuing with a discussion of projective identification within the analytic relationship, I want to briefly review Klein's development of this concept.

In a fascinating second paper on projective identification, Klein (1955) discusses a French novel, *If I Were You*, by Julian Green, as a way of elaborating her thesis that through the processes of projection and introjection the individual is able to build up a coherent, complex identity and is able to move beyond the fragmented experiences of hatred and destructiveness of the paranoid-schizoid position toward a capacity for love and integration in the depressive position. This paper is quite interesting for a number of reasons, including Klein's emphasis on the importance of the internal good object in developing the capacity to love and the importance of omnipotence in the individual's development.

> Here I wish to go somewhat beyond my paper on "Schizoid Mechanisms." I would suggest that a securely established good object, implying a securely established love for it, gives the ego a feeling of riches and abundance which allows for an outpouring of libido and projection of good parts of the self into the external world without a sense of depletion arising. The ego can then also feel that it is able to interject the love it has given out, as well as take in goodness from other sources, and thus be enriched by the whole process. In other words, in such cases there is a balance between giving out and taking in, between projection and introjection. [p. 144]

The hero of Green's novel, Fabian,

> is unhappy and dissatisfied with himself, in particular with his appearance, his lack of success with women, his poverty and the inferior work to which he feels condemned. He finds his religious beliefs, which he attributes to his mother's demands, very burdensome, yet he cannot free himself from them. His father, who died when he was still at school, squandered all his money gambling, and on a "gay" life with women, and died of heart failure, thought to be the result of his dissolute life. Fabian's pronounced grievance and rebellion against fate are bound up with the resentment against his father, whose irresponsibility had deprived him of further education and other prospects. These feelings, it appears, contribute to Fabian's insatiable desire for wealth and success, and to his intense envy and hatred of those who possess more. [p. 145]

Klein uses this novel as a powerful illustration of the process of projective identifications, commenting that at the end of the story, Fabian's experiences of "the characters into whom he had turned himself are all present in his mind before he dies and he is concerned about their fate. This would imply that he rejects his objects, as well as projects himself into them" (p. 170). In addition to being an explication of her theory of projective identification, illustrating the processes of projection, identification, enactment (becoming the other and having the other become the self), and introjection, this paper dramatizes the inner experience of paranoia.

The devil teaches Fabian a magical formula through which he can invade and take possession of other people's material and spiritual possessions. However, Klein seems to have difficulty locating the character of the Devil in her system. Initially she sees him as the seducing, dangerous, bad father; however, this interpretation does not work, because he is also the one who facilitates Fabian's transformation from the paranoid-schizoid position to the depressive position. I believe that her difficulty in understanding the character of the Devil reflects a conflict between her earlier one-person model and the developing two-person model of projective identification. Although she consistently describes a dialectic process of projection and introjection, her interpretations tend to define a narrow interpretive role for the analyst, who does not become a full participant in the dialectical process of projection, enactment, and introjection. Klein's emphasis is on the receptivity of the other (the analyst) in processes of projective identification as a function of the patient's experience of a common ground between him- or herself and the analyst, suggesting that for an analyst to be available for projective identification, he or she must be experienced as having those negative qualities that are being projected. The next generation of Kleinians, particularly Bion and Betty Joseph, developed an explicit two-person perspective on processes of projective identification with concepts such as the container and the contained, reverie, and the importance of enactments in the transference–countertransference relationship. From this two-person perspective, the Devil may be thought of as representing the therapist, an object with whom Fabian can freely identify his ruthless, greedy, grandiose, and destructive parts without feeling guilt or shame.

The experience of projective identification is an inevitable aspect of intimate relationships and can be both an intensely uncomfortable and anxiety-filled experience that thrusts the individual into a paranoid world of persecution and grandiosity, or it can be a creative experience of mutuality and playfulness, creating the symbolic experiences of the depressive position. The critical issues in understanding projective identification in psychoanalysis, psychotherapy, and life is that the other (the therapist, parent, lover, friend) becomes deeply affected by the split-off parts of the individual as they become involved in the dialectical process of projective identification.

PROJECTIVE IDENTIFICATION, ENACTMENT, AND CLINICAL PROCESS

From a clinical perspective, the analyst is both a passive participant, being invaded and controlled by the patient's evacuated unconscious fantasies, and an active participant, being receptive to the projective identifications and affectively and cognitively elaborating the patient's projected fantasies. Ogden (1982) describes the analyst's initial passivity in relation to the patient, who is organizing and controlling the dramatic enactment of his unconscious fantasies.

> If we imagine for a moment that the patient is both the director and one of the principal actors in the interpersonal enactment of an internal object relationship, and that the therapist is an unwitting actor in the same drama, then projective identification is the process whereby the therapist is given stage directions for a particular role. In this analogy it must be borne in mind that the therapist has not volunteered to play a part and only retrospectively comes to understand that he has been playing a role in the patient's enactment of an aspect of his inner world. [p. 4]

Ogden presents a schematic view of the process of projective identification and describes three phases in which the analyst moves from a passive position of being taken over to an active position of joyfully participating in the elaboration of the patient's disowned unconscious fantasy.[3] In the first phase of projective identification, the patient or the infant needs to rid itself of a part of the self, an internal object, through the fantasy of splitting it off and putting it into the other. In the second phase, the patient or infant exerts both external and internal pressure on the other to identify with, to be, or to enact the patient's

---

3. Ogden, like most American authors, seems to use the word *fantasy* to represent all inner imaginative processes, while the British authors, following Klein, tend to use *phantasy* when referring to unconscious processes, and *fantasy* when referring to more conscious imaginative productions. I will use the language of each author and allow the context to define the type of psychic experience.

unacceptable unconscious fantasy. This second phase of projective identification differentiates the Kleinian perspective from a more traditional view of projection as a defense because it requires the involvement of the other through identification with and an enactment of the patient's unconscious fantasy. There are three possible ways that the therapist can experience the patient's projective identifications: (1) The therapist (parent) may remain impervious to the patient's projections, which would result in the patient (infant) feeling isolated, dead, and crazy. (2) The therapist (parent) may momentarily take in the projection and quickly reject it, encouraging a premature differentiation of self–other patterns, leaving the patient (infant) feeling filled with toxic material that is experienced as the core of his or her identity. (3) The therapist may accept the patient's or infant's projection, dedifferentiating the experience of self and other, and experiencing the projection as his/her own in a process of introjective identification. The Kleinian literature distinguishes the concepts of introjective identification, enactment, acting in, and acting out in the following way: acting in and acting out are thought of as an evacuative, defensive, or drive discharge activity, often representing an imperviousness to the patient's projective identifications, while introjective identification and enactment represent a process of identification and reverie, through which the analyst is open to the patient's projective identification in a complementary process of concordant identification (Racker 1968).

Introjective identification sets the stage for the third phase, in which the therapist or other experiences him/herself as a part of the other's unconscious fantasy. In this phase the therapist's participation can and often does include long periods of intense anxiety and defenses against paranoid experiences (Newirth 1990), including feelings of being controlled or of being out of control, desires to flee the situation, or preoccupations with trivial aspects of the analyst's life, including list making, counting money, and keeping track of minutes and patient hours. However, this process of introjective identification opens up the possibility (through reverie) of a deeper understanding of the patient and the transformation of the concrete paranoid experiences of hatred, phobic dread, and destruction to becoming elaborated as symbolic experiences of identity, which can be reinternalized by the patient as strengths and as valued aspects of the self.

INTERPRETATION, ENACTMENT, AND PROJECTIVE IDENTIFICATION

Bion (1959) describes both the communicative and the potentially constructive aspects of projective identification between infant and parent or between analyst and patient:

> Projective identification makes it possible for the infant (patient) to investigate his own feelings in a personality powerful enough to contain them. Denial of the use of this mechanism, either by the refusal of the mother (analyst) to serve as a repository for the infant's (patient's) feelings, or by the hatred and envy of the infant (patient) who can not allow the mother (analyst) to exercise this function, leads to a destruction of the link between infant (patient) and breast (analyst), and consequently to a severe disorder of the impulse to be curious on which all learning depends. [p. 314]

Ogden (1982) illustrates the analyst's struggle with the projective identifications of being greedy and inadequate, which were first expressed in the patient's accusations that the analysis was worthless, a waste of time and money. These accusations resulted in the analyst being unable to maintain the parameters around time and money because he felt guilty that he was not giving the patient his money's worth. Ogden describes the analyst's overcoming his feelings of anxiety and self-disgust as a critical part of the more active process of introjective identification and reverie:

> For the analyst, the first step in integrating the feeling of greediness was perceiving himself experiencing guilt and defending himself against feelings of greed. He could then mobilize an aspect of himself that was interested in understanding his greed and guilty feelings, rather than trying to deny, disguise, displace, or project them. Essential for this aspect of psychological work was the analyst's feeling that he could have greedy and guilty feelings without being damaged by them. It was not the analyst's greedy feelings that were interfering with his therapeutic work; rather, it was his need to disavow such feelings by denying them and by putting them into defensive activity. As the analyst became aware of, and was able to live with, this aspect of himself and his patient, he became better able to handle

the financial and time boundaries of the therapy. He no longer felt that he had to hide the fact that he was glad to receive money given in payment for his work. [p. 19]

Having come to this position of being able to enjoy his greed and desire, the analyst was able to enact this transformation of the experience of greed, expressing enjoyment in his desire for money and recognizing the value of his contribution to the patient when the patient next accused him of being the unseemly greedy one.

This process of introjective identification involves several simultaneous transformations in the analyst as the recipient of the patient's projective identifications. There is a transformation from passive to active, from being flooded with unpleasant experiences, part object identifications, paranoid anxieties, and defenses, and the experience of thoughts as unacceptable ("not-me"), concrete, and real, to acceptable ("me"), playful, symbolic, and possible, and from a phobic quality of avoidance of the patient to a pleasurable quality of enjoyment of the enactment of the previously unacceptable unconscious fantasy. The analyst's active, playful, perhaps even joyful enactment of the patient's unconscious rejected fantasy represents a critical step in the transformation of externalized paranoid unconscious fantasies to symbolic depressive fantasies, which facilitates the patient's reinternalization and integration of previously fragmented and frightening aspects of their identity.

In focusing on the transformation of projective identifications from concrete to symbolic organizations, interpretation becomes a complex process involving identification, dedifferentiating the qualities of person, place, and time. This process of transformation involves the analyst's affective and symbolizing activity involving an identification with the patient's disowned unconscious fantasies. Joseph (1988), in discussing the clinical and technical implications of projective identification, elaborates on the difficulty of the interpretive process:

> Sometimes it [projective identification] is used so massively that we get the impression that the patient is, in fantasy, projecting his whole self into his object and may feel trapped or claustrophobic. It is in any case a very powerful and effective way of ridding the individual of contact with his own mind; at times the mind can be so weakened or so fragmented by splitting processes or so evacuated by projective

identification that the individual appears empty or quasi psychotic. . . . For example, bearing in mind that projective identification is only one aspect of an omnipotent[4] balance established by each
individual in his own way, an interpretive attempt on the part of the
analyst to locate and give back to the patient missing parts of the self
must of necessity be resisted by the total personality, since it is felt
to threaten the whole balance and lead to more disturbance. [p. 140]

Joseph is suggesting a critical idea that the patient's resistance and
phobic dread of interpretations are a result of experiencing the analyst's
words as concretely destructive attacks that are premature attempts to
force a reinternalization of projected aspects of the self before the patient has developed the capacity to symbolize experience through enactments and the interpretation of enactments in the analysis. Because
it is difficult for the analyst to know at any moment in the analysis
whether the patient's projective identifications are aimed at communi-
cating a state of mind that cannot be verbalized or at invading, controlling, and attacking the analyst, he or she must be prepared to understand all experience that occurs within the analytic situation through
processes of introjective identification, the dedifferentiation of the transference–countertransference experience, and subsequent enactments.
This complex process of self-analysis is described by Joseph (1988) in
her developing understanding of a patient's projective identifications,
providing a valuable illustration of the effort involved in the process of
introjective identification that precede any attempts at interpretation:

First, the nature of the communication, which I could understand
primarily through my counter-transference, through the way in which
I was being pushed and pulled to feel and react. We see here the
concrete quality of projective identification structuring the countertransference. It seems that the way N [the patient] was speaking was
not asking me to try to understand the sexual difficulties or unhappiness but to invade me with despair, while at the same time unconsciously trying to force me to reassure myself that it was all right, that
interpretations, now empty and hollow of meaning, were meaning-

4. Joseph does not make the distinction between omnipotence and grandiosity
that I made in the previous chapter, and I would suggest that in this context she is
describing the manic defense of grandiosity.

ful and that the analysis at that moment was going ahead satisfactorily. Thus it was not only the despair that N was projecting into me, but his defenses against it, a false reassurance and denial, which it was intended I should act out with him. I think that it also suggests a projective identification of an internal figure, probably primarily mother, who was felt to be weak, kind, but unable to stand up to emotion. In the transference (to over-simplify the picture) this figure is projected into me, and I find myself pushed to live it out. [p. 146]

INTROJECTIVE IDENTIFICATION AND ENACTMENT

Harold Searles (1979), an American analyst, developed a clinical approach integrating Kleinian object relations theory within the context of interpersonal psychoanalysis. Searles has an uncanny ability to describe the complexities of the analyst's subjective experience within the evolving psychoanalytic situation. His approach is to describe, or more accurately map, the changing landscape of the affective, perceptual, cognitive, and linguistic experiences of both individuals within the evolving analytic relationship. His rich descriptions of the changing landscape of the psychoanalytic relationship introduced the study of subjective experience and predate by a generation current interest in intersubjective phenomena. Searles departed from the more traditional ego psychological and interpersonal concepts of structures and adapted Erikson's (1950) concept of identity in an attempt to provide a theoretical structure for his clinical observations. At times he used the concept of identity as a one-person experience (i.e., "This is who I am"), while at other times he emphasizes its two-person meaning as it relates to processes of internalization and the evolution of a sense of self ("I am you and you are me"). His use of the concept of identity involves a sensitivity to the paradoxical aspects of using this concept both to represent a singular sense of self and simultaneously to join together two separate beings into a single affective experience. It is this second meaning that Searles developed as the concept of introjective identification involving the analyst's active identification and imaginative elaboration of experiences that are the result of projective and introjective processes between the patient and himself.

In most discussions of countertransference the analyst is seen as either passive in relation to the patient's projective identifications (Racker 1968) or as encircled (Levenson 1985) by the interpersonal demands of the patient, which the analyst uses to understand and interpret the transference and its antecedents. From this perspective, countertransference can be understood as the analyst's response to the press of the patient's transference. In this reactive model of countertransference, the patient can be thought of as both active and unconscious (the past is enacted in an unconscious form), and the analyst is in the complementary position of being passive and conscious. However, in addition to responding to the press of the patient's transference, Searles introduces into the analytic discourse his primary experiences of identifications and his experiences of love, hate, hope, and despair. In contrast to other views of countertransference, Searles's position suggests that the analyst is both active and conscious while the patient continues to be thought of as active and unconscious.

Searles defined four progressive stages or relational organizations in the evolving psychoanalytic relationship that describe the subtle texture of the processes of projective and introjective identification: pathological symbiosis, autism, therapeutic symbiosis, and individuation. Within each stage, he describes the patient's mode of organizing experience and the analyst's experience of connection with the patient. Searles (1979) describes these relational organizations in the following way:

> The individual who at the beginning of therapy gives us to understand that his characteristic mode of relating to other persons is dominated by the ego defense of pathological symbiotic relatedness, forms with us a relationship in which he is part of a whole person, and we [the therapist] are the other, complementary part. This is in contrast to the autistic patient, who functions as though he himself, or contrariwise the therapist, were the whole—the single conceivable and perceivable and palpable—world. Pathologically symbiotic relatedness also contrasts with therapeutically symbiotic relatedness in many regards. Whereas in pathological symbiosis the patient and therapist form two relatively fixed, complementary parts of a whole system, in therapeutic symbiosis both persons function in thoroughgoing and rapidly changing flux and interchangeability, with all parts of the potentially whole and separate persons and, far beyond that, whole and separate worlds, flowing from and into and between, and

encompassing, both of them. Also the affective tone of therapeutic symbiosis is one of liveliness or contentment or fulfillment, while that of pathological symbiosis is one of constriction, incompleteness, unfulfillment, or inner disturbance to the point of threatened insanity. . . . The pathologically symbiotic patient either coercively puts parts of himself into the therapist, or coercively evokes the therapist's attempts to complete his [the patient's] self, manifested as poignantly needful and incomplete. [p. 134]

During the autistic phase of the treatment the analyst's attempts at transference interpretation meet with a thoroughly defeating response. Either the patient essentially ignores them, or responds with such devastating derision and contempt as to make one feel crazy for having uttered them, or he finds them so deeply and destructively disturbing that it may require him the bulk of the hour to digest, as it were, this foreign body and expel it and restore thus his temporarily damaged autistic world to its state prior to this rude introduction. All this makes the analyst feel thoroughly stupid and useless; but the patient has unconsciously thus to destroy or ignore what the analyst offers him, in order to keep repressed his own infantile need toward the analyst as mother who is far more than a mere person—who is the whole functional world for him. To hear and accept and utilize the analyst's interpretation would mean, for the patient, the relinquishment of his only known world, in exchange for one which feels entirely unknown to him, namely that comprising the analyst. [p. 150]

Searles's structural approach to the psychoanalytic process suggests that within each successive stage or relational organization from pathological symbiosis to the autistic stage and to the stage of therapeutic symbiosis, the analyst and patient are joined in complicated and changing states of mutual identification and regulation. In this map of the structure of the analytic relationship, the movement between the autistic stage and that of therapeutic symbiosis is extremely important for the development of new internal structures in the patient and defines the analyst's active suggestion in the process of introjective identification. I believe that the critical reorganization of the relationship from the autistic stage to the stage of therapeutic symbiosis is a function of the analyst's capacity to identify with the patient, which Searles describes as the patient becoming the analyst's whole world. Searles has written extensively about the importance of the process of introjective identification in both human development and clinical theories. He has emphasized the essentially healthy, "permissible" aspect of the parent's and analyst's dependency on the child or patient and the mutuality of growth in their respective identities over the course of childhood or of treatment. For instance, [he] pointed out that we identify with our patients not only in terms of the so-often-emphasized transitory identifications which arise from an empathic sensing of the patients conflicts, which are of essentially communicative value in furtherance of the patient's treatment, but also we identify with the healthier elements in our patients, in a fashion which entails enduring constructive additions to our own personality. [p. 53]

Searles ends his observation on the importance of introjective identification with a statement of his own anxiety and concern: "I continue to be impressed with the intensity of the felt taboo, for me at least, upon the analyst's identifying deeply with the patient in this fashion. . . . One tends to shy away from such experiences as evidence of a forbidden and frightening 'being in love' with the patient" (p. 53).

Searles illustrates this dialectic of the analyst's, supervisor's, or parent's growth through identification with the child, patient, or supervisee in his discussion of the relationship between supervisor and supervisee:

I sometimes find that I try to get the supervisee to live up to my own ego-ideal aspiration, in the hope that if I can help one after another supervisee to practice what I preach, then these supervisees will be tangible persons with whom I can identify, so that hopefully, I may someday have the courage and skill, myself, to do with patients what (so I tell them from my vast experience) they "obviously" should set about doing. My point is that sometimes all this works successfully for both the supervisee and me as well as for the patient, and sometimes it does not; there is a continuum between clearly pathological and healthy processes here. [p. 55]

I have conceived of the analyst's experience of introjective identification during the movement between the autistic stage and that of therapeutic symbiosis as the analyst speaking in a different voice, that of a subject expressing the analyst's unconscious fantasies, in contrast to the traditional analytic voice, which is that of an object in which the analyst represents the rules and experiences of reality. The shift in the analyst's experience of him/herself from that of an object to that of a subject and the reorganization of the analytic relationship through an active process of introjective identification involve multiple dimensions of power and levels of symbolic discourse. Searles's focus on the dimension of power and the level of symbolic discourse reflects his interpretation of the paranoid position. Issues of power are reflected in his attention to both his and the patient's aggression, hostility, and destructive fantasies as well as in his view that the patient is as likely to provide help for him as he is for the patient. Searles's work involves a symmetrical definition of power in the psychoanalytic relationship. An important part of the reorganization of the relationship involves a choice to the more narrow, literal, and concrete protosymbolic representations of the language and experience of the paranoid position. This voluntary and controlled regression in the level of symbolic discourse is critical, albeit frightening, in the shift from the therapist as an object, functioning in the social role of doctor, representing the reality principle, and the therapist as a subject, in which the patient becomes the central affective locus of one's identity and emotional self.

Searles describes the developing experience of the analyst as subject:

> For the resolution of the patient's autism to occur, the analyst must do more than to function as a more reliable protective shield for the patient than the latter's biological mother was during his infancy and early childhood [in the manner Khan (1963, 1964) has described]. First the analyst must have become increasingly free in his acceptance of the patient's functioning as his—the analyst's—maternally protective shield. In my own way of conceptualizing it: to the extent that the analyst can become able comfortably and freely to immerse himself in the autistic patient as constituting his (the analyst's) world, the patient can then utilize him as a model for identification and regards the acceptance of such very primitive dependency needs and can come increasingly to exchange his erstwhile autistic world for the world consisting of, and personified by, the analyst. This progression of events is in actuality composed not of discrete once and for all shifts forward, but rather of blended and ever oscillating processes as that at any one moment the exoskeleton is being provided by the analyst, and at the next moment by the patient, and, increasingly, by both at once and at one. [p. 189]

CLINICAL ILLUSTRATION: THE WINGS OF ICARUS

This case illustrates the processes of projective and introjective identification, the shift from the position that included countertransference resistance and the analytic experience of being an object to that of identification, reverie, and being a subject, which followed the reorganization of the analytic relationship from the stage of autism to that of therapeutic symbiosis. In this example the movement from the isolation and destructiveness of the autistic stage, in which interpretation was not possible, to the stage of therapeutic symbiosis involved the analyst's becoming conscious of both his and the patient's multiple paternal identifications. I want to underline the fact that this was an emotionally challenging experience, which was filled with primitive experiences of devaluation, aggression, and abandonment.

The patient, a woman in her late 30s, had been in treatment for a number of years. The reasons that she had come to treatment involved difficulties in her marriage, discomfort and alienation from her body and her sexuality, long-standing lethargy and depression, and a sense of hopelessness, ineffectiveness, and disconnection in the world. She often experienced herself as an impersonal object with little sense of affective involvement, subjectivity, or agency. The patient was the youngest of four daughters, and I thought that as the last child it had been expected that she would be a son. A significant historical event was her father's death during her adolescence. Early themes in our work focused on her sense of separateness from her husband and issues involving her mother's nonresponsiveness to her (which became more extensive as she developed sexually). The initial focus of treatment was on her feelings of a lack of specialness and feeling like one among many "groupies" waiting for me, while I was seen as a self-impressed Elvis impersonator. As this transference issue of her importance became resolved, her sexual fantasies came to the fore. Concurrent with these transference changes was her increased sense of herself as a sexual and competent person and a decrease in her sense of lethargy, depression, and impotence. Throughout this period of treatment, we were functioning in a traditional interpretative frame.

The aspect of the treatment that I will focus on involved what I have come to see as a period of autism, which became reorganized, through processes of introjective identification, into a period of thera-peutic symbiosis. As the sexual transference–countertransference situa-tion developed, the patient began to experience me as cold, mechanical, and abruptly shifting our focus away from the immediate treatment context to external events. From my perspective, I felt confused and frus-trated that the patient was not hearing and responding to my interpre-tations and comments, and that she frequently arrived late and used the time for more and more superficial discussions of everyday situations in her life. What had been an intimate and productive analytic relation-ship seemed to become a dull, closed, mutually judgmental, and critical relationship. During this time the patient would occasionally call and leave a message requesting an additional appointment. Several times over a period of months I either waited several days, or completely failed, to return her call. This lack of responsiveness was unusual for me in rela-tion to patients, although not always so with colleagues and friends. The patient was devastated by my lack of response to her. It confirmed her earliest fantasies and made her feel that our relationship was phony and that I did not care about her. I was quite upset by the situation and felt that my explanations were rather superficial. I was shocked at my lack of empathy and compassion for this patient, with whom I had a very meaningful relationship. I was verbally and cognitively dumbstruck by my own behavior. I felt extremely guilty about having hurt the patient by not responding to her calls and at having no reasonable explanation for my actions. The patient felt devastated and alone and I felt isolated and extremely guilty. This unconscious acting out would seem to reflect an early phase of projective and introjective identification.

I have come to think of this set of events in the treatment as a de-veloping crisis in the autistic stage of treatment. The crisis reflected the convergence of the forces and frustrations of the autistic stage and si-multaneously allowed the potential resolution of the crisis into a rela-tionship involving therapeutic symbiosis. Searles (1979) describes the experience of intense paranoid anxieties that occur in the analyst during the autistic stage: "Any analyst, however well analyzed he has been, ex-periences considerable anxiety at least on occasion in this phase of the work. As time goes on he tends to become related less and less to the patient, and more and more to his own increasingly regressed, archaic, self-punitive superego. The patient so tenaciously requires omnipotence of him, and his own superego increasingly finds him not qualified for

benevolent omnipotence, but as qualifying for the only other alternative—malevolent omnipotence" (p. 151).

I found myself feeling and being increasingly isolated, with little
to say that seemed significant, and feeling dull, uncreative, and malevolent. As the intensity increased, I found that the patient began to take
on the importance of being my whole world, that what transpired between us defined who I was. It was unclear whether I was containing
her or she was containing me. Relief of my countertransference guilt and
anxiety came with increased focus on my own identifications and the
ability to abandon the safety of the position of the object: the one who
knows. I was a subject in the relationship, I was responsible for having
injured the patient, and I was flooded with my own associations, memories, and fantasies. In this process of introjective identification I became
aware of my associations to my distant, unresponsive, critical, and depressed father, and my inability to separate myself from this identification in my responses to this patient. At the time, I did not share these
associations with the patient because they occurred largely in regressed,
concrete cognitive modes. I felt embarrassed, distrusting, and quite isolated from the patient. I experienced her as my cold, distant, disapprov-
ing father. Finally, it seemed that this period of treatment did not allow
for a constructive, collaborative use of interpretation. I felt that what-
ever I would say would be seen as an excuse; my father's word "phony"
rang in my ears.

During this period the patient began a session talking of her literal
fear of flying as she anticipated an upcoming vacation. In a half-serious
and half-amused way, the patient focused her anxiety on what kept the
plane in the air and why it did not fall down and crash. My initial internal response was to minimize her anxiety and to empathetically explore
in an interpretive way what this anxiety meant to the patient: separation
from me, loss of control, sexual excitement, fear of success, exhibitionism, and grandiosity. All of these were reasonable explanations. Although
not a conscious thought at the time, it is noteworthy that my father had
an intense fear of heights. Suddenly I had a flash of insight. I thought,
she needs a good father, someone who could reassure her that she will
be safe and to explain to her what keeps the airplane in the air. This
experience of insight, as I believe frequently is the case, involved recognizing (or is it re-cognizing) what is known, what is apparent, in a new
and intensely affective, personal, and subjective experiential frame. In

the voice of a father talking to an anxious child, I explained the amazing dynamics of flight, how the curve of the wing causes the plane to lift off the ground. I picked up a piece of paper and blew across it, demonstrating the principle of lift and how the plane stays in the air. The patient began to cry and felt quite touched by this experience. It was an experience of being held, an enactment of the positive identification that had been absent for a long time. On one level she understood that the plane would stay in the air and that she would be safe and no longer alone. Shortly after this she was also able to begin a real process of mourning for the father whom she did not have, which allowed her to integrate important aspects of her subjective experience.

From a theoretical perspective I see this as a symbolic enactment or projective identification occurring within the dimension of therapeutic symbiosis; it was as if suddenly we were on a different plane, one where affective communication and a dialectic of mutual growth and understanding were possible. The work shifted from the isolation and tension of the autistic stage to the more fluid constructive and interpretive modes of the stage of therapeutic symbiosis. I believe that this shift was contingent upon the process of introjective identification, including my ability to understand and experience my identification with my father and to allow the patient to represent my whole affective world. As always, the question of whether this was a necessary sequence comes to mind. Would a different therapist with a different history have been able to avoid this painful and somewhat lengthy sequence of events, of resistance, of countertransference failure, guilt and anxiety, and then the reorganization and an enactment of the unconscious fantasies with the analytic relationship? I think that with a different therapist the content might have been different; however, I believe that the process of structural change that is at the heart of psychoanalysis and psychoanalytic therapy inevitably calls for the intense subjective participation in the enactment of unconscious fantasies by both the analyst and patient as they negotiate the different relational organizations inherent in the processes of projective and introjective identification, which have been described by the Kleinians and mapped by Searles.

5

Power in the Psychoanalytic Relationship: Symmetrical, Complementary, Metacomplementary

Power, a critical dimension in all human relationships, has been largely ignored in psychoanalytic theory and practice. Two factors explain this lack of interest in issues of power in psychoanalytic theory. Concepts of power focus on political, social, and class issues, rather than on the preferred explanatory models of biology and natural science. Theorists who have introduced sociopolitical concepts of power into the psychoanalytic discourse have presented their theories in the context of critiques of society's impact on the individual, where pathology is defined as a distortion of social rather than biological being. Adler (1932), Fromm (1947), Horney (1937), Sullivan (1953), May (1972), and Marcuse (1955) each presented theories that focus on issues of power in the social context, and each of these theorists has been marginalized in contemporary psychoanalytic theory. The second explanation for the lack of consideration of issues of power in psychoanalytic theory is that in the traditional one-person model of psychoanalysis, issues of power, including questions of equality and mutuality between patient and analyst, have been thought of as elements of the analytic frame, invariant structures within which questions of power were understood as the patient's resistance, reflecting transference issues around authority, dependence, and infantile wishes. Freud's metaphor of the analyst as a surgeon defined the analyst's authority and power in the classical one-person perspective describing (or inscribing) the explicit inequality or asymmetry of the expert doctor in relation to the ill patient, the need to stand against and eliminate the clearly defined pathological bodies, whether an infection or an unconscious infantile wish, and the need for an aseptic or psychologically neutral environment in which the doctor's personal style is minimized in relation to the standard technique. Many aspects of the analyst's attitude and technique can be understood within the context of this asymmetrical power relationship, where the analyst maintains the superior position, representing the reality principle, while the patient is in the subordinate position, representing the pleasure principle.

As contemporary theory has progressed from the one-person perspective of the classical drive model to the two-person relational perspective (Gill and Hoffman 1982, Greenberg and Mitchell 1983, Kernberg 1993, Mitchell 1988), it has lost the certainties of the asymmetrical definition of power of the traditional model of psychoanalysis. Concerns with redefining power in the two-person model of the psychoanalytic relationship are central to questions of the therapeutic effect of the relationship, enactment, the positive and negative aspects of countertransference, issues of self-disclosure, and the fundamental symmetry and asymmetry of the psychoanalytic relationship. However, contemporary theory has not yet developed a comprehensive model of the analytic relationship that addresses the complex issues of power inherent in the two-person relational model of the psychoanalytic relationship.

Klein (1975), unlike her politically oriented contemporaries, conceptualized the central dimension of power in human relationships from a purely psychological perspective. The paranoid-schizoid position can be understood as the development of the capacity to express power and agency through the development and symbolization of unconscious fantasies of greed, envy, sadism, and aggression. In the paranoid-schizoid position, the transference–countertransference situation is organized through enactment and concrete experiences around dimensions of power, for example: "Do you control me or do I control you?" "Do I put this in you or do you put it in me?" "I am the victim, you are the abuser." "You always take advantage of me." "You are greedy and want my money." Projective identifications often involve conscious awareness of power, aggression, and destructiveness as the individual externalizes aspects of the self through projecting it into the other and then condemning, rejecting, or controlling the other as the embodiment of the disowned aggressive aspects of the self.

Many contemporary psychoanalytic theories have failed to appreciate the central importance of power in Kleinian theory and have prematurely attempted to accommodate her radical insights into the traditional forms of the psychoanalytic relationship. Schafer's (1994) conclusion that traditional Freudian and contemporary Kleinian technique are essentially similar ego psychological approaches to treatment illustrates this trend toward minimizing theoretical differences and collapsing vastly different analytic approaches into the traditional model of the psychoanalytic relationship. Similarly, discussions of asymmetry, symmetry, and mutuality (Aron 1996, Burke 1992) in the psychoanalytic relationship have focused on the traditional, one-person dimension of the analyst's self-disclosure (of countertransference and other personal information) rather than on a Kleinian focus on power, sadism, and aggression in the psychoanalytic relationship. The emphasis on transference and countertransference as a source of information, rather than an enactment, reflects an ego psychological emphasis on discursive language, understanding, and defenses against awareness as contrasted to an emphasis on performative language, issues of power, and the enactment of dominance and submission in the psychoanalytic relationship. Unfortunately, discussions of power in the Kleinian literature have often seemed complicated and anachronistic because of the use of concepts drawn from instinct theory to describe the complex intertwining of projective and introjective experiences of power, aggression, and the pleasures and pains of sadomasochistic triumph in relationships.

THE PARANOID-SCHIZOID POSITION: FROM DEATH INSTINCT TO POWER

Klein felt that Freud's concepts of the life and death instincts provided the best structure to explain the constant struggle that she observed in her child patients as they attempted to both destroy and preserve their objects (Rosenfeld 1971). She believed that a primary anxiety arises from the operation of the death instinct, which is manifested as an unbearable fear of annihilation, of nonbeing, and is split off and projected into external objects, where it is experienced as persecutory anxiety. For Klein, this struggle with destructiveness is not a reactive experience, a response to either deprivation or frustration, but rather something arising from within the structure of being human, a part of our existential state that needs to be confronted, integrated, and developed. Although Klein's (1957) thinking evolved from this simple formulation of instincts to a more psychological concept of aggression, the experience of greed, envy, destructiveness, aggression, and power remained the cornerstones of her theory of the paranoid-schizoid position, a universal aspect of being human, and a basic element in the evolving transference–countertransference relationship, accounting for many of the difficulties patients experience in the process of change.

Rosenfeld (1971) vacillates between the language of instincts and drives and that of envy, which reflects the ambivalence of many Kleinian authors in their attempts to give up the anachronistic language of a one-person instinct theory for the more fully psychological language of a two-person theory focused on the dynamics of envy, greed, aggression, and power as the central dimension of the paranoid-schizoid position. This ambivalence is reflected in the following:

> She [Klein] also stressed that through investigating these early (destructive) processes in the transference she became convinced that the analysis of the negative transference was a precondition for analyzing the deeper layers of the mind. It was particularly in the negative aspects of the early infantile transference that Melanie Klein came up against primitive envy, which she regarded as a direct derivative of the death instinct. She thought that envy appears as a hostile, life-destroying force in the relation of the infant to its mother and is particularly directed against the good feeding mother because she is not only needed by the infant but envied for containing everything which the infant wants to possess himself. In the transference this manifests itself in the patient's need to devalue analytic work which he has found helpful. It appears that envy representing almost completely undiffused destructive energy is particularly unbearable to the infantile ego and early on in life becomes split off from the rest of the ego. Melanie Klein stressed that split off, unconscious envy often remained unexpressed in analysis, but nevertheless exerted a troublesome and powerful influence on preventing progress in analysis. [p. 244]

The trend in contemporary Kleinian literature (Feldman 2000, Joseph 1982, Segal 1997) is to view the death instinct as a metaphor for a deep endogenous structure that reflects the experience of psychological and emotional death, and of how meaning, creativity, need, gratitude, and love are attacked, undermined, retarded, and deadened. Segal (1997, as cited in Feldman 2000) points out that the individual can follow either of two directions: "One, to seek satisfaction for the needs: that is life promoting and leads to object seeking, love and eventually object concern. The other is the drive to annihilate: the need to annihilate the perceiving experiencing self, as well as anything that is perceived" (p. 53). Feldman (2000) elaborates this idea, describing the goal of the death instinct as eliminating "anything that give rise to admiration, dependence, rivalry and particularly envy" (p. 54).

Joseph (1982, 1988) describes the experience of the death instinct in terms of character structure. She discusses pathological organizations in which patients are addicted to near-death experiences, to being barely alive, and to filling their objects with either masochistic despair or complementary unbearable sadism. In describing the clinical work with these patients, she describes the extremely frustrating passive indifference of the patient to the analysis, which she contrasted with the analyst's experience of containing the split-off and projected experience of being active, interested, and alive. Joseph (1988) describes this evolving transference situation that may go on for years:

> The patient comes, talks, dreams, etc. but one gets the impression of very little real active interest in changing, improving, remembering, getting anywhere in the treatment. Slowly the picture builds up. The analyst seems to be the only person in the room who is actively concerned about change, about progress, about development, as if all the active parts of the patient have been projected into the analyst. If the analyst is not aware of this and therefore does not concentrate his interpretations around this process, collusion can arise in which the analyst carefully, maybe tactfully, pushes and tries to get the patient's interest or tries to alert him. The patient briefly responds only to withdraw again and leave the next move to the analyst, and a major piece of psychopathology is acted out in the transference. The patient is constantly pulling back towards the silent kind of deadly paralysis and near complete passivity. When these lively parts of the patient remain so constantly split off it means that his

whole capacity for wanting and missing, feeling disturbed at losing, etc., the very stuff that makes for whole object relating is projected and the patient remains with his addiction and without the psychological means of combating this. To me, therefore, the understanding of the nature of this apparent passivity is technically of primary importance with these patients. Moreover, it means that with such splitting off of the life and instincts and of loving, ambivalence and guilt is largely evaded. As these patients improve and become more integrated and relationships become more real, they begin to feel acute pain sometimes experienced as almost physical—undifferentiated but extremely intense. [p. 320]

PASSIVE AND ACTIVE ORGANIZATIONS OF THE PARANOID-SCHIZOID POSITION

Observations of these qualities of affective deadness, passivity, and the masochistic triumph of patients devoted to the destruction of analytic progress suggest the need to conceptualize two organizations within the paranoid-schizoid position. The passive paranoid position describes the experience of patients who have projected their aggression into external objects and who experience themselves as passive, helpless, and filled with despair, victims of the cruelty of both the analyst and of others, helpless and imprisoned in the world. In contrast, the active paranoid position describes the experience of the patient who has internalized aggression as a grandiose defense against objects and is in the process of deadening all need, meaning, and creativity in self and in others. The individual in the active paranoid position is devoted to, although consciously disavowing, the triumphant gratification of replacing the analyst's psychic reality, his or her words, thoughts, creativity, and optimism, with one dominated by paralysis and terror. We may think of the analysis of the psychological death instinct as the transformation of the passive paranoid position, the patient's experience of being a victim, filled with despair and impotence, to the active paranoid position, in which the patient can fully experience aggression, grandiose denial of dependency, and pleasure in the exercise of control and power rather than the persecutory fears of domination and retaliation. The transformation of the passive to the active paranoid position is a necessary experience if the patient is to begin to reinternalize evacuated aggression and become capable of experiencing the reparative and symbolic capacities of the depressive position.

The destruction of the patient's and analyst's capacity to think, substituting repetitive, concrete acting out, or acting out through noncommunicative use of language, is indicative of the passive paranoid position. Joseph (1988) describes this deadened, isolated, paranoid-schizoid use of language in one of her patients:

> A [the patient] in the period that I was trying to explore in him this dedication to masochism, described one day how he had been upset the previous evening because K [his girlfriend] had been going out with someone else. He realized that on the previous evening he had, in his mind, been rehearsing what he might say to K about this. For example, he could talk about how he could not go on with her like this, while she was going around with another man; how he would have to give up the whole relationship; he could not go on like this, and so and so. As he went on speaking about what he would say to K, I got the feeling, not only from the ideas but from his whole tone, that he was not just thinking what he might say to K, but was caught up in some kind of cruel dialogue with her. Slowly then he clarified the ideas that he had had, and how he was going over things in his mind. On this occasion and indeed on others, he realized that he would be saying something cruel, for example, and that K in the phantasy would reply or cry or plead or cling, she would become provocative, he would get cruel back, etc. In other words what he had been calling "thinking about what he would say" is actually actively being caught up in his mind in a provocative sado-masochistic phantasy, in which he both hurts and is hurt, verbally repeats and is humiliated, until the phantasy actively has such a grip on him that it almost has a life of its own and the content becomes secondary. [p. 316]

This destructive use of language is consciously experienced as an aspect of the passive paranoid position by the patient. Although unconsciously, it is experienced as an active grandiose attack on the analyst's words and mind through editing interpretations, changing a word, becoming overly literal or abstract, being silently contemptuous, destroying meaning, and feeling angry, disappointed, and aggrieved. The patient's passivity involves both the projection of aggression, hatred, and power into the analyst, and simultaneously disavowing the more complex, internal (psychic) experience of the disavowed unconscious sadomasochistic fantasies and enactment, which can provide an active experience of triumph and pleasure. Feldman (2000) focuses on facilitating the patient's recognition of this unconscious pleasure and gratification, allowing for the transformation of the passive to active paranoid position and the internalization of the patient's disowned aggression and power. He illustrates a beginning shift into the active paranoid position with a patient who can simultaneously recognize this gratification experienced as moral superiority while at the same time not fully recognizing the triumphant pleasures of destruction and the grandiose denial of need and dependency. Feldman describes this oscillation between the active and passive paranoid positions in a difficult and frustrating session that he had begun several minutes late and in which the patient was talking about a problem of incompetence with his accountant:

> Mr. B [the patient] claimed to be uncertain about the time we had started. His offer to "split the difference" was also manifest in the ambiguous and partial way he related to my interpretations. What emerged in relation to the accountant was that when it was the other person's failure, he didn't express his criticism directly, but used his observations and his subjective experience in a more hidden way. He now felt that he had something that he could hold over his object, to control and intimidate in a superior, quietly menacing fashion. He had no responsibility: he didn't have to pay, he was "off the hook." His power depended in part on the other person's sense of guilt and responsibility. At times Mr. B was now able to recognize the satisfaction he got from holding his object in such a tormenting grip. More important, however, were the mechanisms by which his internal objects were tyrannized and undermined. As a result they often appeared weak, bed-ridden and vulnerable. It was because of his inevitable identification with such weakened internal figures that Mr. B often found it difficult to make proper use of his capacities. [p. 61]

DESTRUCTIVENESS, AGGRESSION, AND POWER IN THE DEVELOPMENT OF IDENTITY

The Kleinian view of the transference–countertransference situation contrasts the importance of aggression, power, and the enactment of the death instinct with the traditional asymmetrical definition of power in which the analyst is a representative of the reality principle, maintaining paternal authority through interpreting the patient's repressed oedipal wishes. Dewald (1972) presents a classical illustration of the asymmetry of the power relationship as it manifests itself in the structure of the analytic relationship and oedipal interpretations of the patient's dynamics and the transference–countertransference relationship. He focused on his female patient's oedipal conflict, and directed his interpretations of resistance and transference at facilitating remembering and reconstructing the patient's repressed childhood desires and experience. I will present a neo-Kleinian reading of this material and suggest how this perspective would have structured a different approach to the transference–countertransference relationship. My discussion emphasizes the patient's failure at mastering the aggressive and destructive anxieties of the paranoid-schizoid position, and the related difficulties in consolidating a separate and autonomous identity as an adult woman.

POWERLESSNESS AND THE PASSIVE PARANOID POSITION

I will start by contrasting the oedipal interpretations of classical theory with a Kleinian view of the patient's experience of powerlessness, of her evacuated aggression, and the need to transform these passive experiences into an active experience. During the first week of treatment, the patient presented her central concerns as intense anxieties about being an unfit mother and her fear that her mother-in-law would take her children away from her. This concern can be understood as either a derivative of her oedipal wishes and anxieties or as a paranoid anxiety, a fear of retaliation arising from the projection of her aggression and envy. In the following dialogue we see how Dewald's (1972) structures the issues in terms of oedipal dynamics and seems to foreclose issues of aggression, power, and the fear of destructiveness.

> *Patient:* I don't feel as if I'm an adult and a woman and I can't stand it.
> *Analyst:* How do you mean a woman?
> *Patient:* I want to feel equal with you. And this is what I'd like this analysis to result in, but I'm afraid it will never come. . . .

This whole idea of getting understanding—I feel as if I'm less of a person and as if you've completely overpowered me and you've weakened me. I feel that I'm completely defenseless against this and like I'm not a person at all. I'm here and your here and it's like with my father. If there is any understanding between us then we will come together and I'm really nothing. I want to be a person and I want to grow up to be a woman. . . . I feel all repressed again right now. I can't understand what happened. This is an ideal situation, but something happens to me. [p. 36]

Dewald focuses his intervention on what it means to be a woman as opposed to the patient's concerns about being a competent, powerful adult. I would have heard her statements as reflecting feelings of being powerless, of having projected her aggression into external objects, feeling empty and powerless and robbed by her father, although she is able to state her hopes that the analysis would facilitate her development as an equal to the analyst, to her father, and to be able to stand as a separate and autonomous individual in the world. From a Kleinian perspective, her experience of insecurity and inadequacy as a mother and her fear that her children will be taken away from her focuses on her projections of envy and her mother's inability to contain these destructive projective identifications that would have allowed for processes of reverie, introjective identification, and introjection.

The patient quickly learned the analyst's language, which did not make room for themes of aggression and power, telling Dewald that she feels more comfortable and "trusts" him with her sexual feelings as opposed to her angry feelings. This suggestion expresses awareness of Dewald's preference for oedipal themes, translating a potentially wide range of experience into this narrow interpretive band. In the second month of treatment, the patient acknowledged her sadistic use of sexuality as a pleasure in having power over men and seeing their weakness. Dewald recognized how the patient used sexuality for a variety of nonsexual aims: "the control of the other person, the expression of hostility and depreciation of the man" (p. 78). However, rather than addressing the issues of aggression, power, and control, he understands this material as a defense against the development of an oedipal transference neurosis, with him having the desired paternal phallus, rather than as the transference itself. This narrow view of the experience and language of sexuality as repressed desire can be thought of as an avoidance of issues of aggression, sadism, control, and power. I believe that the patient was attempting to express her unacknowledged paranoid anxiety of an awareness of an intensely destructive aspect of herself, rather than an oedipal wish, when she states, "There is no love in there [referring to her internal world], it's all hate."

About a month later, after Dewald canceled an appointment, which caused the patient to feel insignificant, she said, attempting to differentiate sexuality from aggression, "I have a desire to seduce men, and to have all men fall head over heels in front of me, and yet it's all so hostile. I feel this toward you and I have no sexual feelings at all" (p. 131). However, Dewald's need to see himself in the transference as a sexually desirable oedipal object as opposed to an object of the patient's hatred and aggression seems to structure the following interpretation: "So you felt my cancellation was a slur on your femininity. . . . You don't want to feel any sexual feelings toward me because you are so angry at me so you displace all of this to other men" (p. 131).

Dewald consistently avoids the patient's aggressive and angry feelings and fantasies, which are cast within a narrow oedipal framework in which the analyst is the defended against but desired sexual object. This interpretive strategy is maintained, even though the patient frequently describes her destructive, aggressive feelings and fantasies, which I believe reflects limitations dictated by Dewald's use of classical theory and his initial assessment of the patient. Kleinian theory would provide a more veridical understanding of this patient's difficulties—her sense of inadequacy as an adult, and her inability to assert herself and to be an autonomous woman equal to men in social and sexual relations. These difficulties arise out of early issues of aggression, destructiveness, and envy, and the family's failure to contain these projections, which perhaps were experienced as too dangerous and destructive, as well as a family model of using sexuality as a means of expressing aggression, dependence, dominance, and control. The family history contains a great deal of information, including the almost unacknowledged reality that the patient had been sexually abused by her maternal uncle.

IDENTIFICATION AND THE PARANOID POSITION

The fifteenth month of treatment followed Dewald's being away for a week, which he had told the patient about in a way that he recognized as unusual for him and was apparently a countertransference reaction to the patient's announcement of a planned vacation with her husband. Dewald does not comment, to the patient or to the reader, on his understanding of this countertransference, which seems to reflect separation anxiety and destructive envy that he expressed in a literal assertion: "I'm going on a trip also." I think it would have been helpful if Dewald understood his countertransference as an experience of projective identification through which he could have elaborated the parallel experience of the patient's anxieties, where separations are seen as dangerous abandonment evoking the anxieties and defenses against need and destructive envy. Although recognizing that his unusual behavior was a countertransference response to the patient, he chose to maintain a neutral stance and inquire into the memories and affects aroused by his action.

The patient's use of introjective identification as a means of reparation and in dealing with her own destructive fantasies is clear in her response to Dewald's absence. After describing her paranoid fantasies that Dewald was in the hospital and her husband was having affairs during this absence, her affect became calm and she said, "There were three other people who came to me for help this week with their problems. I identified myself with you, and suddenly I began to love you! I got such a good feeling from helping them" (p. 400). The patient continued to describe her positive feelings and then returned to her thoughts about her husband's affairs. Even considering the explicitness of the patient's attempts through introjective identification to repair her frightening, destructive projections, Dewald continued to maintain an oedipal interpretative strategy, choosing to inquire about her feelings about her husband's sexual acting out rather than her identification, maintaining the split between the "good father–analyst" and the "bad father–husband." This inquiry reflects his strong preference for the interpretive line of the classical oedipal conflict, but it also is a limitation in his ability to understand the importance of identification as a reparative, symbolic act.

At the beginning of the next session the patient clearly expressed identification with her mother: "I feel just like a deserted housewife. I hate it!" (p. 403). Dewald's interpretation focused on the absent but desired father rather than on the failed identification with the mother: "You seem to be identifying with your mother, and to feel that your father has just returned to you." The patient, frustrated in her attempt to clarify the split in her identification with her mother as a whole person independent of the relationship with the phallic father, stated, "There are two possibilities for me, either to feel that way or to be a whore. I'd rather be my mother." Dewald inquired, "Why do you have to be either one?" This seems naive, and minimizes the importance of both the patient's identification with her mother as well as the need to integrate her good maternal object with her bad maternal object in an attempt to make reparation and consolidate her identity as a woman independent from her relationship with father, analyst, and phallus. Throughout the remainder of the session, Dewald seemed unable to inquire into the issue of her identification with her mother. It is as if he can only see this relationship between the daughter and mother as an extension of the oedipal triangle. Dewald's continued interpretation of the triangular oedipal dynamics and his inability to see the patient's desperate need for an identification with her mother presented a significant difficulty in understanding the patient and in providing appropriate analytic interventions.

A neo-Kleinian approach would understand the patient's processes of introjective identification as an effort at reparation, a therapeutic symbiosis, through which she attempts both to heal her mother by internalizing the "bad maternal object" and to merge with her in an attempt to affirm her mother's life. However, because of her mother's apparent limitations, there is primarily an experience of a pathological symbiosis in which the patient must contain the mother's split-off, projective identification of being a bad woman filled with destructive feelings. The patient can only be a whore, a "bad sexual object," the woman as an object of the man's desire. For this patient, the fantasy of the bad sexual object was usually associated with men as she had projected these fantasies onto her husband and the analyst. It would seem that sexuality would then be experienced as a split-off, destructive male part-object that would further confuse and interfere with the development of her identity as a woman.

There are three dimensions that are confused for the patient and result in her inability to form an autonomous, integrated identity of herself as a sexual woman. These part-object identifications with her mother involve a dimension of power and control expressed as sadism, a voyeuristic dimension in which sexuality is always experienced from the perspective of an external or objective observer, and a dimension of dependency expressed as either weakness involving a need for others or strength through withholding and being isolated. These destructive identifications with her mother—the sadism, voyeurism, and withholding—are expressed in the following statement by the patient: "I have a feeling that I'm being like my mother. It's as if she says, 'This is my power over men because they are so weak and so sexual.' I can keep my own sexual feelings in and then I have him and he's nothing" (p. 411).

Dewald's difficulty in conceptualizing the potentially reparative function of identification and his use of triangular oedipal interpretations interfered with the patient's developing sense of her female identity and is reflected in the following interpretation: "The feeling of being protective toward your mother suggests that there is also a wish to have your mother for yourself and that maybe you feel jealous because your father has her" (p. 453). This interpretation suggests that there is little value in being a woman, a daughter, or a mother except as it exists in relation to a man and to the father's penis. It is interesting that the final interpretation before the treatment was terminated was that the patient's deepest desire was to return to her mother by being identified with her father's penis and being able to enter and become one with mother through intercourse. This is an interesting fantasy; however, it is a fantasy from a man's perspective and one that denies an independent value to women, to mothers, to the breast, and to dyadic as opposed to triangular relationships.

One of the problems with the framework provided by the classical oedipal theory that is illustrated in Dewald's presentation is that it maintains both the themes and structures of paternal authority, dismissing issues of aggression, envy, destructiveness, and the need for multiple identifications with aspects of both mother and father. In Kleinian theory (Birkstead-Breen 1996, Sayers 1989) and in feminist developments of relational psychoanalysis (Benjamin 1995, Dimen 1991, Harris 1991), concepts of identity represent relational structures or unconscious fantasies involving complex integration of aggression, power, and a complementary and interlocking series of gender definitions independent of libido theory and the constraints of traditional oedipal relationship. Winnicott (1971) has an often overlooked contribution to discussions of sexuality and gender in which he focuses on processes of identification and the bisexual nature of the individual's unconscious experience. Khan (1974) illustrates Winnicott's theory of bisexuality in a case of a young woman that is quite similar to the case presented by Dewald. Khan presents a neo-Kleinian perspective and focuses on the internal process of identity formation in a young woman who initially talked a great deal about her frequent deadened sexual affairs. Khan came to understand this sexual activity as both a component of her male identification (an identification with her stepfather's penis) and more importantly as a way of protecting her fragile, undeveloped, and far more subjectively real female self.

Dewald's patient's difficulty in achieving an independent identity as a woman and mother reflects early failures in projective and introjective processes in her family, resulting in her inability to separate from the pathological symbiotic identifications (Searles 1979) with her childhood objects. Searles uses his notion of pathological symbiosis to describe aspects of the processes of projection and introjection in which the child takes on those split-off, unacceptable components of the parents' identity in the hope of magically healing the pathological aspects of the parents so that the child can then become a separate and individuated person. Winnicott (1977) also presents a similar approach to processes of projection and introjection, suggesting the importance of the analyst's active process of introjective identification in working with the pathological effects of splitting and the failure to integrate aggression, destructiveness and envy. In his work with a child who was frightened of her destructive (paranoid) potential, he identified himself with the disowned greedy impulses and allowed the child to experience him as being the greedy and potentially destructive one. Rather than being the good analytic object in contrast to the bad historical object, he became the bad object, allowing this child patient to experience her destructiveness in an object strong enough to contain it.

POWER IN THE PSYCHOANALYTIC RELATIONSHIP

Contemporary psychoanalytic theory (Aron 1996, Kernberg 1993, Renik 1996) has focused a great deal of attention on the analytic relationship, attempting to address the transference–countertransference relationship as one that has been mutually constructed and becomes the stage for the enactment of the patient's unconscious fantasies. Within these different contemporary approaches, questions of the analyst's authority and prerogatives have received attention largely from the perspective of the patient's and analyst's expectations around issues of authority, in which there has been a trend toward a more egalitarian view of the analytic relationship. These approaches have not addressed the issues of power as a derivative of Klein's concept of the death instinct and the essential deep structures of aggression, destructiveness, and envy as aspects of the paranoid position. In this section I present a neo-Kleinian approach to issues of power in the psychoanalytic relationship.

Aron (1996) makes a valuable distinction between issues of mutuality involving shared information and issues of power as reflected in asymmetry and symmetry or equality and difference in the analytic relationship. This dimension can be described as who sets the rules of the relationship. In relation to this dimension of power, he argues for an asymmetrical structure in the analytic relationship, maintaining the rule-making function and the maintenance of the analytic frame as the analyst's sole prerogative. However, Aron's position presents a dilemma for contemporary technique as he attempts to integrate mutuality, which he sees as an important aspect of the two-person model, while simultaneously defining the relationship as asymmetrical, reflecting the assumptions of the one-person model in which issues of power are defined through the analyst's role as the paternal authority. Does the patient have a right to ask or demand that the therapist do something or to talk about a particular aspect of the therapist's life? [See Aron's (1996) example of the magazine and Gerson's (1996) example of the lie as illustrations of this dilemma.]

Burke (1992) presents a more typical position, in which he ignores the dimension of power and contrasts asymmetry, which he defines as withholding information, with mutuality, which he defines as providing information. Burke advocates a judicial use of self-disclosure as a way of facilitating the analytic process and the differentiation of the historical objects from the new analytic object. He illustrates his argument with a case vignette of a patient who was very critical of the analyst's practice of charging for missed appointments. Earlier attempts at interpreting the patient's confusion between his father and the analyst, who was seen as "operating in the same 'self protective, hostile and small-minded' manner as the patient's father" (p. 251), did not seem to resolve this intense negative transference. Burke suggests that this impasse was resolved when the analyst provided the following information that he believed facilitated the differentiation between the historical object and the new analytic object. In response to the patient's continued barrage of criticism following being charged for another missed appointment, the analyst said, "It is more comfortable to have a set of rules agreed upon in advance than to be cast in the role of judge who must rule on the merits of each absence" (p. 251). This interpretation would appear to express the analyst's intention to differentiate himself from the tyranny of the patient's father by contrasting his beliefs in an egalitarian, contractual relationship with the authoritarian relationship of the castrating paternal object. However, this strategy sidesteps the basic issues of power and the patient's moralistic, aggressive attacks on the analyst, who was seen as another unfair authority who arbitrarily set the rules of the relationship. From a Kleinian perspective, this sequence can be thought of as representing an enactment of the patient's failure to integrate his aggression in the paranoid-schizoid position, which is projected into the analyst where the feelings of greed and aggression are condemned. This view of the issue as one of projected aggression presents a contrast to an essentially ego psychological focus on the reality of fees for missed appointments and information about the difference between the fair-minded analyst and the tyrannical father. We can understand this set of transactions as the enactment of an unconscious fantasy of power, envy, and aggression as it becomes enacted as a set of concrete transference–countertransference experiences that may be defined as the unconscious fantasy of a greedy thief (son, analyst, patient) who needs to be controlled and limited by a fair and benevolent judge (father, analyst, patient). Like most unconscious fantasies, or their representations as identity structures, the two complementary positions—the greedy thief and the fair and benevolent judge—are fluid, with each person (son, father, analyst, patient) taking on each position in the unconscious fantasy and in the enactment. This fantasy reflects splitting and the disavowed aggression of the paranoid-schizoid position, so that it is difficult to say who is the victim and who is the persecutor.

This paradox of power in the psychoanalytic relationship involves an interesting and complex layering of victim and persecutor as we focus on the question of who is controlling whom. On the surface it would appear that the patient is powerless and feels hurt, abused, and angry at being charged for missed appointments by the analyst. However, one can readily imagine the analyst's experience of frustration, of being forced to explain his actions to the patient, of having to step outside of his preferred mode of interpretation and justify his own behavior before a judge who questions his fairness. In terms of the manifest content, it is the patient who is submissive and the analyst who is dominant; however, on the level of action it would seem that the patient is dominant, although claiming to be submissive, and the analyst who appears dominant is now submissive. The positive effect of the analyst's explanation is not a function of providing the patient with additional information ("I am different from your father"), but rather, like the wolves in Konrad Lorenz's (1966) classic example of dominance and submission, it is the experience of the simultaneous assertion of power and the disavowal of power that allows the patient and analyst to address through a concrete enactment the multiple levels of the paranoid experiences of dominance, submission, sadism, aggression, and power in the analytic relationship.

Bateson and his colleagues at the Mental Research Institute (Ahumada 1991, Etchegoyen and Ahumada 1990, Watzlawick et al. 1967) conceptualized multilayered relationships in which control is expressed through the simultaneous disavowal and assertion of power as a metacomplementary relationship. They saw all relationships and all communication as involving a dimension of power and a dimension of information and developed a taxonomy of these relationships—how they are structured and organized through verbal, nonverbal, and contextual aspects of communication. They described three patterns of relationships based on the dimension of power or control. The first is a relationship of symmetry, which is defined as a relationship of equals. The second is a relationship in which each individual has different prerogatives, statuses, or rights, and is defined as a complementary relationship. The traditional, asymmetrical, one-person model of psychoanalysis, in which the analyst defines the rules of the relationship and defines the analytic frame, can be thought of as an example of a complementary relationship. The third relationship structure, the metacomplementary relationship, involves a complex organization in which the person in the apparent subordinate position instructs, gives permission to, provokes, or forces the other to be in charge or in control, while the person in the apparently superior position is forced to act in accord with the subordinate person's covert commands. The two-person model of psychoanalysis has a liability toward the problems inherent in the metacomplementary relationship because the relationship is simultaneously conceptualized as co-constructed (Hoffman 1991), suggesting a symmetrical or egalitarian relationship, while the analyst still maintains the prerogatives of establishing the rules of the relationship, suggesting a complementary relationship. Because of this conflict between equality and authority, the relationship tends toward a metacomplementary structure in which the analyst and patient become covertly engaged in both the assertion and disavowal of the paranoid themes of power, control, and the establishment of the rules of the psychoanalytic relationship.

Burke's (1992) example collapses the distinction between symmetry defined as mutuality and self-disclosure and the asymmetry of issues of power inherent in the complementary activity of deciding the rules of the analytic relationship. As a result of this covert conflict, the analyst and patient develop a metacomplementary relationship, with each participant presenting himself overtly in the benevolent and persecuted position while covertly attempting to sadistically control the other. Understanding this transference–countertransference paradigm as a metacomplementary relationship shifts the focus from an information exchange and the differentiation of historical and current objects to the paranoid issues of the patient's unintegrated or disowned aggression projected into the analyst, who feels that he is being unfairly accused of being tyrannical and greedy. This transference–countertransference configuration becomes a repetitive and circular enactment of the father–son relationship, with each participant in turn being father and son. The analyst's implicit confession and disavowal of greed can be thought of as a response to the patient's sadistic attack on the analyst, while simultaneously the analyst disowns his own power in the relationship, thus enacting the unconscious fantasy of the dominating father and the weak son in the metacomplementary structure of the transference–countertransference relationship. Metacomplementary relationships may be thought of as enactments within the paranoid-schizoid organization, in which projected and disowned issues of power, sadism, and aggression trap the analyst, who wishes both to be experienced as a benevolent and helpful new object and to maintain the authority of the traditional complementary relationship where the analyst defines reality.

BION AND THE DEVELOPMENT OF SYMMETRY IN THE ANALYTIC RELATIONSHIP

Issues of power and the subtlety of working with the complex metacomplementary communications in the transference–countertransference relationship are illustrated in Bion's sensitive approach to issues of power and control and his capacity to freely act on, or enact, rather than explain, the rules of the relationship in his work with patients (Symington 1990). Bion's development of Kleinian technique reflects a strong emphasis on maintaining a symmetrical relationship, which is embodied in his statements about the analyst's freedom to think and to act independently of the patient's expectations, projective identifications, and attempts at control. It is the analyst's freedom to act and to think his own thoughts that allows him to develop a genuinely symmetrical relationship, a relationship between equals, and to work through the paranoid issues of dominance and control. Symington (1990) illustrates this process in relation to a patient's attempts at metacomplementary control; the patient presents herself as a powerless victim caught in the pathological forces of the past and the disowned urges of her sexual and oedipal impulses. The patient who was presented to Bion in supervision presents the problem that she "wants sex with other men besides her husband, therefore in her view she must be a whore" (p. 96). The patient's relationship with her husband can be understood as a metacomplementary relationship where she assigns him the role of keeping her under control. She is attempting to establish a similar metacomplementary relationship with her analyst, who she implores to control her behavior and to define her experience. She claims to be afraid that if she got a divorce from her husband "she would run around and have sex with all sorts of men—behave like a free whore" (p. 96). The analyst seems to feel uncomfortably trapped into defining the patient's experience and not knowing how to avoid the conclusion that she is a whore. She demands that her analyst tell her whether he thinks that she is or would be a whore.

Bion suggests to the analyst that he "would try to draw her attention to the way in which she wishes to limit my freedom about what I call her. It is just as much a limitation if the patient wants you to give the correct interpretation. Why shouldn't I be free to form my own opinions that she's a whore, or that she's something quite different? Why be angry with me because in fact I am free to come to my own conclusions?" (p. 96). Bion maintains a focus on the implicit issues of power and attempts to playfully establish a symmetrical dialogue with the analyst, through which he can separate the content from the relationship aspects of the transference–countertransference situation. However, because of being dominated by the patient's projective identification and his own issues of power and control, the analyst is unable to shift to Bion's symmetrical position and insists on finding a way to respond to the patient's metacomplementary demands while maintaining his role as the benevolent analyst.

The analyst insists that Bion respond to the patient's metacomplementary demand, re-creating in the supervision experience a parallel to the relationship between himself and the patient. He says to Bion, "Her fear is that your own conclusion will be that she is a whore." Bion responds, "But why shouldn't I be allowed to come to that conclusion?" The analyst continues in a somewhat concrete or literal manner: "So that you conclude that she is a whore—now where are you?" Bion responds in what I would imagine to be a playful way, "But I haven't said that I do. The point I want to show is that there is a wish to limit my freedom of thought" (p. 96).

Although perhaps appearing stubborn, simple, or unresponsive, Bion's interventions can be understood as reflecting an emphasis on issues of power and symmetry in the analytic relationship as well as illustrating the Kleinian view that language and words in the paranoid position represent concrete experiences and action rather than exclusively units of information. Steiner (1994) concisely points out that patients who are functioning at the paranoid-schizoid level are not interested in understanding, but rather experience words concretely; words are "used, not primarily to convey information, but to have an effect on the analyst, and the analyst's words are likewise felt as actions indicating something about the analyst's state of mind rather than offering insight to the patient" (p. 406).

Etchegoyen and Ahumada (1990) extend the importance of the concept of symmetry in contemporary Kleinian theory from the interpersonal dimensions of power between people to include an intrapsychic dimension of power as an internal creative force. They integrate Bateson's conceptualization of symmetrical, complementary, and metacomplementary relationships with Matte Blanco's (1975) conceptualization of the structure of thought and logic in conscious and unconscious experience. Matte Blanco's theory of the mind views consciousness as based on asymmetrical or Aristotelian logic, in which one member of a class of objects is differentiated from the other members of the class, while the unconscious is conceptualized as organized through symmetrical logic, in which experiences are perceived or are created as homogeneous events and are dedifferentiated one from the other so that any member of a set is the same as all others. This difference between the asymmetrical logic of consciousness and the symmetrical logic of the unconscious is illustrated by the difference between the symmetrical language of poetry, passion, and metaphor, where the unique example stands for the universal and infinite, and the asymmetrical language of science, news media, and external reality, where the goal is to separate and differentiate one experience from another.

Matte Blanco's view of the unconscious experience as based on symmetrical logic provides an interesting perspective on Kleinian interpretations, in which there is a dedifferentiation of part with whole experiences, a reversibility of experiences of self and other, and the absence of the distinctions of secondary process thought including that of person, place, time, and sequence. Matte Blanco's conceptualization of the unconscious also explains the Kleinian view of the unconscious in the depressive mode as a source of creativity, power, and reparation, as well as the more typical themes of sadomasochistic control and persecutory anxiety in the paranoid-schizoid position.

CLINICAL ILLUSTRATION:
A CONFUSION OF TONGUES

From a Kleinian perspective, issues of power in the psychoanalytic relationship are reflected in the organization of both the interpersonal and the intrapsychic dimensions of experience. In the interpersonal dimension of the analytic relationship, power is expressed in the rule-making function, which involves the right to determine and define the other's actions and experiences. This relationship may be complementary (asymmetrical) as in the traditional psychoanalytic relationship, where the analyst and patient agree to the tasks and prerogatives that each will have. However, in the contemporary two-person model of the psychoanalytic relationship, the ideas of mutuality and of the co-construction of the relationship suggest a symmetrical or egalitarian organization that often becomes a problem when issues of power are not seen as central and are disowned and externalized through projective identification. This failure to acknowledge the importance of the interpersonal dimensions of power and aggression often results in the formation of a metacomplementary relationship in which analyst and patient alternately disown and accuse each other of being hostile, irrational, and immature, with each participant containing the projected aggression of the other. On the intrapsychic dimension, power is reflected in the individual's capacity to freely function in a symmetrical or unconscious mode of experience and thought. The symmetrical mode of thought allows the analyst, through processes of introjective identification and reverie, to identify with, experience, and begin to symbolize the patient's disowned fantasies rather than to feel compelled to act on and to differentiate his or her presence as a benevolent new object from the historical object through the use of asymmetrical or conscious logic. The capacity to freely use the symmetrical mode of thought allows the analyst, in Bion's words, to think his or her own thoughts, and, I would add, to take pleasure in the resulting fantasies.

The following clinical material illustrates the difficulty in working with issues of power on both the interpersonal level, through the struggle with symmetry, complementarily, and metacomplementarily in the analytic relationship, and the intrapsychic level, where there is a shift into the symmetrical language of the unconscious from the earlier attempts at clarification and interpretation using the asymmetrical language of consciousness.

The patient is a 40-year-old man and the analyst is a woman of approximately the same age. The patient had been in psychoanalytic psychotherapy for approximately one year and was experiencing the analytic situation in a paranoid-schizoid mode that focused on the central question of who will be in control of and dominate the relationship. The sessions reflected the concerns with issues of interpersonal power through the patient's repeated attempts at imposing his reality and language onto the analyst, who simultaneously attempted to impose her reality and language onto his experience. The patient described himself as a very spiritual person, both through his involvement in traditional religious practices and also in terms of his New Age beliefs. He had been confronting the analyst with his spiritual beliefs and explanations as a challenge to her attempts to understand and explain his experiences in terms of her views of psychoanalysis and reality. One persistent issue was that the patient aggressively presented his belief in reincarnation and the influence of unfinished relationships and past lives as an alternative to the analyst's psychoanalytic explanations. The patient's repeated challenges can be thought of as both an enactment of important paranoid themes in the transference as well as a multilevel challenge to the analyst in terms of both the metacomplementary definitions of power and control and her emphasis on the asymmetrical logic of conscious thought in her attempts to encourage the patient's reality testing, the differentiation of past and present, and her view of herself as a benevolent new analytic object.

In supervision, the analyst expressed a great deal of frustration, describing the situation in the following way: "The patient and I had been wrangling about his tendency to conceptualize events, thoughts, and fantasies in his life as spiritually mediated. I had been frustrated by what I saw as a resistance to engaging in an exploration of the psychological meaning of things. He had nearly quit therapy, citing my lack of appreciation for the potentially spiritual aspects of life as the reason for termination." In addition to the frustration that resulted from this power struggle, this was a particularly difficult situation for the analyst because of her own positive feelings about and involvement with religion.

The analyst's initial attempt to respond to the patient's complaints about the asymmetrical, complementary power situation in the analytic relationship involved her failed attempts at "mutuality," which involved increased self-disclosure. She talked about the importance of her own early and current religious experiences, which she thought would reduce the patient's hostility through establishing an empathic link. However, rather than feeling less in conflict with the analyst, the patient responded to her self-disclosure with continued attacks on the structure and language of the analytic relationship. The analyst reported, "The patient was again asserting that there were few coincidences in life and that things happen for a reason, a reason that frequently belongs in the spiritual world. He began to speculate about why we might be working together, suggesting that it was probably important for me as well as for him." However, feeling somewhat desperate, the analyst attempted to regain control through the use of a metacomplementary formulation in which she simultaneously asserted and disavowed issues of power. She said, "Perhaps he was working with me so that he could help me to develop my spirituality." This intervention reflects a metacomplementary attempt to reestablish her authority and power through suggesting that the patient actually be in charge. For the remainder of this session, the patient continued to focus on the importance of his spirituality and the difficulty that the analyst would have in understanding him. The analyst's further attempts at mutuality and self-disclosure did not seem to alter the metacomplementary structure of the relationship or allow for a genuine exploration of the analytic relationship or of the patient's life events. The analyst continued to feel quite frustrated and powerless to affect the patient and the treatment relationship.

In supervision, we focused on the difficulty as a function of the avoidance of the underlying issues of power, dominance, and submission, and how each participant used projective identification to disown and externalize his or her aggression, which resulted in a frustrating and laboring metacomplementary relationship. We also discussed the difference between using the symmetrical logic of the unconscious, in which the analyst could identify with or dedifferentiate herself from the patient's projection, rather than her attempts to differentiate herself from him using the asymmetrical logic of consciousness. I attempted to provide explanations of the different levels of power that were being enacted in this transference–countertransference situation and at the same time to provide a relationship in which we might each be able to enter into transitional states (Newirth 1996) of reverie and play where we could articulate our unconscious, symmetrical fantasies. Supervision during this period was taken up with entering states of reverie in which we each developed and played with various fantasies around themes of power, language, and ancient religions. In the supervision relationship we were able to develop a space in which each of us was able to think our own thoughts without feeling compelled to respond to or control each other or the patient. It is this freedom to think one's thoughts and to enter into transitional states of reverie that leads to the capacity to use the symmetrical thought processes of the unconscious in the development of symbolization and the internalization of the interpersonal and intrasubjective power of the unconscious.

In a subsequent analytic session in which the "patient continued to speculate on the possibilities that the analyst and he might have known each other in one or more previous lives," the analyst was now able to respond to the underlying issue of power, submission, and dominance, and presented the patient with a symmetrical definition of the relationship—one that was framed in the symmetrical language of the unconscious. In this interpretation the analyst no longer felt a need to deny her own power, and she said, "Perhaps long ago you had been a Druid priest and I a priestess and that we still had unfinished business with each other." Using this interpretation, the analyst gave voice to an unconscious symmetrical fantasy of the analytic relationship as one between two powerful omnipotent people, which seemed to result in a change in the affective tone of the session from being defensive and challenging to collaborative. As part of this change in the definition of power and the organization of the relationship, the issues of spirituality and the struggle about which language and system of explanation to use disappeared from the analytic dialogue and the patient began to discuss the extremely shameful experiences of having been sexually molested as a child. It was as if the analyst's assertion of her power in both the metacomplementary organization of the relationship and her reliance on the asymmetrical language of consciousness represented a retraumatization of the patient both in terms of having been controlled, dominated, and sexually molested and also having been asked to deny or negate his experience as not being logical or part of the asymmetrical world of reality. We can understand this patient's interest in spirituality and past lives as an externalization and dissociation of his experience of powerlessness and confusion, which grew out of his experiences of being molested as a child, which resulted in his failure to integrate the power and aggression of the paranoid-schizoid positions into the symbolic capacities of the depressive position.

The patient's sensitivity to issues of power in response to the metacomplementary or asymmetrical aspects of the analytic relationship can be thought of as reflecting a concrete enactment, in the transference–countertransference relationship, of the paranoid issues of dominance and submission and not simply a challenge to the traditional asymmetrical structure of the analytic relationship. The analyst's shift into a symmetrical modes both in terms of the interpersonal issues of power and the use of the symmetrical logic of the unconscious had an immediate and positive effect on the treatment situation. Her interpretation, which perhaps sounds a bit glib, reflected different meanings on several simultaneous levels; it suggests that she was willing to recognize both her own and the patient's power, to recognize that there was an essential equality in the relationship, and to use the metaphorical language of symmetrical internal experience rather than the asymmetrical language of external reality. This shift from the metacomplementary position of disowned power to the interpersonal and intrasubjective symmetrical position allowed for the working through and integration of important issues involving the failure to integrate power as a result of the patient's early traumatic experience.

This case, although more dramatic than most, demonstrates the importance of two aspects of power in the two-person model of the psychoanalytic relationship. The first is the importance of the development of a symmetrical, as opposed to asymmetrical or metacomplementary, relationships in which there is an equality of power and prerogatives between the patient and analyst, and the second is the use of the symmetrical language and logic of the unconscious, which is described by Matte Blanco (1988) and emphasizes the dedifferentiation of current and past experiences, of subject and object, and the articulation of the power, passion, and poetry of the unconscious.

I want to underline the importance of the interpersonal and intrasubjective issues of power in the evolving two-person constructivist model, and suggest the application and further development of the symmetrical organization of both the interpersonal relationship and the form of logic used to understand and interpret analytic experience.

6

The Paranoid Position and the Development of Symbolic Thought

THE CREATION OF MEANING

The third important theoretical dimension of the paranoid-schizoid position is the development of the capacity to think symbolically and to create meaning. The creation of meaning and the nature and development of thought processes have been important themes in Kleinian theory from the early concept of unconscious fantasy (Isaacs 1948) as the fundamental psychological unit in Bion's development of the concepts of projective identification and reverie and Winnicott's development of the concept of transition experience. This concern with the development of cognitive processes is also reflected in another dimension of theory: the paranoid-schizoid and depressive positions are primarily thought of as parallel systems of organizing, apprehending, and generating experience, belief, and knowledge. Kleinian clinical theory has focused on the moment-to-moment development of the patient's capacity to think and to develop symbolic processes in contrast to the inevitable pathological concrete processes of the paranoid-schizoid position. In developing and articulating these cognitive processes that are central to Kleinian theory, it is useful to note that most other psychoanalytic schools do not address these cognitive dimensions directly; rather, the capacity to communicate, to think, to perceive the world, and to understand experience is thought of as a function of maturity and the development of the reality principle, consensual thinking, and the ability to separate emotional considerations from an objective perspective.

From a historical perspective, this interest in cognitive processes was a logical outgrowth of Klein's interest and work in child psychoanalysis. Klein's earliest work with children focused on their inhibitions in learning and the way anxiety interfered with intellectual curiosity and the development of the capacity for fantasy. Klein (1921, 1928) was strongly influenced by the language of instinct theory, and she thought of children's difficulties in learning, their inhibited curiosity, and the absence of fantasies as representing an expression of a conflict between the expression of an instinct and the fear of its consequences, such as impotence or frigidity as an expression of libido. Klein (1928) thought of these cognitive symptoms as inhibitions of the *epistemophilic* instinct. Although the concept of an epistemophilic instinct was quickly dropped, Klein and her colleagues continued to think of these cognitive functions as deep structures, and continued to focus on theoretical and clinical aspects of learning, communication, and the capacity to think and creatively interpret and construct experience. Bion's (1959, 1962) work on learning in groups, on linking, and the concept of K and minus K, represents important developments in the cognitive dimension of Kleinian theory, focusing on the essential processes of creating meaning as a autonomous psychic function separate from adapting to external reality.

This process of creating meaning has often been described as a somewhat simplified duality comparing the concrete thought processes of the paranoid-schizoid position and the symbolic thought of the depressive position. The simplified view suggests a hierarchical relationship privileging the symbolic thought of the depressive position and pathologizing the concrete thought of the paranoid-schizoid position. However, this is not an accurate representation of Kleinian theory, which describes these processes of constructing meaning as oscillating between the destructive elements of the paranoid-schizoid and the integrative elements of the depressive positions. Some of the most important and interesting aspects of the process of creating meaning involve the dialectic between the positive and negative aspects of concrete and symbolic thought in the patient's experience of the world and in the psychoanalytic encounter.

CONCRETE THOUGHT AND
THE PARANOID POSITION

The dialectical movement between concrete and symbolic thought can be considered a continuing state of oscillation between destroying old meanings and creating new meanings in the deepening processes within the psychoanalytic relationship and the growing experiences of anxiety and projective and introjective identification. Segal (1979) describes her work with a patient in which there was a movement to the more concrete experience of the paranoid-schizoid position as a result of his displacing aggression from the analyst who was experienced as a bad internal object on to substitutes in the external world:

> Thereupon the numerous persecutors in the external world were dealt with by scotomization. That phase of his analysis, which lasted several months, was characterized by an extreme narrowing of his interests in the external world. At that point also his vocabulary became very poor. He forbade himself and me the use of many words, which he felt had the power to produce hallucinations and therefore had to be abolished. This is strikingly similar to the behavior of a Paraguayan tribe, the Abipones, who cannot tolerate anything that reminds them of the dead. When a member of the tribe dies, all words having any affinity with the names of the deceased are immediately dropped from the vocabulary. In consequence, their language is most difficult to learn, as it is full of blocks and neologisms replacing forbidden words. [p. 165]

Segal's comments underline the importance of attending to the patient's concrete use of words and the subtle distinctions in the paranoid organization of experience in which words and things are treated as if they are bad objects that must be avoided for fear that they will be destructive or poisonous. This paranoid mode of experience can subtly appear in patients' concrete use of language through attributing a reality to the spoken word that seems separate from internal thought processes; for example, a patient may indignantly quote himself or an other, saying, "I said . . ." or "You said . . ." as a way of disowning the thought and placing it in the external world of facts.

This critical distinction between the symbolic and the concrete experience of words is captured by Philip Roth in *Portnoy's Complaint,* when Portnoy describes his first awareness of language as a symbolic experience in which words are used to communicate internal experience and to connect people in pleasurable states rather than in the paranoid-schizoid mode of his childhood memories in which words were used to attack and manipulate the family members (Newirth 1994).

> "Did I have a good night's sleep? Why, yes! I think I did! Hey—did you?" "Like a log," replies Mr. Cambell. And for the first time in my life I experienced the full force of a simile. This man, who is a real estate broker and an alderman of the Davenport town council, says that he slept like a log, and I actually *see* a log. *I get it!* Motionless, heavy *like a log!* "Good *morning,*" he says, and now it occurs to me that the word "morning," as he uses it, refers specifically to the hours between eight A.M. and twelve noon. I've never thought of it that way before. He wants the hours between eight and twelve to be good, which is to say, enjoyable, pleasurable, and beneficial! We are all wishing each other four hours of pleasure and accomplishment. Why that's terrific! Hey, that's very nice! Good morning! And the same applies to "Good afternoon"! And "Good evening"! And "Good night"! My God! The English language is *a form of communication!* Conversation isn't just a crossfire where you shoot and get shot at! Where you have to duck for your life and aim to kill! Words aren't only bombs and bullets—no they're little gifts, containing *meanings!* [Roth 1969, pp. 220–221]

The persistence of concrete thought processes of the paranoid-schizoid position and the absence of true symbolic language and experience in the depressive position are often unseen elements in the psychoanalytic and psychotherapeutic work in which there is confusion, misunderstanding, ineffective interpretations, and intense experiences of negative therapeutic reactions. Often we fail to recognize the pervasiveness of concrete thought processes in the seemingly logical and functional discourse of the patient, who, although being quite successful in the world of material reality and the world of objective experience, is unable to negotiate the world of psychic reality and subjective intimate relationships. These patients often experience themselves as an object, a thing in a world of things.

Basch-Kahre (1985) presents an interesting discussion of the hidden aspects of concrete thinking and of the difficulty in progressing past these early representational and organizational processes in patients who have psychosomatic and borderline problems. She conceptualizes these archaic thought processes as operational thinking, which is concrete and logical, with no room for feelings, metaphors, or symbols. She believes that operational thought processes cannot "become integrated with other patterns of thinking in persons who have experienced early and severe trauma" and whose thought "becomes hypertrophied at the expense of other thinking patterns in the inability to verbalize feelings and understand metaphors" (n.p). She underscores the important point that logic and the capacity to think abstractly are qualities that are independent of the patient's capacity to use symbolic thought, and that individuals may have the capacity for high levels of abstraction in their ability to understand and solve objective, mathematical, and technical problems while continuing to function concretely in their personal and subjective experience. Basch-Kahre suggests that "when working with borderline patients, one regularly finds that chaos hides behind the exaggerated logic of their operational thinking," which is "brought about by splitting, projective identification and introjection" (p. 461). She focuses on the difference between the patient's ability to use logical and abstract processes in reference to external or objective events (material reality) and the ability to use symbolic process in relation to intimate relationships and the development of the internal world of fantasy and emotion (psychic reality). This distinction between abstract thought and symbolic thought is important from both a theoretical and a clinical perspective. Theoretically, it suggests that there is not just a single dialectic between concrete and symbolic thought, but that there are two sets of dialectics: one that refers to the dimensions of psychic reality and one that refers to the dimensions of material reality. Psychic reality comprises the world of intimate relationships, identity, and emotion, and it is here that thinking oscillates between concrete and symbolic experience, while material reality comprises the external, objective world where thinking oscillates between a similar set of dimensions—that of being literal and abstract.

Winnicott (1971) addresses a similar concept that he conceptualizes in terms of a spatial organization in which experience can be located either in the external objective world or in the internal subjective world. Winnicott presents a carefully reasoned argument about the subtle difference between the concrete thought processes of the false or objective self organization and the capacity for symbolic thought in the patient who is a subject, a true self. Winnicott illustrates symbolic thought processes as located internally in psychic reality through the analysis of a patient's dream, which involves the mutual development of meaning through the implicit and explicit discourse with the other. He describes a concrete or literal experience located outside of the person in material or external reality, citing a patient's daydreaming as concrete, ruminative, and not differentiated from the experience in itself, resulting in paralysis rather than self-directed action in the world. In differentiating processes of concrete and symbolic thought, Winnicott states, "Fantasying was about a certain subject and it was about a dead end. It had no poetic value. The corresponding dream, however, *had poetry in it*, that is to say, layer upon layer of meaning related to past, present and future, and to inner and outer, and always fundamentally about herself." Later in the session, he describes the analyst's experience of the difference between concrete and symbolic thought and the difficulty in interpreting externalized experience through commenting on the patient's playing solitaire, which he saw as "a form of fantasying, a dead end, [which] cannot be used by me. If on the other hand she is telling me a dream, 'I dreamed I was playing solitaire'; then I could use it, and indeed I could make an interpretation. I could say: 'You are struggling with God or fate, sometimes winning and sometimes losing, the aim being to control the destines of four royal families'" (p. 36). Winnicott's comments illustrate the analyst's difficulty in interpreting material to patients who organize in the concrete thought processes of the paranoid-schizoid position and either have not achieved the capacity for symbolic thought or are oscillating into a paranoid state. This distinction between concrete or symbolic thought determines the patient's capacity to internalize and make use of the analyst's interpretations through a symbolic integration and emotional elaboration of the analyst's words.

THE CAPACITY FOR SYMBOLIC THOUGHT

The capacity for symbolic thought is an aspect of the depressive position that allows the individual to internalize, integrate, and emotionally elaborate previously evacuated unconscious fantasies. For Klein, the analyst's focus is on helping the patient develop from a limited and limiting concrete paranoid experience dominated by unconscious concrete fantasies experienced as persecutory projective identifications and inhibiting anxieties to the ability to symbolically experience and articulate the previously terrifying unconscious fantasies. Klein (1975) illustrates this process of externalization, symbolic enactment, and the development of the patient's capacity to use symbolic processes in the analysis of a 5-year-old boy (see Chapter 1). It is the capacity to use symbols that underlies the capacity for a different mode of generating meaning in the depressive position.

Segal (1979) notes that the symbolic thought is necessary for communication both with others in the external world and with one's own unconscious fantasies. The symbol is necessary to displace aggression from the original object in order to preserve, restore, re-create, recapture, and regain the original object. Segal describes the importance of an individual's being able to communicate with his/her unconscious fantasies, that is, to be in touch with the unconscious:

> [For] people who are 'well in touch with themselves' there is a constant free symbol-formation, whereby they can be consciously aware and in control of *symbolic expressions* of the underlying primitive fantasies. The difficulty in dealing with schizophrenic and schizoid patients lies not only in that they cannot communicate with us, but even more in that they cannot communicate with themselves. Any part of their ego may be split off from any other part with no communication available between them. [p. 169]

In elaborating the importance of the developing capacity for symbol formation, Segal notes that the person is able to return to earlier unresolved conflicts symbolizing both the repaired whole objects of the depressive position and the persecutory and idealized objects of the paranoid-schizoid position. She illustrates these processes of reparation and symbolization and the oscillation between concrete and symbolic thought in her work with a schizophrenic girl. Segal states that during a period of growth, this patient was able to write a fairy tale about witches, which allowed her to integrate her aggression and to identify with positive elements in her mother, who she had previously experienced as a devouring presence. However, during a period of intense anxieties, the symbolic experience of her fairy tale became concretized and projected into the external world, so that she again felt persecuted and terrified, feeling that she would be attacked by the witches that she had created including her analyst. This oscillation between the concrete experience of the paranoid-schizoid position and the symbolic experience of the de-pressive position allows the individual to find enrichment in the reser-voir of unconscious fantasies and to reexperience the terrors of the past.

SYMBOL FORMATION AND THE PSYCHOANALYTIC PROCESS

In a series of papers, Bion (1959, 1962) developed a theory of thinking and symbol formation that made explicit the role of the other[1] in the development of the process of symbolization. He conceptualized the two-person relationship between parent and child, or analyst and patient, as following a model of the container and the contained. In this model the infant or patient, through projective identification, puts unacceptable, concrete experiences in the other. If the other is reasonably well balanced and able to tolerate the projected unconscious fantasy, he or she can sym-bolize the patient's or infant's experience through processes of reverie, which in time allows the patient or infant to reintroject the unconscious fantasy in a symbolic form. Bion's model of the container and the im-portance of the analyst's or parent's ability to symbolize the projected experience is a complex process that can be thought of as introjective identification of an active process that is complementary to the process of projective identification. Bion suggests that this relationship between the container and the contained can be disrupted through the analyst's or parent's incapacity for reverie, by an inability to contain, identify, and effectively elaborate the projective identifications, or because of the patient's or infant's experiences of intense envy and inability to tolerate the other's capacity to provide a nurturing constructive experience. One of Bion's (1962) contributions is his focus on development of the ca-

1. For example, in the illustration in Chapter 1 of Klein's work with a 5-year-old emphasizing the development of symbolic experience, she participates in a two-person process, articulating and organizing the fantasy of the shopkeeper and customer. See discussion of Searles's work (Chapter 4, this volume) in relation to the analyst's use of introjective identification.

pacity to think and the failures in this process; he describes both positive and negative aspects of projective identification, since these processes are necessary for the development of the capacity to think symbolically, and are used to attack the process of thinking itself. For example, in situations in which the child's projective identifications cannot be tolerated and are evacuated by the parent,

> the development of an apparatus for thinking is disturbed, and instead there takes place a hypertrophic development of an apparatus of projective identification. The model I propose for this development is a psyche that operates on the principle that evacuation of a bad breast is synonymous with obtaining sustenance from a good breast. The end result is that all thoughts are treated as if they are indistinguishable from bad internal objects; the appropriate machinery is felt to be, not an apparatus for thinking the thoughts, but an apparatus for ridding the psyche of accumulations of bad internal objects. . . . The dominance of projective identification confuses the distinction between the self and the external object. This contributes to the absence of any perception of two-ness, since such an awareness depends on the recognition of a distinction between subject and object. [p. 180]

Bion's evacuative model of the mind reflects both the individual's failure to develop the capacity for symbolic thought and the importance of the patient's active, moment-to-moment attempts to disrupt processes of symbol formation and the development of links between patient and analyst and self and other, and in the internal process of linking emotions with thought. These attacks on processes of linking are seen as a function of envy and the inability to tolerate the experience of the good breast: the sense of being cared for, responded to, and identified with by the analyst. In patients who, as a result of these failures in the development of the capacity for symbolic thought, have developed an evacuative process of thinking (Bion 1959), "the attacks on the linking function of emotion lead to an overprominence . . . of links which appear to be logical, almost mathematical but never emotionally reasonably. Consequently the links surviving are perverse, cruel and sterile" (p. 100). In working with these patients, the analyst's task is to be able to contain the ongoing destructive and envious attacks on the analytic processes of linking, reverie, and introjective identification, which can often involve long periods of painful countertransference experiences of feeling and being the evacuated bad object.

MODELS OF SYMBOLIC EXPERIENCE

Kleinian theory places the development of thinking, symbol formation, and the ability to use symbolic experience at the center of the analytic process. The Kleinian view of symbolic experience, reverie, and the development of symbolic enactment is quite different from the traditional view of symbols and interpretation, in which unconscious symbols are thought of as representations of repressed primary process wishes that can be translated into secondary process conscious thought. In 1916, Ernest Jones (as cited in Rose 2000, Segal 1979) defined the traditional psychoanalytic view of a symbol as a representation of a repressed wish, such as a dream image, which had a relatively fixed meaning. Jones contrasted the symbol as an unproductive representation of an unconscious wish with sublimation, in which there is a resolution of unconscious conflict allowing for the development of compromises and the achievement of satisfaction in the external world. This traditional view of the symbol as an unconscious representation of a repressed wish defines the analyst's function as that of interpreting or translating unconscious symbols into conscious secondary process thought.

Rose (2000) compares this limited view of symbols as representations of repressed wishes and desires with Susanne Langer's concept of multiple types of symbols, which she describes as *presentational symbols* and *discursive symbols*. Langer thought that presentational symbols developed in relation to artistic productions and expressed a mode of symbolic activity that had a different purpose from discursive or verbal symbols.

> The purpose of presentational symbols was to present the pattern of our emotional and experiential life in an evocative and sensual way. Their purpose was not primarily to present ideas as propositions, which was the role of (secondary process or rational) language, but to show the nature of patterns in which we live and the experiences we have. . . . The discursive symbolism of language, on the other hand, conveyed relations and discrimination in the world of objects

through an agreed set of conventional symbols that merely referred to but did not iconically or imagistically present that which it symbolized. [p. 466]

Jacobus (1999), in discussing Klein's development of the concept of symbols and its relation to the work of Lacan and Kresteva, describes the powerful generative, although evanescent, quality of the Kleinian symbol as constituted like a poetic image, in which meanings are multilayered, supersaturated experiences, constantly shifting and expanding in their ability to evoke and create meanings. This distinction between symbols as iconic, poetic, evocative, and capable of generating experience and meaning, and of symbols as representational, denoting information, is useful in deepening an understanding of the Kleinian concept of symbols. The Kleinian concept of symbolic thought as generative of experience, as defining identity through organizing self–other relationship patterns, and as emotionally evocative and iconic suggests the category of presentational symbols in contrast to the Freudian symbol, which functions as a discursive symbol.

Basch (1985), a self psychologist, presents a similar dual theory of thinking and symbol formation in which the process of encoding experience about the external or material world is done in a "semantic" memory system, and information about the self that is germane to the maintenance and enhancement of self-esteem is encoded in an "episodic" memory system. He describes a process like dissociation and projective identification in which pathology is the result of a breakdown of communication between these two parallel systems. Basch discusses the development of an internal barrier that prevents the affective and personal significance of events known in the semantic system from being understood and effectively registered in the episodic or subjective system: "The affective significance that a particular event would and should have for the self is blocked. This protects the person . . . from an overwhelming flood of affects and a subsequent fragmentation of the self system" (p. 39). The person is well aware of the reality of the event, but it is as if he/she is able to say, "Yes, it happened, but, since it has nothing to do with me, why get upset." The experience of the world from the perspective of the semantic system reflects schizoid or narcissistic representations, which are concrete, logical, impersonal. This dual system of encoding information or of thinking and symbol formation describes from a different perspective the distinction that Bion (1961) and Basch-Kahre (1985) described of patients' overinvolvement in positivist, operational thought, which coincides with the logic of external or material reality as compared to the affective and symbolic experience of dreams, poems, and psychic reality.

CLINICAL ILLUSTRATIONS: OSCILLATIONS BETWEEN CONCRETE AND SYMBOLIC EXPERIENCE

The pervasiveness of concrete thought, including the less apparent forms represented by operational thinking, the barrier between the semantic and episodic memory systems, and the concrete, impersonal, and objective preoccupations frequently reported by patients, as well as dissociated experiences and daydreams, often lead to a deadening in the analytic process. Bion (1962) describes an aspect of this phenomenon, the patient's overinvolvement in the external world as a phobic avoidance of the internal world of fantasy, emotion, and living itself. The analyst's experience of the patient's concrete and hyperobjective thought leads to the common countertransference experiences of tiredness, lack of memory, and acting out. To move past these paralyzing concrete experiences of language and thought into a symbolic discourse, the analyst needs to disrupt the frozen, impersonal, objective thought processes through initiating a shift in linguistic and affective experience, utilizing the symbolic equations of the paranoid-schizoid mode from external experience to internal experience. This movement often involves a shift from the hopeless, impotent, and persecuted feelings of the passive paranoid position to the hopeful, pleasure-filled, and omnipotent feelings of the active paranoid position.

Khan (1986) illustrates this shift from a literal and discursive use of language to using symbolic equations, and presentational symbols, in his work with a frustrating patient who speaks in extremely concrete, impersonal, and operational language. Khan describes his strategy as acting through language in order to become engaged with this patient who is a rigid, moralistic, schizoid person. He describes his technique as a verbal *squiggle game* that paralleled Winnicott's (1989) squiggle tech-

nique with child patients that involved his use of evocative and provocative language such as calling this very formal patient by a diminutive
name, "Johnny." The analyst's initiation of a disruption of the deadened,
concrete language in the early processes of symbol formation through
the use of symbolic equations within the analytic discourse can occur
either unwittingly or strategically. The latter involves a purposeful use
of reverie, introjective identification, and symbolic enactment. The following clinical illustrations demonstrate the destructive and constructive effects of the analyst's unwitting disruption of concrete thought
through a symbolic equation, and then a more purposeful use of the
iconic language of the active paranoid position in the development of a
symbolic enactment of the patient's disowned hopefulness. In both cases
there is a reorganization of the analytic relationship from a deadened
concrete experience to a more alive symbolic experience.

B., a very successful attorney, illustrates the contradictions in
thought process inherent in the failure in the development of subjectivity. He was extraordinarily capable of high levels of logical and abstract
thought in his work, where he functioned as an efficient professional,
while at the same time experiencing his few personal relationships in
the most concrete, barren, and paranoid way. The early part of treatment was filled with profound concrete experiences in which he would
painfully describe details of his days, often including the loss of his sense
of psychological and physical cohesiveness, which would result in severe anxiety attacks, phobic reactions, and the terror that he would stop
breathing in his sleep. Similarly, his experiences of the extremely concrete representation of the world, at times would involve a loss of perceptual constancy, so that either his body or my body would become
terrifyingly enlarged or shrunk. My countertransference experiences
during this extended period involved a great deal of tiredness, the loss
of my ability to hold on to meaning, and the fragmentation of words.
These countertransference reactions are examples of what Bion described
as attacks on the linking function, through splitting and projective identification, creating a frightening chaotic paranoid experience within the
transference–countertransference situation. As treatment progressed, this
patient became more involved with individual sports, which he would
participate in along with other players, and allowed us to begin to work
on his disowned issues of competition and aggression, and to experience his developing self as a more cohesive physical and psychological

entity. These activities became a first experience of symbol through which we could enter into a more personal, albeit concrete, emotionally alive analytic conversation. The following experience involved an accidental disruption in the analytic relationship and a regression into more concrete and terrifying thought processes, which helped me to appreciate the omnipotence and the potentially destructive aspects that are involved in the development of symbolic equations and symbolic representations.

Toward the end of a session, B. told me that on his winter vacation he would be going to a ski resort, which coincidentally turned out to be the same resort I was planning to go to at the same time on my vacation. Without consciously thinking about the impact of my statement, although having vague thoughts of exploring his identification and experience of connectedness with me, I spontaneously suggested that we might run into each other while on vacation since we would both be on the same mountain at the same time. During the next several weeks the patient regressed to extremely concrete, anxiety-filled, chaotic language and thought processes, which were reminiscent of the fragmentation and lack of cohesiveness of the early period of treatment. It took a while for me to be able to reconstruct the events that preceded the patient's fragmentation and regression, until I realized that my spontaneous comment was experienced concretely, that we would literally run into each other and each of us would become shattered into bits. Once I was able to think about this and recognize and consider the destructive aspects of my comment, perhaps that I didn't want to share my mountain with him, I could effectively elaborate my fantasies and interpret to him this image of us running into each other on the slopes. In this symbolic elaboration I was able to acknowledge the destructiveness of this image, which seemed to facilitate the patient's reintegration and his ability to function on a more symbolic level in the analytic situation. This is an extreme example in which the analyst's comment led to a major deterioration in the patient's capacity to use symbolic processes and communication.

This experience raises the question of how often, in more subtle ways, patients experience our comments and interpretations as concrete, as commands, attacks, or punishments, and that our words "are felt to be objects or actions, which [are not] easily used for purposes of communication" (Segal 1981, p. 57) but become objects in and of themselves. Bion (1959) writes about the patient's destructiveness in attacking the

analyst's ability to construct links to create symbols and symbolic experience; however, it is also important to keep in mind the analyst's destructiveness in not recognizing that an interpretation has been experienced symbolically. Kristeva (2000) cautions us that the analyst's act
of interpretation and the development of symbolic processes also involve
destructive acts toward the patient, and suggests that "the knowledge
that interpretation is an act of cruelty leads us to carry it out with the
utmost kindness and tact. The care is in the delicacy of the story telling.
It cuts gently into the flesh and thus optimizes the capacity for (symbolic) representations" (p. 786).

The next case example illustrates an intentional use of symbolic equations as a way of facilitating the patient's reorganizing experience from
the concrete, deadened experiences within the passive paranoid position
to the early symbolic experience of the active paranoid position.

D., a successful, hard-working professional, felt that his life was
barren and lacking any intimate relationships. He felt himself to be continuously self-sacrificing, which could be understood as reflecting either issues of castration anxiety or anxieties about his destructive greed.
As the treatment proceeded, he began to develop an intimate relationship with a widow with whom he was able to achieve a great deal more
gratification and joy than in previous relationships. However, as this
relationship progressed, he began to describe his experiences in more
objective terms, focusing on the issues of time and place and expressing
the operational belief that it was only because of her husband's death
that this woman was interested in him. He was only an expedient substitute, a replacement for her dead husband. The patient could not tolerate the sense of hope and the experience of envy and gratitude that
recognizing his need and his happiness would create. He fled to the
concrete and pseudo-logical language of the paranoid-schizoid experience of material reality, destroying his capacity to communicate with his
unconscious fantasies as well as deadening the analytic discourse. My
strategy was not to interpret the obvious oedipal significance of the content of the patient's unacceptable fantasies and his conflicts and their
genetic roots, but rather to facilitate a movement into symbolic discourse
in which the patient's dissociated experience of greed, joy, success, and
omnipotence could be expressed in symbolic language. I enacted the
disowned active paranoid position, expressing through a symbolic equation my identification with his evacuated greedy self. I insisted with

exaggerated affect that I thought it was my work that had led to the relationship and not the former husband's death. In this way I disrupted his concrete, operational representation and expressed the disowned omnipotence, magic, and hopefulness that are critical to the development of symbolic thought. Using language as symbolic equations led to the patient's experience of intense anxiety as he experienced his disowned greed and omnipotence concretely in the analytic relationship.

The analyst's use of symbolic equations, although often disruptive, develops the affective conditions within the transference–countertransference relationship in which the patient can begin to internalize dissociated paranoid fantasies, anxieties, and fears of potential destructiveness. The movement from concrete to symbolic processes almost always needs to be initiated by the analyst, and involves a reorganization of the analytic relationship into a paranoid mode of experience in terms of the level of object relations, thought process, affect, and language use. This regression into a paranoid mode of experience is necessary to unfreeze previous adaptations based on the concrete organization of operational thinking, an overinvolvement with external material reality, and the lack of affect and aliveness. The analyst's active use of symbolic equations, presentational symbols, and a poetic structure represents an important change in interpretive strategy of the analytic process, from an emphasis on secondary process thought and the reality principle to the symbolic articulation of unconscious fantasy and its reinternalization and integration.

7

Transitional Experience
and the Development
of Symbolic Thought

KLEIN, BION, AND WINNICOTT:
A THEORY OF THINKING

The previous chapter developed the Kleinian theory of thinking and
its function in the transformation of concrete to symbolic thought.
Bion's expansion of Klein's theory of thinking with concepts of reverie and the container–contained relationship developed it into an
explicit two-person theory that suggests a postmodern concept of mind,
a set of mental functions that exists both within and between people.
Bion made explicit the implicit two-person structure of Kleinian theory
and focused on the dialectical, mutually constituting aspects of the
transformation of concrete to symbolic thought that is central to the
contemporary neo-Kleinian approach. Bion's concept of reverie describes the central importance of a particular kind of two-person relationship as the basis for the development of the capacity to think and
to use symbolic processes. He connects the parent's or analyst's capacity to contain and elaborate the child's or patient's frightening, unacceptable projective identifications, to detoxify these real concrete experiences, with the child's development of the capacity to use symbolic

processes and, therefore, to be in the depressive position. In focusing on the process of introjective as well as projective identification, he expanded Klein's image of the early feeding situation to include the parent's capacity to detoxify the child's projective identifications. Racker (1968) and Joseph (1975) also use this feeding metaphor in conceptualizing the patient's relationship with the therapist's words and his or her interpretations. They see the patient's responses to their interventions as reflecting a concrete experience of their words as milk, which can be either taken in or spit out. The patient's concrete responses to the analyst's words are symbolic equivalents (Segal 1978) of the patient's capacity to take in the analyst's good milk or to spit out the analyst's poisoned milk.

Bion's focus, much like Klein's, was on the disruptive effects of anxiety on thought processes and the necessity for the analyst or parent to contain the unmanageable anxiety that was inherent in the evacuated contents of the child's or patient's unconscious fantasies and projective identifications. Bion suggested that there are constructive as well as destructive aspects to processes of projective identification, and the relationship between the paranoid-schizoid and the depressive positions is both dialectical and reversible. He indicated this dialectical relationship with reversible arrow in the term $Pa{\leftrightarrow}D$. Bion conceptualized thinking as a creative and transformational process and not simply a hierarchical, linear system in which thought becomes successively more accurate representations of reality.

Winnicott, like Bion, developed the Kleinian theory of thinking; however, he focused on developmental aspects of thinking and on the intermediate or proto-symbolic aspects of thought that occur between concrete thought or symbolic equations and true symbols. Winnicott's theoretical and clinical concepts extended Kleinian thinking into a radical, two-person psychology that focused on constructive aspects of unconscious experience. Winnicott viewed the unconscious as a source of creativity, which is expressed through experiences of illusion, magical thinking, and omnipotence. This chapter develops Winnicott's concept of transitional experience within the context of the Kleinian theory of thinking and symbol formation, and Bion's concept of reverie.

Winnicott's relationship with Klein and his contributions to the development of object relations theory involved complicated personal, political (Grosskurth 1986), and theoretical issues, often involving his desire for affirmation and connection that was thwarted by Klein, Joan Riviere (his former analyst), and other colleagues. Winnicott had worked with Klein as a supervisor and was strongly influenced by her ideas, which form the basis for his theoretical and clinical work. The following touching letter (Rodman 1987), written on November 17, 1952, expresses his frustration with the rigidity of the Kleinian group in London, as well as a commitment to her ideas. This letter also offers a glimpse into his therapeutic approach of personal involvement and a constructive identification with the bad object.

Dear Melanie:
  I want to write to you about last Friday evening's meeting, in order to try to turn it into something constructive.
  The first thing I want to say is that I can see how annoying it is that when something develops in me out of my own growth and out of my analytic experience I want to put it in my own language. This is annoying because I suppose that everyone wants to do the same thing, and in a scientific society one of our aims is to find a common language. This language must, however, be kept alive as there is nothing worse than a dead language.
  I said that what I am doing is annoying, but I do also think that it has its good side. Firstly, there are not very many creative people in the Society having ideas that are personal and original. I think that anyone that has ideas is really welcome and I always do feel in the society that I am tolerated because I have ideas even though my method is an annoying one.
  Secondly, that I feel corresponding to my wish to say things my way there is something from your end, namely a need to have everything that is new restated in your own terms.
  What I wanted on Friday undoubtedly was that there should be some move from your direction toward the gesture that I make in this paper. It is a creative gesture and I can not make any relationship through this gesture except if someone comes to meet it. I think that I was wanting something which I have no right to expect from your group, and it is really in the nature of a therapeutic act, something which I could not get in either of my two long analyses, although I got so much else. There is no doubt that my criticism of Mrs. Riviere was not only a straightforward criticism based on objective observation but also it was colored by the fact that it was just exactly here that her analysis failed with me.

I personally think that it is very important that your work should be restated by people discovering in their own way and presenting what they discover in their own language. It is only in this way that language will be kept alive. If you make the stipulation that in future only your language should be used for the statement of other people's discoveries then the language becomes a dead language, as has already become in the society. You would be surprised at the sighs and groans that accompany every restatement of the internal object clichés by what I am going to call Kleinians. Your own statements are of course in quite a different category as the work is your own personal work and everyone is pleased that you have your own way of stating it. . . .

You will see that I am concerned with something which I consider to be much more important than this paper of mine. I am concerned with this set-up which might be called Kleinian which I believe to be the real danger to the diffusion of your work. Your ideas will only live in so far as they are rediscovered and reformulated by original people in the psychoanalytic movement and outside it. [p. 34]

Winnicott expanded Kleinian theory through his focus on the positive and negative influence of "the environmental factors": the importance of the other in development and in the therapeutic relationship. This shift from Klein's implicit two-person theory to an explicit, radical, two-person theory is reflected in the metaphors Klein and Winnicott used to describe the relationship between infant and parent. Klein's metaphors of the good and bad breast maintain a focus on drives, feeding, and primitive fantasies of nurture and destructiveness, while Winnicott's metaphor of being held suggests normative social relations, focusing on the sensory and affective experience of holding while simultaneously suggesting multiple aspects of the relationship.

In his clinical work, Winnicott developed an active, affectively involved and less interpretive technique that focused on three transformational processes: holding, the enactment of the transference, and the interpretation of transference experience (Khan 1974). For Winnicott each of these transformational processes contributes to the patient's growth and development. Holding facilitates a sense of going-on-being, a psychosomatic unity and self-cohesion, that is similar to Ogden's (1986) autistic-contiguous position and Kohut's concept of self-cohesion (Trop and Stolorow 1992). His emphasis on analytic experience, and enacting the transference–countertransference relationship, is related to Winnicott's (1945) early concept of realization and his papers on hate (1949, 1963) in the countertransference, in which he emphasized the importance of interpersonal contact for experience to become affectively real. This emphasis on experience and enactment of the transference–countertransference relationship is a proto-symbolic organization that allows for the symbolization of unconscious fantasies and the development of transitional experiences. The third element, the process of interpretation, allows for the verbal and affective integration and recognition of unconscious fantasies within the context of the depressive position in which the patient is able to experience concern for both the self and the therapist. Winnicott's writing and his approach to therapy focused on the patient's developing the capacity for symbolic thought while being aware of the entire range of concrete thought (symbolic equations), to proto-symbolic thought or transitional experiences, and finally to true symbols.

Winnicott (1971) presented a carefully reasoned argument illustrating the subtle difference between concrete thought processes and the capacity for symbolic communication (see Chapter 6), and how thoughts can be experienced as either external and objective events, that is, as concrete symbolic equations or as internal subjective experiences, as true symbols representing the multiple levels of personal and affective meaning of subjective experiences. Hanna Segal (1994) poignantly describes this difference between concrete and symbolic thought as one between the "as-if world, which is fantasizing" unproductive concrete thought, and the "what-if world, which is the world of imagination" (p. 615), creativity, and symbolic thought.

WINNICOTT'S CLINICAL AND THEORETICAL APPROACH

In viewing Winnicott's work in the context of Kleinian theory, it is helpful to keep two aspects of Winnicott's personal history in mind. First, Winnicott's upper-class, British background encouraged a different personal style and relationships than did Klein's middle-class, Eastern European, Jewish background. Winnicott's preference for experience-near, descriptive language rather than dense, metapsychological language is probably related to his sense of upper-class reserve and modesty.

Second, his theoretical and clinical work is predicated on his early experience as a pediatrician and his consultations with children where he developed the *squiggle technique*, which allowed Winnicott (1989) to dramatize his young patient's inner conflicts through a projective process that involved spontaneous drawing or doodling and a simultaneous process of interpretation. The squiggle technique involved a series of drawings that Winnicott would alternate with the child, each presenting a squiggle for the other to interpret and elaborate. This sequence of alternating drawings and interpretation would become a fluid dialogue of the newly symbolized and partially disowned unconscious fantasies in the context of a joyful and playful relationship between an adult and a child. This process of creating a sequence of drawings elaborated into a conversation about inner experience preceded and is probably the basis for Winnicott's development of therapy as a proto-symbolic, performative activity rather than one focused on information exchange and insight. Winnicott's (1971) development of transitional experience and play as a central aspect of the analytic relationship can be thought of as a more active two-person development of Bion's concept of reverie.

Winnicott did not see himself as a theory builder developing an integrated theory or a coherent model of the mind. His theoretical contributions included the development of the concepts of *true self* and *false self,* the *holding environment, illusion, omnipotence, transitional experience,* the *use of an object,* and the development of the concept of the person as simultaneously a subject and object. Three themes emerge in his work and evolve into progressively more sophisticated ideas: a radical two-person perspective on both human development and the psychoanalytic relationship, a dialectical view of the self as simultaneously an object and a subject, and an emphasis on creative experiences, particularly those of illusion, play, and transitional experience.

The first theme, a radical two-person perspective, suggests that intersubjective or interpersonal experience is always a construction of both participants and exists in a middle ground between each person's inner subjective experiences. This radical two-person perspective is illustrated in Winnicott's (Ogden 1992) often quoted phrase, "There is no such thing as a baby," Winnicott's evocative way of suggesting that baby and mother constitute or construct each other's experience, which cannot be separated from their relationship. Ogden (1994) and Benjamin (1995) each developed Winnicott's idea as a critical element in their theories of intersubjectivity, suggesting that subjectivity and intersubjectivity are different from each individual's self experience and represent a new psychological organization—the analytic third. The concept of the analytic third suggests that subjectivity and intersubjectivity are extensions of Winnicott's concept of transitional experiences defining as symbolic relationships.

Winnicott's radical two-person perspective differs from many current constructivist approaches, such as self psychology (Stolorow et al. 1987), which emphasize a phenomenological perspective, with each participant having his or her own perception and experience that is understood and accepted, leading to a consensual understanding of the relationship events that function at an intersection in time. These differences in concepts of subjectivity reflect the difference between a discursive view of language and a performative view of language. Winnicott's development of a radical two-person position focuses on a performative view of language—the creation of experience—rather than on a discursive view understanding experience. His approach to language and treatment is similar to Lacan's (Dor 1999) emphasis on *being* rather than on having the phallus, the other's desire, and on Klein's and Bion's view that the other is always trying to control and influence the way we experience ourselves and the world.

A second theme in Winnicott's work is of a dialectical relationship between two internal organizations of experience, one that is adaptive to external reality and in pathology molds the individual around the impact or demands *impingements* from the external world, and one that reflects psychic reality, is emergent, utilizes primary process thought, and reflects a personal, authentic, true, or subjective self.[1] In his earlier conceptualizations he thought of this dialectic as that between a true and false self, which suggested a hierarchical relationship and one that seemed to privilege the development of the true self. As this concept evolved, it became clear that the false self was not simply a pathological structure but was necessary to mediate the external world, which led to the development of the concept of the person as both subject and object. Winnicott's work suggests that we spend much of our life being

---

1. Although Winnicott uses the concept of self, I suggest that his concept actually reflects an early version of the concept of subjectivity, because the self always exists in a dialectical relationship with another person.

objects and that the development of subjectivity is an achievement. This view is similar to Martin Buber's (1974) existential theory of two parallel, potential organizations of experience, the I–it position, defining a relationship with objects, and the I–thou position, defining a relationship with subjects. Winnicott's theory suggests that relationships can be organized within one of four categories, reflecting whether each person is experiencing himself and other as an object or as a subject. The organizations of experience are object–object, reflecting a formal objective relationship dominated by a sense of being an object in the external world of impersonal relationships; subject–object, in which the other represents a transference object, someone to satisfy needs or is experienced as a source of terror and persecution; object–subject, reflecting a traditional caregiving arrangement in which the caregiver maintains his or her sense of objective authority and knowledge, and the patient is understood as being in personal need; and subject–subject, reflecting intimate relationships in which each person is focused on his or her own and the other's internal experience and each defines the other's whole present world. Winnicott described the usual transference relationship in which the patient organizes his or her experience with the analyst through historical schemas as that of a *subjective object*, and the experience with the analyst in which the patient can recognize the analyst as having his or her own internal experience as that of an *objective subject*. Winnicott's conception of analysis was as a developmental process in which the patient progressively becomes more able to organize experience in each of the four intersubjective modes, developing the capacity to experience the analyst as an objective subject, one who has his or her own internal experience and who the patient can express concern to for the pain endured in the course of analysis.

The third theme is Winnicott's belief in the importance of creativity, illusion, omnipotence, and magic as positive elements in human experience and growth. Winnicott had a unique appreciation of the nonrational and nonpurposive aspects of life, which became the basis for his development of the concept of transitional objects and transitional experience, suggesting that play and creative or artistic productions are aspects of life that are independent from biology, drives, adaptation, and survival. Phillips (1988) attempts to capture Winnicott's playfulness, describing him as a circus clown who is quietly and unobtrusively present until suddenly he springs into action and does a cartwheel or some other prank that causes the audience to laugh and then become conscious of their own humanity. Winnicott attributes a dual purpose to the early mother–infant interaction involving both physical sustenance and the development of the illusion of omnipotence. If the mother is able to present her breast (her self) to the infant without the infant's experiencing frustration, the infant will develop the idea that he or she has created the breast, which is experienced as an illusion of omnipotence. For Winnicott, the illusion of omnipotence is critical for the development of the sense of subjectivity, and, like Klein's concept of the internalization of the good breast, it is the source of hope throughout life. From this initial experience of creating the mother and her breast, the child is capable of creating other illusory experiences in the world. The next set of illusory experiences involves a progressive development of transitional objects, special things that contain meaning and provide a sense of omnipotent control over the world of external objects. Winnicott describes transitional objects as being neither purely internal nor purely external objects, but as defining a new middle, illusory space to experience between parent and child and between self and other. Winnicott notes that it is critical that these transitional objects be understood not within the objective rules of external reality but as having a life of their own. He emphasizes that the transitional object is not a substitute or sublimation that stands for an absent mother, but rather something that children are able to use in developing their own subjective world where they are not simply anxious infants dependent on their mother's return but can be anyone they imagine. This sense of personal power or omnipotence contained in transitional objects is often experienced by parents when they wish to leave home and their child cannot find his or her favorite toy; everyone in the family becomes controlled by the task of finding "Mr. Red," so that the parents may freely leave the house. The child whose transitional objects are not recognized and respected does not develop the capacity for imagination and play, and often becomes addicted to external stimulation.

Transitional experience (Winnicott 1971) reflects "an intermediate area of *experiencing* to which inner reality and external life both contribute. . . . It does not refer exactly to the little child's teddy bear or the infant's first use of the fist (thumb, fingers) . . . [but is] concerned with the first *possession*, and with the intermediate area, that which is objectively perceived" (p. 2). Winnicott's idea of the transitional object as a first possession reflects an initial experience of agency, of being in control in the inner world of relationships and not simply as pushed and pulled by inner and outer forces of an objective world. These early transitional objects become the precursors of adult transitional experiences, experiences that provide belonging, comfort, power, creativity, and a sense of omnipotence, which may involve personal rituals in intimate relationships, experiences of identity, ideals, art, literature, and religion. Winnicott uses the concepts of transitional objects, transitional phenomena, and transitional experience to describe the development of the individual's capacity to use symbolic thought, to infuse objective experience with personal meaning.

ENACTMENT AND TRANSITIONAL EXPERIENCE

Winnicott (1971) found that for many patients, interpretation, the communication of rational explanation, and objective understanding of his patient's history and current experience did not facilitate change, and that in these situations it was necessary to develop an experiential dimension in treatment. In referring to the limits of interpretation and of rational, objective understanding in his clinical work, Winnicott commented, "In this kind of work we know that even the right explanation is ineffectual. The person we are trying to help needs experience in a specialized setting. The experience is one of a *non-purposive state*" (p. 55). Winnicott seems to be referring to patients who are too focused, too earnest, and too self-critical in their mission to be cured, to overcome their symptoms and problems. Although these patients might be quite successful in the external world, they can be thought of as arrested in a paranoid-schizoid state where they evaluate everything as good or evil, right or wrong. For patients in this state, relationships are experienced as functional, part-object organizations in which each individual has a specific purpose. Winnicott focuses on the patients' failure to develop the capacity for symbolic thought and believes that the core of analysis and of psychotherapy is facilitating the patients' development of this capacity, which involves suspending the goal-directed, functional orientation of treatment and entering into the nonpurposive states of transitional experience and play. Winnicott describes the patients' treatment goals:

Schizoid people are not satisfied with themselves anymore than are extroverts who can not get in touch with the dream. These two groups of people come to us for psychotherapy because in one case they do not want to spend their lives irrevocably out of touch with the facts of life, and in the other case because they feel estranged from the dream. They have a sense that something is wrong and there is a dissociation in their personalities, and they would like to be helped to achieve unit status (Winnicott 1960) or a state of time-space integration in which there is one self containing everything instead of dissociated elements that exist in compartments, or are scattered around and left lying about. [p. 67]

Winnicott (1971) believes that psychoanalysis and psychotherapy involve utilizing the nonpurposive states of play, including the development of transitional experiences, in which the analyst strategically suspends the reality principle, dedifferentiating past and present, reality and fantasy, and linear assumptions of cause–effect sequences. In this intentional and strategic suspension of the reality principle, Winnicott substitutes the principles of play, in which purpose does not involve the achievement of a goal, explanation, or understanding, but rather the articulation, affective intensification, and mastery of different transference–countertransference organizations that are manifestations of the patient's unconscious fantasies. Winnicott's use of transitional experience and play suggests a postmodern view of the analytic process, in which the goal is the capacity to generate meaning, to articulate and symbolize experience.

Winnicott (1971) views psychotherapy and psychoanalysis as a specific example of the broader category of play, which he understands to be a universal aspect of all human cultures. For Winnicott, play involves the opportunity to affectively integrate experience as one does in dreams, poetry, art, the theater, and religion. Viewing the analytic situation as a subset of play involves the analyst's choice to primarily focus on psychic reality in comparison with a focus on external reality and the patient's capacity to differentiate experiences in terms of past and present or reality and fantasy. Winnicott's focus on play also defines an intersubjective field: "Psychotherapy takes place in the overlap of two areas of playing, that of patient and that of therapist. Psychotherapy has to do with two people playing together. The corollary of this is that where playing is not possible then the work done by the therapist is directed towards bringing the patient from a state of not being able to play into a state of being able to play" (p. 38). He states that "the precariousness of play belongs to the fact that it is always on the theoretical line between the subjective and that which is objectively perceived" (p. 50). For Winnicott, play involves the capacity to use symbolic thought and to experience the self as a subject. Fonagy (1995), who was influenced by Winnicott, presented an interesting series of studies supporting Winnicott's observations about separate dimensions of thinking, which are represented by play and by reality-oriented thought. He found that in play situations children are capable of thinking in new and creative ways and are able to process and integrate affective relational experiences. Kristeva (2000) has also thought of experience as organized along two dimensions: a linguistic dimension that is organized through social rules, and a rhythmic dimension that involves aspects of play such as humor, dance, song, and communal and personal rituals.

CLINICAL APPLICATION OF TRANSITIONAL PHENOMENA

In his descriptions of transitional experiences within the context of normal development, Winnicott emphasized the importance of the parent's not challenging the child's creation of a transitional object and the parent's ability to join in the elaboration of these subjective and illusory experiences. However, in his descriptions of the use of transitional experience in the psychoanalytic relationship, Winnicott suggests that the analyst often has the more active and strategic role of introducing and enacting the dissociated countertransference images or fantasies that become the nucleus for the development of transitional experience in the analysis. The analyst's use of his own countertransference experiences and fantasies in the development of transitional experiences involves a shift from the classical interpretive frame of reference that emphasizes the clarification and differentiation of aspects of objective reality to focusing the analytic discourse on the development of early symbolic experience. Unlike interpretations that organize experience in a functional sequence of causal relationships, transitional experiences and transference–countertransference enactments organize the world in the surrealistic perspective of magic, dreams, poetry, and art.

Because transference–countertransference enactments and transitional experiences use concrete, proto-symbolic modes of communication, including action, it is important to differentiate these concepts from the more traditional concept of acting out. Freud (1914b), in his paper "Remembering, Repeating, and Working Through," recognized the communicative importance of the patient's action as a means to recover repressed memories and as a key to the construction of unremembered past events. The concept of acting out was subsequently understood as the patient's discharge of drive affect through action and as an avoidance of awareness through action outside of the analytic relationship. In contrast to the traditional concept of acting out, therapeutic enactments, such as those described by and derived from Winnicott's work, involve the analyst's putting into action a critical aspect of the patient's dissociated experience; it is the analyst and not the patient who acts. The purpose of these enactments is to contain, frame, or create an intense affective experience, and not to remember a past experience. Enactments develop the affective conditions through which the patient can internalize dissociated aspects of experience, which frequently involves paranoid anxieties and fears of potential destructiveness. In enactments, the analyst initiates a reorganization of the analytic relationship into a paranoid mode of experience in terms of the forms of affect, language use, and thought process. This reorganization into a paranoid mode of experience seems to be a necessary, albeit regressive aspect of the development of the capacity to use symbolic processes and the integration of dissociated experience. Enactments are often emotionally painful and confusing experiences for both patient and analyst; they are not "play acting" or a corrective emotional experience where the analyst presents a lesson through example to the patient. Analytic enactments often involve intense affective regressions, loss of boundaries, and the stable objective sense of separateness of analyst and patient as they become enmeshed (Newirth 1990) in a paranoid transference–countertransference experience.

Winnicott (1977) illustrates the analytic use of enactment and transitional experience in facilitating the development of a patient's capacity to integrate disowned aggression and the capacity for symbolic thought in "The Piggie," an account of the psychoanalytic treatment of a very inhibited little girl. In this treatment situation, Winnicott joyfully takes all of the toys for himself and announces that he is the "greedy Winnicott," enacting the patient's dissociated greedy destructive and fearful fantasy. In his insistence that he is the greedy Winnicott, enacting the disowned greedy part of the patient, Winnicott takes an important step beyond the use of countertransference as a source of information or interpretation. He enacts his countertransference fantasy, which might also be thought of as an example of a projective identification, becoming a transitional object for the child, the disowned greedy one (like the cookie monster on *Sesame Street*), embodying the patient's private, dissociated experience in a recognizable living form. In his enactment of the greedy one, Winnicott reorganized the objective relationship of patient and analyst into an intersubjective experience that utilized the early cognitive processes of splitting and manic omnipotence.

Initially the patient was made anxious by Winnicott's insistence that he was the greedy Winnicott, and insisted that he was "Dr. Winnicott," her good therapist. The patient's resistance to Winnicott's use of transitional experience is a common reaction, reflecting anxiety related to the suspension of the reality principle and the movement into the paranoid modes of thought, which are aspects of play and the proto-symbolic experiences of enactment and transitional experiences. However, the patient eventually responded to Winnicott's implicit invitation to play in a similar, playful way, and was able also to be the greedy one. Through this development of mutual play, a transitional experience developed that allowed the patient to symbolize her aggressive, greedy feelings without fear that she would destroy herself, Winnicott, or her family. The transitional object of the disowned greedy one was played out repetitively, including transitional experience of being loved, punished, mourned, and reborn. Through the development of this transitional experience, the child developed the capacity for symbolic thought and could experience greed and aggression without fearing that she would destroy the world.

Winnicott presents another more complicated illustration of the use of transitional experience in the analysis of a man who had been in treatment for many years. Although this is a fairly dramatic example, it is important to keep in mind that it developed within the context of a therapeutic stance of play and the analyst's enacting of countertransference fantasies. In this situation the enactment starts out as a verbal statement describing Winnicott's fantasy and becomes a fully developed transitional experience in which patient and therapist accept the presence of an embodied transitional object in a dream-like experience of psychic reality. It is helpful to differentiate the enactment of a single proto-symbolic experience and a transitional experience in which the enactment becomes integrated into the relationship as a complex intersubjective element similar to Ogden's (1994) concept of the analytic third.

Winnicott (1971) describes his patient speaking in his usual way "about penis envy" when Winnicott surprised himself and said, "I am listening to a girl. I know perfectly well that you are a man but I am listening to a girl, and I am talking to a girl. I am telling this girl: 'You are talking about penis envy'" (p. 73). This interpretation involves several interesting elements that are unarticulated aspects of Winnicott's theory. First, the interpretation reorganizes the experience into a paranoid mode of thought by using splitting into two separate experiences of the patient: his subjective girl self and his objective male self. Second,[2] Winnicott uses a repetitive, rhythmic language that seems more like an evocative poem, rather than a traditional interpretation that is informative, differentiating fragments of experience and functioning as an explanation of two spatial or temporally separate events.

Winnicott reports that there was an immediate acceptance of his interpretation; however, the following exchange between Winnicott and the patient structured this interaction within the locus of transitional experiences rather than as a traditional interpretive/explanatory approach to treatment. The patient said, "If I were to tell someone about this girl I would be called mad." I think that this comment, although involving recognition of his disowned subjective experiences of himself, as a girl and as mad, also represents a resistance to Winnicott's invitation to enter into a transitional realm through maintaining a safe, objective relationship of being the patient with Winnicott, assigned the role of the good, insightful analyst. I believe that this attempt is directed at avoiding the loss of boundaries inherent in Winnicott's intervention and is an example of a resistance to the regression implied by movement into a transitional experience. Winnicott

---

2. It is very helpful to read this interpretation out loud, to get a sense of the repetitive use of the word *girl*, and how it becomes a rhythmic experience, like a child's verbal game or a ritualistic chant. It also can be thought of as a invitation to regress to a nonrepresentational use of language and an experience of play.

does not relinquish his position, continuing to enact his identification/ merger with the crazy part of the patient and saying, "It was not that *you* told this to anyone; it is I who see the girl and hear a girl talking, when actually there is a man on my couch. The mad person is myself" (p. 74). Winnicott continues to use paranoid modes of thought, as he did with his child patient, identifying with the disowned, pathological experience of being mad and not allowing himself to be placed in the objective frame of the interpreting, helpful analyst.

Directly responding to the patient's resistance through maintaining his identification and the enactment of the "mad one" allowed for the mutual development of the more complicated transitional experience of the patient as subjectively both a girl and a boy. This girl who had previously been only an unconscious fantasy, part of the patient's private life, became recognized in the transitional experience between the patient and Winnicott; they were able to talk about her, and to her, experiencing her as a living participant in the analysis with her own reactions, needs, and intentions. Their mutual recognition of this girl's influence on the patient's life and the playful way that she became integrated in the treatment is like a family's acceptance of a child's invisible playmate; her existence was not challenged, interpreted, or objectified.

Winnicott's theory involves a dialectical relationship between the self experienced as an object and the self experienced as a subject. In his controversial paper, *The Use of an Object*, Winnicott (1969) presents the thesis that it is the analyst's capacity to expose himself to and survive the patient's destructiveness that allows for the development of subjectivity and the capacity to use symbols. Often, as in the two examples cited above, this process involves the analyst's identifying with the patient's disowned destructive, mad, and bad projective identifications, involving destructive criticism and persecutory attacks from the patient, and his or her internalized critical objects or personal ideals. The development of this subject-to-subject relationship requires that the analyst be free to express his subjective, countertransferential experience and that he can tolerate the anxiety of loss of self, which results from being destroyed in both his and the patient's fantasies. Ogden (1995) presents a series of cases in which he describes the long periods experiencing deadness and debilitating persecutory fantasies before being able to symbolize the projective identifications with his patients, which we may understand as examples of surviving the patient's destructiveness as a critical part of the treatment.

CLINICAL ILLUSTRATION: THE GREEDY ANALYST

This case illustrates the analyst's enactment of a transference–countertransference fantasy that developed into a complex transitional experience and remained part of the treatment for many years. This series of enactments, of nonverbal play and transitional experiences, occurred in parallel with more traditional psychoanalytic processes of understanding, empathy, and interpretation. The patient, a physician in his mid 30s, had been seen in psychoanalytic psychotherapy for approximately four years. At the point that he entered treatment, he had been both successful and reasonably satisfied with his career. His stated reason for beginning therapy was his increasing unhappiness about his inability to develop an intimate relationship. His difficulty in intimate relationships did not stop him from having close friendships with men and women and a busy social life. He was seen as a loyal, interested friend who was also often critical and argumentative, and lacked generosity. The presenting problem—the difficulty in forming a love relationship—was complicated by the fact that the only love relationship he had had was a homosexual relationship during college. This relationship continued after college. He ended it because of concerns about his parents' reaction as well as his concern about a homosexual lifestyle. At the point that he began treatment, he had not been involved in either homosexual or heterosexual relationships since he had ended the relationship with his lover.

This lack of a love relationship left him feeling an inner emptiness and lack of intense involvement that neither work nor friendship seemed to fulfill. He said that he was prepared to develop either a heterosexual or a homosexual relationship; however, he felt unable to proceed with either choice. In his fantasies he was attracted to both men and women, although the types of people chosen were somewhat different in his heterosexual and homosexual fantasies. His homosexual fantasies involved primarily looking at handsome, athletic-looking young men who he assumed were gay because of their dress—jeans and leather jackets. His heterosexual fantasies were similarly voyeuristic and centered on black and Asian young women. These fantasies were not involved in his frequent masturbation, which seemed mechanical and self-soothing as opposed to a sexually engaged activity. He regarded physical love with either men or women to be "animalistic," particularly if it did not involve an intensely romantic and monogamous commitment. Over the years he had attempted to make love with several women, mostly friends, and, although physically capable, he had not felt either passion or emotional arousal during foreplay or while having intercourse. It seemed to me that his concern was premature over whether he was homosexual or heterosexual, but rather that he was presexual and that the issues of choice of partner were less important than his capacity to relate to someone in a sexual and affectionate way.

He was the younger of two sons in a Jewish middle-class family that had lived in suburban New York. Although a fairly close family in terms of being concerned and involved in each other's lives, on a personal level the family seemed unemotional, cold, and distant, with little physical affection. The patient maintained a close relationship with his brother, exchanging phone calls and frequent visits; however, he reported that they would be embarrassed to kiss or hug each other as well as to ask personal questions. Because his mother worked in the family retail store, he had to take care of himself during much of his childhood, cooking and doing his own laundry. The patient reports never having felt like most of the other boys in the neighborhood. He was not athletic, and he was somewhat shy and isolated, although he had a few good friends.

The family suffered a major setback during his preadolescence when his father became unable to support the family because his business went into bankruptcy. This was an extremely trying time for the patient and his family, and their economic problems were exacerbated by his mother's rageful attacks on his father. Mother accused father of squandering his money on other women, as well as continuously saying that he was inadequate as a man because he could not support his family. The patient had an extremely painful memory of his mother's coming into his room in a rage and taking his piggy bank and saying that she needed his money to feed the family because his father did not provide her with money. During the three-year period subsequent to the bankruptcy, the mother refused to sleep with the father, and he slept in a separate room. The patient reports that during this period his mother would frequently attack and belittle his father, who "acted like a saint," never responding with anger in return.

Initially, treatment was dominated by the patient's strict moral attitudes; he expressed criticisms about sexuality and pleasure, and a pervasive cynicism, describing most people as too lazy to work. He had a very difficult time being in therapy, referring to both himself and other patients as "sickos" and attacking me and the institution of psychotherapy as taking advantage of patients and fostering unconscionable dependency. My initial impression was of a man who denied his feelings, who externalized his negative experiences, and who was dominated by paranoid anxieties around greed, aggression, and destructiveness. He experienced his feelings and desires in an extremely concrete form, often attributing to others his feelings and desires, which he would then criticize and attack. He was dominated by rigid superego values and had a obsessive-compulsive personality organization. He narrated his history, which he felt proud of, and was concerned lest I turn him against his mother. His father had died several years before he entered therapy, and he only had the highest praise for him. There was a surprising lack of anger in his speech, although there were regular notes of sarcasm and criticism of the therapeutic process and me. In addition to the experience of an inner void that had brought him into treatment, there was also a great deal of conscious guilt toward his ex-lover, who he thought continued to suffer as a result of the patient's abandonment.

Toward the end of the first year, the patient began to bring an individually wrapped chocolate donut and a drink into the sessions. It seemed that out of a sense of compulsive politeness he offered me the donut and asked if I would like some. There was no feeling of generosity in this offer. I had a sense of a formal child who was carrying out parental instructions with the belief that his offer would be politely turned down. My fantasy was that taking a piece of his donut would be seen as an extremely selfish, greedy, aggressive, and boorish act that would be revolting to his extremely controlled and strict superego. I also thought that a central dynamic issue for this patient was his projection of greed and envy into others and his condemnation of the aggression that he then found. In any case, I decided to accept the offer and to break off a piece of his chocolate donut. As expected, he was surprised and annoyed at my bold gesture, but said nothing, and I also said nothing.

It surprised me when he brought a chocolate donut to the next session and then to each subsequent session. In each session he would repeat his reluctant offer, as if for the first time, and I would repeat my casual acceptance of the donut; what started as an enactment of what I thought of as a moment of his dissociated greed and aggression became a mutually constructed ritual, a transitional experience, that we both enacted as exaggerated, playful ceremonies of hunger, greed, selfishness, dominance, and submission. At times, he would make hostile comments, for example, "Hungry tonight?" or "Did you think that I might forget your donut?" This transitional experience of eating the donut became an important part of the sessions; although one could trivialize the experience, it began to contain a great deal of implicit, shared subjective meanings that remained unverbalized as we continued to enact this concrete set of proto-symbolic transitional experiences. In a different analytic orientation, this enacted transference–countertransference situation would have been quickly interpreted, made explicit, and put into an historical context of explanation and understanding. I chose not to do this, believing that it was important for the patient to continue with the experience of playing with aggression and greed in a context in which neither of us was destroyed, and that this transitional experience would allow him to develop the capacity to use symbolic processes in addressing his inner experience of need and sexual desire. In Winnicott's (1971) discussions of transitional experience, he often notes that it is important not to question the origin or meaning of the transitional experience because doing so shifts the level of organization from that of the development of early symbolic experiences in the paranoid-schizoid position to an objective, rational mode of discourse. It is crucial to stay within the paradox implicit in the transitional experience of literally being fed, feeding, and loving, while being greedy, aggressive, and hating without actually destroying the other. This paradoxical experience of greed and distruction of feeding and being fed seemed to be at the core of this transitional experience.

There was a great deal of tension and affect contained in this transitional experience. It was as if each time there was an unasked question as to whether I would be greedy and he would be condemning of my selfish behavior. I made no interpretations, but simply, or not so simply, enacted this transitional drama, until in one session the patient angrily asked, "When do you start to bring the food?" Perhaps as a function of resistance, he sarcastically suggested that if my office mates and I were not so cheap we would set up a buffet in the waiting room. I made a minimal comment, not wanting to leave the transitional experience for the implied conversation about power and sharing, and said, "I only eat what is offered to me. I don't bring food. That's not part of what I offer." I wanted to keep my response within the scope of the transitional experience, believing that the issues of greed and aggression were still being developed and that he wanted to negotiate a fairer approach to this feeding situation so as to avoid his own experiences of greed and aggression; it was as if he was asking me to please stop being greedy so as to avoid an awareness of his own unconscious experiences of greed.

Although my participation in this transitional experience might sound glib, it was accompanied by significant countertransference anxieties that required scrutiny and self-analysis to contain the affects and fantasies that grew out of these enactments. My countertransference anxieties focused on two issues or fantasies. The first had to do with my being a sadistic, exploitative, and greedy individual who was acting out and should not be allowed to do treatment. The second countertransference anxiety or issue had a more paranoid flavor and involved thoughts that my colleagues, a projection of a critical part of myself, would see me as engaging in a homosexual seduction, or engaging the patient in an implicit homosexual relationship. An important part of treatment from this neo-Kleinian perspective involves the analyst's capacity to contain the dissociated anxiety of the patient and to be able to imaginatively elaborate these unspoken anxieties, to maintain the enactments and not exchange the subjective discourse of the transitional experience for a discourse in an objective and interpretive language.

The analytic work continued in parallel to this evolving transitional experience. The first set of major changes in the patient's concerns involved his homosexual and heterosexual fantasies. His homosexual fantasies became more overtly aggressive and somewhat sadistic. His heterosexual fantasies were elaborated in a similar way, with his becoming sexually demanding and sexually aroused in his fantasies. His homosexual fantasies began to recede and would emerge during times of loss of self-esteem and anger. He also became able to experience anger as he remembered childhood experiences and was able to hold a less constricted and defensive view of his childhood. In his relationships with people, both at work and with his friends, he became more aggressive, more assertive, and more generous. For example, he found himself surprised when he stopped resenting paying for dinner for the women he had begun to date.

As the treatment progressed, he began to define himself as a heterosexual and become more intimately and affectionately involved with several women. It was difficult for him to move from these intimate and affectionate relationships to one in which he could imagine having intercourse as a pleasurable experience as opposed to an obligation and a performance about which he would be rated. This sexual anxiety allows for an interesting illustration of a more general use of transitional relatedness in treatment. In talking about his sexual anxieties about being judged by women, I expressed my countertransference fantasy of his wish to be the gold medal winner in an Olympic event of making love. He immediately found my imagery engaging and we elaborated this transitional fantasy together using the image of a sexual Olympics to transform his passively experienced paranoid anxieties about being critically attacked into an active paranoid fantasy in which he could experience his desire to be the greatest sexual performer, the most powerful man, the gold medal winner, and be able to dominate a now-submissive woman.

The transitional experience of eating a donut continued and went through several changes both in the form of the ritual and in my sense of the meaning that these enactments contained. For a reason unknown to me, rather than a chocolate donut he began to bring a large chocolate chip cookie that was machine wrapped in plastic, as a colleague[3] said, "shrink wrapped." He found it difficult to unwrap the cookie, and would ask me to do it for him. I seemed more able to undo this wrapper than he was, and so he would present the cookie to me and ask me to undo it. After opening the wrapper, I would hand the cookie back to him, and he would then offer it to me to break off a piece for myself. He seemed to enjoy this version of the transitional experience and the hostility of the previous period seemed to be changed into affectionate chiding about why I would never take a first bite and had to wait for his offer and how he had to watch that I did not take too much.

In one session, shortly after the transitional experience had occurred, he was talking about an anxiety experience with a woman who he felt

3. I wish to express my gratitude to Dr. Bruce Tuchman for his many helpful comments.

was too interested in him and in having his children. It was as if much of the unverbalized aspects of the transitional experience began to make sense, and I interpreted his fear that someone would want to devour him and steal his sperm and his children. He was very moved by this interpretation and became tearful, remembering many comments from his childhood when both his parents and other members of the extended family would imply that the women in the family only needed the men to provide them with babies, and that after that service they were useless. It seemed to me that there was a strong cannibalistic feeling in both his memories of his family and in each of our fantasies. The parallel to the current form of our transitional experience is rather clear in that it involved his recognition that I would not steal his cookie, even after he placed it in my hands.

Subsequently, his anxiety with women became considerably reduced and he developed a relationship that was both affectionate and sexual. He had also become able to express in treatment gratitude for the progress he made and pride in his growth. We continued to share the cookie; however, he suggested that he might begin bringing in two cookies and that we might each have our own. This suggestion seemed to reflect his gratitude at having worked through his feelings of greed and anger; perhaps it is simply a wish on my part, but I suspect it also reflected a fantasy of being able to have a child and to experience himself as a full and generous person. The treatment continued for approximately two more years. The transitional experience disappeared as the focus of treatment became his relationship with a woman to whom he became engaged and subsequently married.

Winnicott suggests that transitional experiences, after outliving their usefulness, tend to fade into the background, leaving behind the capacity to use symbolic thought and to develop further transitional experiences. My understanding of this transitional experience remained largely uninterpreted as a proto-symbolic, transitional experience in the analysis. This complex set of actions and unverbalized meanings represented a process of enacting the patient's dissociated experiences and facilitating the development of his capacity to symbolically experience greed and aggression through the development of a transitional experience. I believe that it was the patient's concrete, paranoid experience of greed and aggression that was at the core of his arrested development and his inability to be a sexual and loving adult in an intimate relationship with another person. I believe that the evolving transitional experience of eating the donut and later the cookie enabled us to enact and play out the multiple meanings of greed, envy, the destruction of the object, and finally the reparation and re-creation of the object. In the paradox created through the transitional experience I could be both greedy and trustworthy and he could be both sadistic and generous. This case illustrates the use of the concepts of play, enactment, and transitional experience involved in a mode of psychoanalytic relatedness directed at developing the capacity for symbolic thought, which is experiential, conscious, and paradoxically purposeful. The paradox involves the analyst's choice to utilize the processes of play and transitional relatedness, which Winnicott describes as being without a purpose, but can be understood as utilizing a different structure of thought from the usual interpretive and explanatory approaches that are based on linear, goal-directed processes that attempt to differentiate experience in terms of person, place, and time.

8

The Unconscious and Interpretation

The development of a two-person relational paradigm in psychoanalysis has resulted in a shift in the central focus of psychoanalytic treatment from the analysis of unconscious wishes and impulses to the analysis of current relational patterns. Contemporary psychoanalytic practice (Kernberg 1993, Schafer 1994) that developed within this evolving two-person constructivist perspective has focused on the analysis of the transference–countertransference interaction as a way of addressing the patient's maladaptive repetitive childhood patterns. In this important shift to a two-person psychology, the unconscious has been redefined as either inaccurate childhood patterns of relationship that distort current experience, or as current relational patterns that remain outside of awareness. In this chapter I will argue that the rejection of the classical notions of the unconscious and the shift from a drive-centered to a relationship-centered psychology have led to privileging rational over irrational experience and a return to Freud's early topographic model in which the structures of consciousness and unconsciousness are defined simply through the presence or absence of awareness. I suggest a model of the unconscious based on the Kleinian theory of thinking and symbol formation integrated with Matte Blanco's (1975) mathematical model of consciousness and unconsciousness as different modalities of organizing and generating meaning and experience. This neo-Kleinian model views the unconscious as an expanding structure of mind, a set of functions that generate the powerful forces and modes of thought traditionally associated with the unconscious and that act both as the center of psychopathology and as a source of energy, hope, and creativity.

In his poem "Sleep," Winnicott (C. Winnicott et al. 1989) describes his concept of the unconscious as a life-giving center of energy, a source of comfort, creativity, energy, and power that captures an essential dimension of the neo-Kleinian concept of the unconscious.

> Let down your tap root
> to the centre of your soul
> Suck up the sap
> from the infinite source
> of your unconscious
> and
> Be evergreen [p. 17]

INTERPERSONAL AND RELATIONAL APPROACHES TO UNCONSCIOUS EXPERIENCE

The concept of the unconscious as a psychic structure developed from Freud's (Breuer and Freud 1895) discovery that his hysterical patients were able to remember experiences under hypnosis or through using free association that explained their symptoms and freed them from the inhibitions, fears, wishes, and disowned actions encoded in childhood. This early view of the unconscious as repressed or dissociated experience was expanded and reified into a metapsychological structure, the unconscious, with Freud's development of the concept of the sexual etiology of the neurosis. This movement from a descriptive, topological model to the dynamic tripartite structural model defined the unconscious as a structure, a place, a basement, a dungeon, or a locked vault that represented Freud's biological and anatomical concept of structure, as well as the cultural view of the antagonism between the wildness of nature and the ethical, lawful, controlled requirements of civilization.[1] The concept of the unconscious as a place within the mind has been a very appealing concept in psychoanalysis, because it answers the unanswerable question of where memory, desire, and dreams are when they are not in our awareness. However, this view of the unconscious as primitive space in the mind serves another purpose: it maintains the nineteenth-century scientific view of consciousness and rational thought conquering the dark, irrational aspects of human experience. This scientific goal can be thought of as parallel to the political, patriarchal agenda of an entitlement to dominate the feminine and the non-Western world.

Fromm (1970) criticized the failure of contemporary psychoanalysis to pursue "the most creative and radical achievement of Freud's theory [which] was the founding of a 'science of the irrational'—i.e., the theory of the unconscious" (p. 16). He believed this failure was a result of conservative political forces in the development of the psychoanalytic movement that focused on increasing control over the profession and conforming to the bourgeois constraints of society. Fromm thought that Freud's revolutionary concept of the unconscious was modified as a result of the conservative development of the profession of psychoanalysis, and that the theoretical shift from an id psychology to ego psychology that emphasized the patient's adaptation to reality was an isomorphic transformation of the political structure of the profession into its theoretical and clinical dimensions.

Fromm's radical critique of the development of psychoanalysis is echoed in current debates on how to define psychoanalysis. These debates often focus on the importance of the "extrinsic criteria" (Gill 1994) of psychoanalysis: the frequency of sessions, the duration of sessions, and the use of the couch. Gill argues that more important than these extrinsic factors in the psychoanalytic situation are the "intrinsic factors" of the psychoanalytic situation, which involve "the intent to analyze the interaction as much as possible" (p. 63). Gill poignantly states his posi-

1. *Civilization and Its Discontents* articulates Freud's view of the antagonism between nature and civilization. Popular ideas of werewolves, Frankenstein, and Jack the Ripper all represented this antagonism between nature and civilization. Ibsen's plays, which were written at the same time, deal with themes that parallel Freud's work, although, unlike Freud, he seems to suggest that evil resides in society rather than in the animal part of the self. Erich Fromm (1941) echoes similar themes in his classic work, *Escape from Freedom*.

tion: "What I am struggling against is the rote acceptance of the idea that an analysis can be conducted only with at least four or five sessions a week and on the couch. . . . I want the frequency to be the *least* that is compatible with an analytic process for a particular patient so that analysis can be made available to more people" (p. 76, italics added).

Gill suggests a radical, postmodern approach to the psychoanalytic situation, emphasizing the analyst's active engagement with the patient and the importance of interpretation and explication of the analyst–patient interaction as the critical dimension of psychoanalytic treatment. However, at the same time that he presents a postmodern approach to analytic technique, he presents a conservative approach to the unconscious as a structure of mind, defining it as distortion, as the source of pathology, and as the core difficulty in adapting to reality. He argues that the analysis of the interaction is the effective means of addressing the patient's pathological transferences, which are rooted in childhood experience; the analysis of the interaction becomes the means of transforming the irrational past into the rational present. The following statement illustrates both the radical and conservative elements in Gill's argument:

> The analyst will remember that he is always interacting with the patient and that the interaction is so complex and multifaceted that it is fatuous to think he can always be aware of what is going on. The analyst will work toward the establishment of a psychoanalytic situation . . . in which, however they temporarily stray from it, analyst and patient both remain committed to the idea that the proximal goal is to understand the relationship, not only to engage in it, while the distal goal is to understand the patient's psychopathology in the light of the patient's development. [p. 116]

This view of the unconscious as the repository of historical, pathological, irrational, interpersonal, or relational schemas has encouraged the development in contemporary psychoanalysis of a view of the unconscious simply as meanings outside of awareness rather than as a structure of the mind that is a source of energy and encompasses the irrational as an important counterforce to the rational. This contemporary view of the unconscious as relational schemas outside of awareness has resulted in the emphasis in contemporary technique on the rational analysis of the transference–countertransference relationship in a process that

increasingly resembles discriminant learning theory. In this contemporary approach to unconscious experience, interpretations are focused on
differentiating the analyst (a contemporary object) from the patient's
historical objects.

Hirsch and Roth (1995) reviewed contemporary literature on the
unconscious and present the current interpersonal and relational views
of the unconscious as unarticulated schemas of past interpersonal relationships. They point out that for many contemporary authors the central dimension of the unconscious and of the treatment is the patient's
"rigid patterns of relating that truncate a more dimensional experience
in living. Specifically people's difficulties result from their adhesion to
loved ones of the past with whom they are embedded and from whom
they cannot separate" (p. 271). These authors, in harmony with Gill and
many other contemporary theorists, state that the goal of treatment is
"to demystify the analyst in the transference and thereby also demysti-
fying the family in the patient's internal world" (p. 273). From this perspective, psychoanalytic cure involves correcting the distortions of the
past, which leads to the recognition of inappropriate historical patterns
in the current situation. Insight and the differentiation of the historical
objects from the current analytic object allow the patient to make the
more appropriate, realistic choices. This relational position, which emphasizes the patient's developing a less distorted and more realistic perspective on current life events and then being able to make rational
choices, has also been the focus of many contemporary Freudian analysts (see Renik [1995] for example).

This view of the unconscious as unarticulated relational patterns
and the treatment corollary of the patient's learning a more realistic or
functionally accurate view of self in relation to others, of differentiating
the repetitive, self-destructive relationship patterns through a current
relationship with the analyst, is the central theme in many contemporary psychoanalytic approaches. For example, the control–mastery approach develop by Weiss and Sampson (Sampson 1992) describes two
aspects of effective treatment. The first involves insight into the pathological beliefs (relational patterns) and the problems to which they give
rise, and the second involves the patient's unconsciously (that is, outside of awareness) testing his/her beliefs in relation to the analyst. The
critical treatment events are whether the patient perceives the analyst's
behavior and attitudes as disconfirming the belief he is testing. Sampson

breaks with the tradition of emphasizing the singular importance of verbal interpretation and points out that "direct experience with the analyst sometimes may lead to significant analytic progress even without interpretation" (p. 519). The unconscious is defined as the individual's repetitive relational patterns, which are outside of awareness; issues of energy, specific content such as sexuality and aggression, or different modes of organizing experience such as primary and secondary process thought or concrete and symbolic thought are not considered in this and similar positions.

Levenson (2001) critiques our preference for a narrow band of rational conscious thought, which we view as the center of awareness. He contrasts this limited psychoanalytic understanding with the expanding perspectives of cognitive science and of neuropsychology, which view consciousness as an epiphenomenon in the much more complex system of mental activity:

> We are shifting to a more holistic concept of brain functioning. The unconscious, many of us now believe, is where most everything happens. Consciousness becomes an epiphenomenon, a bubble of awareness. For Freud, content was pushed *down*, kept out of awareness. For so-called cognitive scientists, consciousness—in its common usage—is simply a selective awareness of unconscious functioning, pulled *up* into awareness. It is true that things may be kept out of consciousness via "selective inattention" or, more strongly, repression. But both activities require, as Sartre (1956) pointed out, an elaborate unconscious perception and a strategy to prevent emergence *into* awareness—not, one notes, to repress *out* of awareness. I do appreciate that this is a considerable oversimplification, but I am trying to delineate a paradigmatic distinction. [p. 245]

Levenson highlights and critiques the linguistic reifications that maintain the concept of the unconscious as a limited, basement-like place in the mind, where ideas and experiences are pushed into, rise up from, and are constantly moving in and out of. Levenson's focus on this directional language comes close to a parody of the language of psychoanalytic interpretation, in which the unconscious is seen as a literal mental space rather than a series of organizational functions and metaphors.

THE UNCONSCIOUS IN KLEIN, WINNICOTT, AND BION

Andre Green (1995), in a critique of contemporary psychoanalytic theory and technique, raises the ironic question, "Has sexuality anything to do with psychoanalysis?" He argues against the current emphasis on the analysis of repetitive relational patterns to the exclusion of references to sexuality and the unconscious. His discussion of sexuality suggests that our difficulty in developing a contemporary concept of unconscious experience is a result of literal interpretations of Freud's concept of sexuality and drive. He argues that the essence of Freud's concerns with sexuality involves the capacity for "pleasurable enjoyment" and the ability "to feel alive and to cathect the many possibilities offered by the diversity of life, in spite of its inevitable disappointments, sources of unhappiness and loads of pain" (p. 874). Green's emphasis on pleasure and aliveness are attempts to address the absent concepts of drive and energy, which were thought of as a core aspect of unconscious experience. Green wants to return to a multidimensional concept of unconscious experience that includes concepts of energy, pleasure, passion, and aliveness.

Winnicott, Bion, and other Kleinian analysts are often confusing in their use of the concept of the unconscious, because they continue to use the one-person, metapsychological language of Freud's structural model, implying that the unconscious is a literal structure containing instincts, drives, energy, and fantasies. However, their dramatic, poetic descriptions of clinical process suggest a two-person perspective, with the unconscious viewed as a transformational system that creates new internal and external experiences, meanings, and an enlivening source of energy. Hanna Segal (1994) illustrates this second metaphorical perspective, using a children's story, *Haroun and the Sea of Stories*, written by Salman Rushdie, as a parable for the psychoanalytic endeavor and the structure of unconscious experience. She describes the unconscious as having the characteristics of either deadness, when its contents are evacuated into external reality, or aliveness, creativity, and joy, when experienced as internal symbolic fantasies. She describes the universal struggle to resolve the "inner conflict between creativity and the anti-creative forces" (p. 612) in the development of the unconscious through the integration of love and hate, and the evolving capacity to use symbols.

The concept of the unconscious suggested by Segal, Winnicott, Bion, and other Kleinian analysts involves a view that the unconscious is a developing set of functions[2] that organize experience in progressively integrated and symbolic forms. This developmental view of the unconscious is radically different from the static view of the unconscious as a container for either drive derivatives or childhood relational schemas. The development of the unconscious as a generative or transformative system that has the capacity for creativity and an evolving sense of aliveness is described by Eigen (1981) as a critical outcome of the analytic process. He describes the unconscious as the capacity to make a passionate commitment to life, which he calls "faith," defined as a "way of experiencing which is undertaken with one's whole being, all out, with all one's heart, with all one's soul, and with all one's might" (p. 413). He contrasts this passionate dimension of the unconscious with theories that emphasize ego mastery, introjection, and successful adaptations to the external world. He is critical of contemporary approaches in which the analyst attempts to become a new, more realistic internal object, replacing the patient's historical, pathological objects. Eigen describes this dimension as a development of his reading of Winnicott, Bion, and Lacan, who "maintain the critical importance of not confusing creative experiencing with introjection (or internalization) of mother and father images or functions" (p. 431). For Eigen, "the sources of creative experiencing run deeper than internalization and goes beyond it. . . . One discovers that the primary object of creative experiencing is not a mother or father but the unknowable ground of creativeness as such. Winnicott, for example, emphasizes that what is at stake in transitional experiencing is not a self or object (mother) substitute, but the creation of a symbol, of symbolizing experience itself" (p. 431). The Kleinian and Winnicottian view of the unconscious suggests that more important than the patient's internalized childhood relational patterns is the development of the capacity to integrate internal experience in an intense, committed, alive, creative, and symbolic form. This developmental dimension

2. Roy Schafer (1976) presents a similar critique of the reification involved in psychoanalytic concepts and suggests the use of "action language" so that it becomes clear that psychoanalysis is addressing issues of action and disowned action. However, his critique eliminates differences between conscious and unconscious experience and actions, focusing on the individual's choice, rather than on different functions or processes.

of the unconscious, implicit in Klein's and Winnicott's two-person perspective, is reflected in the person's evolving capacity for pleasure, joy, a passionate commitment to life, and the capacity to create symbolic and transitional experiences that are an expanding source of power and energy.

DIMENSIONS OF UNCONSCIOUS EXPERIENCE

The Kleinian concept of the transformation of concrete external experience into internal symbolic experience suggests two separate dimensions of unconscious experience and language. The first is the dimension of concrete and symbolic experience, which Klein described as critical components in the paranoid-schizoid and the depressive positions. The second is the dimension of conscious and unconscious thought and language, which has been typically thought of as a function of the location, whether located in the internal world or in the external world or as a tautology in which something is conscious because it is spotlighted with awareness. Segal's (1981) postscript to her paper "Notes on Symbol Formation" illustrates these two dimensions, comparing different forms of failure in the use of symbolic thought. In the first example, she describes a young man who was usually able to function in the depressive position but under times of stress "tended to use massive projective identification accompanied by regression to concrete levels of functioning" (p. 80). In this example, his unconscious, internal, persecutory experiences are projected into the external world where he experiences them as real, concrete, and terrifying events.

> He came to one session very perturbed because on waking up he had a hallucinatory experience. It differed from hallucination only insofar as he clung desperately to the belief that it must be the product of his own mind. When he woke up he felt that his head was solid and he saw a motorcycle riding into his head. The rider had a kind of mask on, which made his head look like a finger. He felt terrified and thought his head would explode. Then he looked at his own index finger, and got frightened because his finger looked like a gorilla. He emerged from the state of acute anxiety only when he made himself remember the previous session, in which he was disturbed by the very intrusive noise of motorcycles outside the consulting room windows.

He thought the motorcycles were connected with my son. He associated the gorilla with a psychotic boy who was described in a paper as looking like a gorilla. The finger he associated to anal masturbation, about which he had spoken a few days earlier. His anal masturbation was always associated with violent projective identification into the anus of the analyst/mother, as described by Meltzer (1966). We could analyze that the motorcycles outside the window represented his own intrusive self identified with his finger and penis, projected into an external object—the motorcycle—and intruding into him. It is important in this connection that there was an external world and actual intrusive object into which this projection fitted. It repeated a childhood situation in which there was, in fact, a very intrusive older sibling interfering with his relation to the mother even when he was a tiny baby. Thus his projections were concretized for him in the external world. [p. 61]

In this first example, we can experience the patient's terror as he wakes from this nightmare, uncertain about his reality and slowly recovering his ability to symbolize his experience through a self-analytic process. This example suggests a temporary regression to concrete thinking in a person who is able to experience a full range of functioning from concrete to symbolic thought.

In her second example, Segal describes her work with a very disturbed patient who often experienced Segal's words and interpretations as concrete external things invading her, which seemed to be a corollary of her experience that her body was a lump, which was accompanied by intense fears of cancer. Segal describes a mode of concrete thought that is a function of the patient's evacuation of all mental contents so that she experiences the world in an impersonal, abstract way similar to the description of operational thinking (Basch-Kahre 1985) discussed in Chapter 6:

But there was an opposite phenomenon. Her speech could be called completely abstract. She spoke most of the time in metaphors, clichés, and technical terms. She often generalized in a way that left no meaning. Sometimes she spoke for a long time, and I realized she had said nothing concrete or real that I could get hold of. At the same time, I could observe how she emptied my words of all meaning as if she listened to an interpretation and immediately translated it into some philosophical or psychoanalytic abstract term, often distorting its meaning completely. The underlying fantasy was that she entered me and emptied me of all contents and she felt equally emptied by me. Stealing was an ever recurring theme.

In those modes of functioning, one can see a disturbance between the container and the contained (between the self and other). When she was overly concrete, the projected part was overly identified with the container (the other). When her communication was empty of meaning, the container and the contained had a relation of mutually emptying one another. . . . This mutually destructive relation between the part she projected and the container (the other) seemed to be related to envy and to narcissism. Nothing was allowed to exist outside of herself which could give rise to envy. [p. 62]

These illustrations present two very different experiences of failures in symbolic thought; the first involves being trapped in the nightmare experience of the paranoid position flooded with primary process experiences, while the second reflects the deadened world of empty words, abstraction, objectification, a pathological experience of being trapped in the external world, of only being able to think in terms of the reality principle and secondary process thought. The examples reflect different analytic dimensions of the transformation of concrete into symbolic experience, although both involve the analyst or the (m)other's use of reverie, therapeutic enactment, and transitional experience.

We can now begin to think about this transformational process as involving two separate dimensions: a movement from the concrete thought of the paranoid-schizoid position to the symbolic thought of the depressive position, and simultaneously a movement from an external to an internal locus of experience, or from conscious to unconscious experience.

MATTE BLANCO: A MATHEMATICAL MODEL OF CONSCIOUS AND UNCONSCIOUS EXPERIENCE

Because of the poetic and literary language of many contemporary Kleinian and Winnicottian analysts, it has been difficult to develop a contemporary concept of the unconscious as a two-person relational structure. This preference for literary and spiritual language reflects both a critique of the mechanistic language of traditional psychoanalytic theory as well as a reflection of the personal qualities of many analysts, who found the constraints of traditional one-person theory incompatible with their experiences as psychoanalysts. Matte Blanco, a Chilean analyst who studied with Klein, has made an important contribution to the clarification of the concepts of conscious and unconscious experience. He conceptualized the conscious and unconscious mind, or primary- and secondary-process thinking, in terms of mathematical theory. He suggested that the categories of conscious and unconscious thought represent different sets of rules for organizing, transforming, and generating experience. He thought of conscious or secondary-process thought and language as organized around a principle of asymmetrical logic: an Aristotelian system of logic that is concerned with and creates differences involving the differentiation of time, person, place, sequence, and causality. Asymmetrical logic is the logic of consciousness, of external experience and material reality. It is the logic of science, news media, business, discursive writing, and traditional strategies of psychoanalytic interpretation directed at increasing the patient's awareness of difference in the areas of time, space, causality, and the experience of people as separate, whole objects. In the asymmetrical mode, the analyst may attempt to differentiate the historical object from the current analytic object, as in the statement, "I am not your mother." Matte Blanco thought of unconscious experience or primary process thought as defined by symmetrical logic, logic that effaces difference, dedifferentiates the experience of time, person, place, sequence, and causality. This form of logic creates similarities or identifications between people and defines the world in terms of absolute or singular affective experience. This is the logic and language of dreams, poetry, and drama, and is the basis for the analytic processes of reverie, enactments, empathy, and transitional experience. In the symmetrical mode, the analyst may attempt to efface differences in the dimensions of person, place, time, sequence, and causality, creating a dream-like world of affective meaning as in the statement, "I am your mother."

Matte Blanco (Rayner 1981) defined the operation of the two sets of logical functions or ways of organizing experience in the following way:

> Consciousness is defined by asymmetrical logic and is concerned with, and operates to form discrimination of differences; the unconscious is defined by symmetry and is concerned with registering and creating sameness, identity or homogeneity. Asymmetrical logic

(Fink 1995) allows the conceptualization of time and space and the differentiation of the whole and its parts. It is ruled by the laws of contradiction or antinomy, negation, causality, numerical, spatial and temporal sequence, and the ability to distinguish between subject and object. Thus it is possible to conceive of time, the idea of past, present and future; in terms of space, the here and there, inside and outside, left and right, below and above, external and internal world, self and non-self, etc.; and in terms of whole and parts, the idea of part objects versus complete objects formed by many parts, leading to concepts of individuality, identity. [p. 137]

In symmetrical logic the distinctions of time, space, part and whole, and subject and object are effaced; all relationships are equal to their converse, and therefore there cannot be concepts of sequence, time, or space. Matte Blanco thought the equation of a part with the whole and the tendency to experience emotion at all-or-nothing levels is related to a specific quality of symmetrical logic and of the unconscious; that the unconscious operates as if it is a series of mathematical infinite sets. The psychological experience of an infinite set is "limitlessness, of there being no end, no boundary, no constriction, no control, a lack of negative feedback and so on" (Rayner 1995, p. 56). Although Matte Blanco's theory, because it is based on a mathematical model, can sound quite abstract, these infinite, limitless, or absolute experiences are commonplace and easily recognized. For example, dreams, poetry, art, ideals, love, friendship, and feelings of purpose and identity all reflect the experience of absoluteness or singularity or infinite sets, which define the affective and cognitive experience of symmetrical experience. Joy, terror, creativity, a passionate commitment to life, and dreams all represent the experience of infinitude, as does a love poem that compares one's lover to absolute or infinite experiences such as the depth of the ocean or the expanse of the universe.

Matte Blanco describes his theory as *bi*-logic, because experience almost always involves a layering of symmetry and asymmetry. Although conceptually we can separate symmetry from asymmetry, as a rule thought processes are intertwined, mutually limiting, dialectically organized structures that can be arrayed from highly asymmetrical to highly symmetrical. For example, Rayner (1995) illustrates the dialectical relationship between symmetrical and asymmetrical logic with the following illustration that echoes Winnicott's theory of play and transitional experience:

A child may lie on the beach lapped by the waves and declaim "I am a stone." If he is playing he will know very well that he is not a stone but the point of the game is that he is a stone. This is a paradox inherent in any make believe play. Without symmetry there is no metaphor and with no metaphor there is no make believe play. But without the self having a containing framework of awareness of asymmetrical relations play breaks down into delusion. The child becomes a stone. This occurs in psychosis of course and also normally in dreams. It is muted in affective states and in neurotic anxiety when a person may feel he has turned to stone but knows very well consciously that he has not. [p. 37]

Matte Blanco's theory distinguishes symmetry and asymmetry, primary- and secondary-process thought, from qualities of awareness, suggesting a more complex and accurate way to describe experience through freeing us from the phenomenological equation of consciousness and awareness. This theory distinguishes the phenomenology of consciousness or awareness from the function of consciousness, which is of making discriminations in the external world of person, place, time, and causality. As a result of distinguishing the phenomenology of awareness from the function of conscious and unconscious thought, this theory presents a different way to conceptualize pathological and constructive aspects of consciousness or asymmetrical thought and unconsciousness or symmetrical thought process. Although not within the purview of this book, recent brain research supports the idea of two independent functional systems, one that has been identified with dream states and one identified with waking experience.

CLINICAL ILLUSTRATION: ALL MEN ARE EXPLOITING CAPITALISTS

In this clinical example, a patient's unconscious, symmetrical experience of greed is externalized and projected into her husband and all men, and organizes her relationship with her analyst. This psychoanalytic fragment (Rayner 1995) illustrates the complexity of the relationship between symmetrical and asymmetrical experience in the transference–countertransference relationship. A woman patient says to her male analyst while talking about "her husband with dismissive abandon: 'He's the same as all you men, of course, an exploiting capitalist'" (p. 34). In equating her husband and the analyst with all men and with capitalism and exploitation of the powerful by the weak, there is a lack of discrimination between people, a concretization of experience, and a projection of her own sense of greed and perhaps sadism on all men experienced as a singular concrete experience, a symbolic equation. In Matte Blanco's bi-logical terms, this reflects a symmetrization of the historical, current, and transference relationship, while also expressing an evacuation of these active paranoid qualities of greed and aggression. It would not be surprising for many contemporary analysts to inquire about, comment on, or interpret this transference with the expectation that the patient become able to differentiate, to make conscious the implicit distortion, or to bring asymmetrical logic to her historical and current relationships. Such an interpretive approach, "making the unconscious conscious," is characteristic of many contemporary theories and suggests a view of the unconscious as symmetrical distortions, with the analyst's function that of differentiating the historical objects from the current analytic experiences. From that perspective, the goal of analysis would be to have the patient use an asymmetrical framework to organize her experience; in classical language, the goal is to make the unconscious conscious.

An alternative neo-Kleinian approach that integrates the work of Klein, Winnicott, Bion, and Matte Blanco would understand this patient's transference as generated from the paranoid-schizoid position in which the experience is both concrete and evacuated into the external world, where it is experienced and organized using asymmetrical logic. The neo-Kleinian analyst would focus both on the dimension of concrete and symbolic thought and on that of asymmetrical and symmetrical thought, attempting to increase the degree of symmetry as a way to address the patient's evacuation (projective identification) of the dissociated, concrete unconscious experience, and through a playful transitional focus attempt to symbolize this transference experience. In the neo-Kleinian interpretive strategy, the focus is not on facilitating the patient's ability to differentiate past and present, becoming conscious of the differences between the various men in her world, but on dedifferentiating (Newirth 1989) her experience as an exploited person and the exploiting other. The analyst would attempt to introduce or switch to a symmetrical organization of experience in order to facilitate the integration of the patient's disowned aggression, greed, and power, which she has projected into her husband, the analyst, and all men. To facilitate a beginning enactment of a symmetrical experience of the transference, the analyst might have said, "Yes, we men are a greedy and exploitive lot," not denying the patient's projection but beginning to symbolize it through a symmetrical enactment of the patient's fantasy. Instead of attempting to differentiate the past and present, or the analyst, husband, and the historical objects, the continued development of symmetrical enactment or interpretations would come to include the patient in this infinite set of greedy and exploitive humans. Through a symmetrical strategy of interpretation, the analyst would explicitly identify himself with the patient's dissociated aggression as well as acknowledging her view that all men, and perhaps, in a wider symmetrization, all women, are greedy and exploitative. The goal is not the differentiation of past and present but the dedifferentiation of the transference and countertransference so that they are experienced as part of the same infinite set.

This example illustrates the complex interweaving of symmetrical and asymmetrical logic, as the unconscious and conscious organizations of experience interpenetrate and control each other in the same way that gravitational fields of adjacent planets control and influence each other's movements.

A NEO-KLEINIAN MODEL OF THINKING

The following model or schematic presents an integration of Matte Blanco's bi-logical theory of asymmetrical and symmetrical thought processes with the Kleinian dimensions of concrete and symbolic thought. This model assumes that these two dimensions of thought, consciousness and unconsciousness, and paranoid-schizoid and depressive organizations, are independent aspects of the process of thinking orthogonal dimensions, which describes thought as a two-dimensional process. The diagram in Table 8–1, a matrix of psychic experience, integrates these two dimensions: the Kleinian concepts of the paranoid-schizoid and the depressive positions, which focus on concrete and symbolic thought, and Matte Blanco's bi-logical concepts of symmetrical and asymmetrical logic, separating the internal world or functionally uncon-

Table 8–1. Matrix of psychic experience

	Symmetry	Asymmetry
The paranoid-schizoid position: concrete thought processes	1. Body symptoms 2. Nightmares 3. Persecutory anxiety 4. States of terror 5. Falling through space 6. Synchronic time	1. Obsessional states 2. Collection of details 3. Literal responses 4. Fragmentation anxiety 5. Splitting or slicing reality 6. Diachronic time
The depressive position: symbolic thought processes	1. Dreams and creative fantasies 2. Empathy 3. Poetry 4. Dedifferentiation of self and other 5. Transcendence and ecstatic experience 6. Synchronic time	1. Abstract thought 2. Inferential process 3. Discursive writing 4. Genetic, transference interpretations 5. Differentiation of time, place, and person 6. Diachronic time

scious experience from the external world of functionally conscious experience. This diagram describes, in schematic form, four possible ways of apprehending, organizing, and generating experience: paranoid or concrete symmetrical experience, paranoid or concrete asymmetrical experience, depressive or symbolic symmetrical experience, and depressive or symbolic asymmetrical experience. The four categories of experience are illustrated through examples of the different experiences that are apprehended or generated in each category.

Time is a central element in the dimensions of asymmetrical and symmetrical logic. In both quadrants of symmetrical organizations of experience, time is defined as synchronic, that is, either as all time existing at this moment or as time functioning in a cyclic form, a repeating cycle, such as the four seasons, or the daily cycle. In both quadrants of asymmetrical organization of experience, time is defined as diachronic, that is, as historical or linear time made up of discrete, equal units that function in an additive model. These two forms of time are critical both in experience and in how we organize and understand the psychoanalytic process. For example, Lewin (2001), in studying how time is used in the interpretive strategies of different analytic schools, found that each school conceived of the relationship between time and the analytic process differently and used time differently in its interpretive strategies. Contemporary Freudian analysts interpret time as going from the synchronic time of unconscious and immature experience to the diachronic time of mature, objective experience. American relational analysts often interpret time as going from diachronic to synchronic and then back to diachronic time as they move between external events to the transference–countertransference experience and back to external experience. Kleinian analysts almost always organized time as going from diachronic experiences of history to synchronic experiences of the enactment or interpretation of unconscious fantasies.

In the paranoid-schizoid position, symmetrical quadrant experiences are concrete, persecutory, and undifferentiated or symmetrized. Experience is located in the internal world and affects tend to be experienced as overwhelming, infinite, and absolute. For example, body symptoms might include psychic pain experienced as intense physical pain and compulsions to cut or mutilate parts of the body. Persecutory states of being trapped, as in nightmares, falling through space, or the experience of being isolated, alone in a black hole, persecutory fantasies, and literal experiences of terror seem to go on forever, linger, and are hard to dispel.

These experiences contrast with the paranoid-schizoid asymmetrical organization of experience, which is also concrete, located in the external world as both a function of projection and the evacuation of the contents of mind, and also represents ways to apprehend experience in the material world. In this quadrant are obsessional processes, which include the splitting or slicing of reality into smaller and smaller units. Often patients functioning in this mode need to present every detail of the week without noticing links between reported experiences or between the past and the present, and experience language in the most literal forms.

In the asymmetrical depressive quadrant, the person locates experience in the external world, is able to differentiate experience in terms of time, place, person, and causality, and is able to use symbolic processes. (It may be more useful to think of the symbolic processes in the depressive asymmetrical quadrant as abstract thinking to differentiate it from the symbolic thought process in the depressive symmetrical quadrant.) In this quadrant we find all kinds of abstract thought, inferential processes, and the usual form of genetic, transference interpretations. In this quadrant experience has specific denotations.

In the depressive symmetrical quadrant we find dreams, creative fantasies, metaphors, and poetry all of which present symbolic experience as located within an individual, which contain meanings that are fluid, expanding, and multileveled. Here we find a dedifferentiation of self and other as in empathic experiences, moments of identification, and the transcendent and ecstatic experience associated with some religions that describes both the loss of self and merger with God or the universe. It is interesting to contrast the experience of transcendence and ecstasy found in the depressive symmetrical quadrant with the states of terror and falling through space of the paranoid-schizoid symmetrical quadrant as an illustration of the difference between concrete and symbolic experience.

The matrix of psychic experience (Table 8–1) provides a schematic for a neo-Kleinian understanding of how experience is organized, apprehended, and generated; it is useful in locating individual experience and in understanding aspects of psychopathology and of treatment.

Matte Blanco (1988) explains how bi-logical structures, which are the result of processes of projective identification, become largely asymmetrical; that is, when experience is evacuated from the internal world to the external world, it moves from an organization of symmetrical logic to an organization of asymmetrical logic. He writes describing Melanie Klein's view of projective identification:

> "Much of the hatred against parts of the self is now directed towards the mother" (Klein 1946a, p. 300). . . . In this case one gets rid of the hatred towards the self by displacing it on to the mother. Note therefore that at this point Klein is referring to a thoroughly *asymmetrical process*. When impulses remain projected into objects in the environment they become organized with asymmetrical logic and treated as if they are part of the external world. However, the process of projective identification also leads to the disappearance of the limits between self and (m)other, i.e. to a *symmetrization*. [p. 145]

Matte Blanco describes the process of projective identification as one that entails both asymmetry and symmetry, which suggests why processes of projective identification are ineffective, maintaining forms of pathological relatedness because of the inability to escape from the evacuated parts of the self that can only be treated as if they are not me. Matte Blanco's description of projective identification can be thought of in terms of the matrix of psychic experience as the individual externalizing a symmetrical experience of hatred to an asymmetrical experience of being hated, although each is experienced in a concrete mode. The evacuation of inner, symmetrical experience through projective identification creates an unstable bi-logical structure in which the individual becomes attached to, becomes one with, the unwanted hated object, which becomes asymmetrically experienced as a part of the external world, forming a persecutory relationship to the object from whom the individual is unable to escape.

PSYCHIC TRANSFORMATION: WORDS, REVERIE, AND SYMBOL FORMATION

Bion's (1962) concept of the mother or analyst's use of reverie and Winnicott's (1971) concept of transitional experience (Newirth 1996) describe a process through which evacuated unconscious contents and projective identifications, which are experienced as asymmetrical, external, concrete events (beta elements), are transformed into new internal symbolic experiences (alpha elements) through the use of both symmetrical logic and the movement from the paranoid-schizoid position to the depressive position. This dual movement in the analyst's internal experience and words represents a critical aspect of the neo-Kleinian interpretive strategy, which allows the patient to internalize the evacuated experiences as symmetrical and symbolic fantasies. Table 8–2 integrates the analyst's interventions as a third dimension in the matrix of psychic experience. In this context the analyst's interventions can be organized within either symmetrical or asymmetrical logic and within either the paranoid-schizoid or the depressive organization of experience. The function of the analyst's speech is to initiate the development of transformational processes that facilitate the patient's ability to move between the different quadrants of the matrix. Each quadrant has positive and negative aspects, and psychopathology can be understood as the patient's inability to move between the different quadrants, being stuck or fixated in one quadrant; being stuck in the paranoid-schizoid symmetrical

Table 8–2. Matrix of psychic transformation

	Symmetry	Asymmetry
The paranoid position: concrete thought processes	1. Body symptoms 2. Nightmares 3. Persecutory anxiety 4. States of terror 5. Falling through space	1. Obsessional states 2. Collection of details 3. Literal responses 4. Fragmentation anxiety 5. Splitting or slicing reality
Analyst's speech	*Reverie and transitional experience*	*Interpretations and secondary process explanation*
The depressive position: symbolic thought processes	1. Dreams and creative fantasies 2. Empathy 3. Poetry 4. Dedifferentiation of self and other 5. Transcendence and ecstatic experience 6. Synchronic time	1. Abstract thought 2. Inferential process 3. Discursive writing 4. Genetic, interpretations 5. Differentiation of time, place, and person 6. Diachronic time

quadrant would result in a psychotic-like experience, while being stuck in the depressive asymmetrical quadrant would result in an affectively deadened, obsessive disorder.

In Table 8–2, the dimension of the analyst's speech represents strategies of psychic transformation or interpretation. (I use the concept of strategy to define the broad intent of the analyst's interpretive efforts.) There are two broad strategies represented in the matrix: a neo-Kleinian approach that focuses on the analyst's use of symmetrical thought and speech in processes of reverie, and the development of transitional experiences, which dedifferentiate the distinctions among person, place, time, and causality; and a traditional approach that focuses on the analyst's use of asymmetrical thought and speech in the development of interpretations and explanations, which differentiate the experience of person, place, time, and causality.

We may think of reverie as the analyst's internal process through which the patient's projective identifications are transformed from concrete, asymmetrical paranoid experiences of external reality to symbolic, symmetrical depressive experiences. Ogden's (1995) paper, "Analyzing Forms of Aliveness and Deadness of the Transference-Countertransference," is an excellent example of a neo-Kleinian approach to the transformation of concrete, asymmetrical experiences that are experienced through processes of projective identification and transformed into symbolic symmetrical experiences through the analyst's processes of reverie. Transitional experiences are enactments in which both analyst and patient participate in the mutual development of transference–countertransference fantasies in the process of transformation of the concrete, asymmetrical paranoid experiences to symbolic, symmetrical, playful experiences within an intersubjective or intermediate field.

The neo-Kleinian concept of the unconscious, which can be located in the symmetrical quadrants of the matrix and represent sources of energy, creativity, passion, and joy are particularly important in our contemporary age when many patients seem to be imprisoned in the asymmetrical world of external reality and have not developed the capacity for make believe, for play, for joy, for creativity, and for a passionate commitment to life. Psychoanalytic technique that focuses on discriminating the historical distortions in the current transference–countertransference relationship ignores the positive and powerful importance of the unconscious as a capacity for symbolic and symmetrical experience. Focusing on the development of the symmetrical and symbolic aspects of the unconscious takes the opposite therapeutic tack from those contemporary approaches that encourage a differentiation of the historical from the current analytic objects. This approach involves a volitional shift in the therapist's interpretive strategy from asymmetrical interventions, which, through objective or rational discourse, attempt to make the unconscious conscious, to interventions that are directed at the development, elaboration, and internalization of unconscious experience, which we might think of as making the conscious unconscious.

9

The Pathology of Consciousness: Asymmetry and Failure in the Development of Subjectivity

Grotstein (1995) describes a paradigm for the development of the pathology of consciousness, which is the result of a gross failure in the parents' ability or willingness to accept the child's projective identifications and use reverie to transform the child's externalized asymmetrical experiences into symmetrical, symbolic experiences that can be reinternalized by the child. Grotstein thinks of these children as "orphans of the real" because they are doomed to live only in the external world of asymmetrical experience. As a result of the failure in the transformation of their projective identifications, these "orphans of the real" live in a world filled with externalized, persecutory objects over which they have no control, or in a world of deadened, meaningless facts and impersonal abstract rules. Winnicott's (1969, 1971) development of the concept of self as an *object*, in contrast to the self as a *subject*, is an attempt to describe the experience of the individual who feels trapped in the external world of asymmetrical experience, a thing in the world, only able to react to the pushes, pulls, and impingements of others, having no capacity to express will, intention, joy, or connectedness to others. The experience of being trapped in a world of asymmetrical experience and of having little ability to utilize symmetrical processes in the organization of experience is a way to understand failure in the development of subjectivity. This failure in the development of subjectivity is a critical problem in analytic theory and technique that is best described in contemporary poetry, theater, and art, as well as in sociopsychological works such as *The Culture of Narcissism* (Lasch 1978).

PSYCHIC TRANSFORMATION

The matrix of psychic transformation (see Chapter 8) presents a structure with which to conceptualize different forms of psychopathology, different analytic strategies, and a method to track different modes of organizing, apprehending, and generating experience. This matrix integrates the Kleinian theory of thinking and the development of symbolic thought, Bion's development of the concepts of projective and introjective identification and reverie, Winnicott's theory of transitional experience and enactment of transference–countertransference fantasies, and Matte Blanco's (1975, 1988) model of conscious and unconscious thought. A key element in this model that is derived from Matte Blanco is separating the phenomenological quality of awareness from the function of conscious and unconscious thought. In this model, the unconscious is not equated with infantile drives and attachments to pathological childhood relational schemata, and the conscious mind is not equated with mature objective thought or the ability to make informed choices and to develop healthy relationships. Conscious thought has the function of differentiating experiences of time, person, place, causality, and sequence, and may be thought of as providing the tools for adapting to external or material reality. Unconscious thought has the function of creating similarities, identifications, intense emotional relationships, and a sense of individuality, subjectivity, purpose, and connection.

The matrix of psychic transformation presents a model for apprehending, organizing, and generating experience, schematically divided into four functional organizations of experience and two strategies of psychoanalytic intervention. The four modes of experience are the concrete symmetrical mode, the concrete asymmetrical mode, the symbolic symmetrical mode, and the symbolic asymmetrical mode. Each mode of experience is involved in healthy and pathological organizations of experience. Psychopathology can be understood as a function of being stuck in one of the four modes of organizing experience and the inability to access the other modes of experience. In health, the four modes of experience function dialectically, defining, limiting, and organizing each other, while in pathology there is a fixation in single mode of experience.

This model allows us to understand psychopathology as existing in each mode of experience and not simply as an intrusion of unconscious derivatives, such as childhood relational patterns or infantile drives on adaptation to external reality. Thus we may conceive of a psychopathology of consciousness as well as a psychopathology of the unconscious. In the psychopathology of consciousness the individual may be stuck in either the concrete or symbolic asymmetrical modes of experience. When a patient is in the concrete asymmetrical mode, the analyst's experience is of being flooded with smaller and smaller details of the patient's life, and the patient is unable to utilize the linking processes inherent in the analyst's empathy and interpretations. In contrast, if the patient is stuck in the symbolic asymmetrical experience, the analyst feels filled with the empty words of an abstract world in which individuality and subjectivity are sacrificed for an objective understanding regulated by sets of impersonal rules of conduct; interpretations become echoed and used to establish new generalized principles that lack affective reality. The psychopathology of consciousness is particularly relevant in addressing the clinical issues in working with narcissistic, schizoid, and borderline patients who live as objects in the external world, feeling an inner sense of emptiness, focusing on external events, being overly literal or abstract and highly resistant to change.

The matrix of psychic transformation also describes a symmetrical and an asymmetrical strategy for psychoanalytic interpretation and intervention. The concept of therapeutic strategy is similar to Schafer's (1983) concept of the analytic attitude: it reflects the epistemological structure of an analyst's theory, in that it describes a general set of intentions that structure the analyst's interventions. The symmetrical interpretive strategy involves the dedifferentiation of the dimensions of time, place, person, and causality, while the asymmetrical interpretive strategy involves the differentiation of the dimensions of person, place, time, and causality. These analytic strategies are associated with different analytic schools and different psychopathological organizations and processes. The matrix suggests that projective identification can be

understood as an externalization or displacement of symmetrical, unconscious concrete experience into the asymmetrical, conscious concrete
mode, where it is experienced as an aspect of external reality. Using an
asymmetrical interpretive strategy, the analyst may attempt to address
externalized or projected experience through asymmetrical interventions,
which focus on distinctions between the patient's experience and the
analyst's experience, or through developing a consensual view of external reality, differentiating the dimensions of person, place, time, and
sequence. Using a symmetrical interpretive strategy, the analyst may
attempt to address externalized or projected experience through symmetrical interventions that dedifferentiate aspects of the projected external experience, collapsing the distinctions of inner and outer, self and
other, here and there, and now and then. The symmetrical interpretive
strategy reflects an evolving neo-Kleinian approach that focuses on increasing the degree of symmetry and the movement from the concrete
symmetrical and asymmetrical organizations of experience to the symbolic symmetrical organization of experience. This neo-Kleinian strategy uses reverie, the enactment of transference–countertransference fantasies, and the development of transitional experiences to focus on the
symmetrical dimension of subjective experience. The analyst, through
the use of symmetrical logic, effacing the differences between himself
and the historical objects, directs his interpretation toward the integration (Steiner 1997) of the aggression, greed, and power that had been
projected into the environment. In describing the symmetrical analytic
strategy, it is important to note that these are not simple behavioral
approaches, or a new version of the corrective emotional experience, but
rather an alternative to analytic strategies that emphasizes the importance of consciousness, both in terms of awareness and the functional
process of differentiating the dimensions of time, person, place, and
causality as the locus of psychoanalytic treatment. The focus of the neo-
Kleinian approach is on understanding how experience is organized,
apprehended, and generated in functional conscious and unconscious
realms, with the unconscious conceived of as a source of energy, passion, commitment, and subjectivity. The neo-Kleinian strategy, like the
work of Klein and Lacan, best fits within a postmodern epistemological
structure in which the goal is the elaboration, development, and generation of meaning rather than clarification and understanding of the
relationships between a past and a current event.

CLINICAL ILLUSTRATION OF ASYMMETRICAL AND SYMMETRICAL PSYCHOANALYTIC STRATEGIES

This case illustrates the relationship between the analyst's strategy of interpretation and experiences of frustration in the treatment of a narcissistic patient who can be thought of as stuck in the concrete asymmetrical world of thought and action. I will focus on the concepts of symmetry and asymmetry as a conceptual framework for understanding the patient's way of organizing, apprehending, and generating experience and how her concreteness is a central dimension of her pathology. The presenting problem in a supervisory consultation was that this patient had frequently and precipitously quit therapy, always returning in four to six weeks. The problem was described by the therapist as the patient's acting out of unconscious relational patterns and the therapist's attempts to make these patterns conscious. The therapist's questions and interpretations reflected her attempts to develop asymmetrical understanding and discriminations in what appeared to be an increasingly frustrating attempt to gain control over a relationship that was experienced as both persecutory and out of control.

The patient lives as a false self, as an object driven to respond in action and concrete thought to her experiences of impingements from a world that she finds to be a dangerous and threatening place. The patient is a successful, middle-management executive in her early 30s who is quite energetic and has a somewhat manic personal style. The patient came to therapy because of generalized unhappiness in her life and an inability to establish a long-term relationship with a man. The supervisory session focused on the patient's flight from therapy, and the therapist's attempt to differentiate her childhood experience from her current experience, and to understand the patient's anger as a reflection of unconscious feelings, displacements of earlier feelings, and a distortion of the current therapeutic relationship. The therapist's interventions suggested the theory that as the patient's anger becomes conscious and differentiated, it will disappear as an inappropriate affect directed at the therapist and a cause of acting out. The therapist's strategy reflects a contemporary view of the unconscious as a container of unarticulated, temporally displaced affects and relational schemas. In describing her concerns, the therapist, who is also a woman, emphasized her own anxiety that after a successful session the patient would not come to the next appointment or might even quit therapy. I thought that the therapist's countertransference anxiety reflected an unconscious, unarticulated transference–countertransference experience of competition, which I thought of as an unconscious, paranoid, envious fantasy that one would destroy the other. Here is a brief segment of the therapy dialogue as the patient discusses her experience of humiliation at the beginning of treatment:

> *Patient:* I feel like I wasted time. I was feeling so, so bad about things that weren't worth it. It was just, um, all through my life, it was just, you know sometimes marching off in my own direction would often profit me in the end, but sometimes it would just, it would have been better to cooperate more, rather than go off on my own. But I know I can do things.
> *Therapist:* Do you think that you do that in here? Like when you leave therapy?
> *Patient:* I like to know that there is an open door. And I think that sometimes I get mad at therapy and I need a break from it.
> *Therapist:* Uh-huh, tell me more about that because you got mad at it last week.

The therapist reiterates the patient's use of asymmetrical logic, differentiating herself as a person from the therapy seen as a separate entity, when she states, "You got mad at it last week." There are many historical precedents for this asymmetrical strategy of splitting the therapist's self from the analytic situation, including Freud's (1909) separation of himself and the rules of therapy in the Rat Man case. However, this split presents an asymmetrical strategy in which to structure the goals of treatment as a process of differentiating the historical objects from current objects, disowning and displacing aggressive affect, and imposing the reality principle. It is particularly important to pay attention to the ways in which we introduce concepts of space, time, and causality in the therapeutic dialogue.

> *Patient:* Yeah (laughs), yeah, um I just feel like it just makes trouble sometimes. It hurts to bring things out. And when you're not feeling 100 percent. . . . After that talk with X [a friend] that bothered me, it just felt that everything came out all wrong. It haunted me a little this week. I felt . . . I felt like I wanted to

just . . . to just tell you. I didn't like it, like, I wanted to just . . . to just tell you. I didn't like it, right away I was going to call you and say I didn't like last week. But then I thought, well, what's she going to do about it. (Laughs) "So you didn't like last week, it's not always easy." It's just it hurts sometimes. It's more hurt.
Therapist: So there's a conflict there.
Patient: Yeah!
Therapist: It seems on the one side you logically see that it's not always going to be easy,
Patient: Yeah, but I show up.
Therapist: But then you feel really hurt at the same time.
Patient: I show up whenever I say I will. I've never stood up an appointment. I show up usually early (laughs).

There follows a brief interchange about the meaning of being early and how therapy is important to the patient, and then the therapist, continuing with her asymmetrical strategy, inquires as to the times the patient doesn't come to therapy.

Patient: Oh, I feel, at first I feel like I feel mad at you and I know it's not her, it's *this.*

It is interesting that at first the patient is able to say that she is angry with the therapist, but then quickly follows the therapist in reorganizing this experience into an asymmetrical form, separating the therapist from the process of therapy. This use of asymmetrical thinking can frequently lead to confusion and increased fragmentation because of the increased use of splitting and slicing external reality into smaller and smaller pieces.

In her next comment the therapist shifts from an asymmetrical to a symmetrical perspective as a way to contain the patient's increased anxiety and fragmentation.

Therapist: Tell me about feeling mad at me.
Patient: Because, well I mean no offense, but like, what does *she* know (laughs). You know, I just have an attitude about you, sometimes, but only sometimes.
Therapist: Tell me more about those times.

The therapist returns to asymmetrical logic in this inquiry, attempting to differentiate the patient's experience of anger in terms of both time and space.

> *Patient:* Like last week (laughs), like what good does that do, like when I left here I was like ooh.
> *Therapist:* But what about it.
> *Patient:* Then I'm like, "P, she's helped you so much so don't think that."

In this last comment, the patient used her own name as she verbalized a conversation that she had with herself, which can be thought of as an example of her need to externalize the dangerous inner experiences of aggression. The patient's conversation with herself is a concrete attempt to maintain the asymmetrical structure of her experience, disowning her aggression in order to define both herself and the therapist as good.

As this session progresses, the patient seems to be experiencing an increased amount of discomfort around her anger, and a greater need to externalize and split her experience of good and bad. The patient then assumes the responsibility for the difficulty in therapy, making herself the bad one, which she attributes to her tendency to "head off on my own, not always to my benefit." This is an important relational schema, which is understood by the therapist and patient as the patient's characteristic way to "ignore everything that is horrible."

The patient's next set of associations was to her aunt, who is very rich and who occasionally and arbitrarily gives her money, but who always indulges herself. The patient explains that the aunt tends to minimize emotional pain and see everything in terms of anger. The patient then switches to how she sees the money she spends on the treatment as an investment, but wishes that the therapist would "dispense some wisdom so I could have some tools in order to have an easier time of it." This set of associations can be thought of as a concrete symmetrical process reflecting an unconscious fantasy of the greedy breast and the empty child; this fantasy is made up of one who has and withholds and one who is empty and helpless. However, because she has difficulty accepting this thought, she externalizes it, projecting it into the therapist. The patient is struggling with her experiences of the therapist as empty and unhelpful and also full and helpful; she is arguing with herself and trying to make sense out of this experience in a logical and rational or asymmetrical way, trying to understand which experience of her therapist is real. She is trapped in the asymmetrical world of objective reality where a person can only be one thing and not at the same time its opposite, a person cannot be both *A* and *non-A* at the same time. This pathology of consciousness, of asymmetrical logic, leads to the continuous fragmentation of the world and confusion about self and reality.

The patient's associations to her rich, arbitrary, and self-indulgent aunt are an obvious displacement from the therapist, which suggests that the patient as struggling with her envy of the therapist, her knowledge, and the supplies that she contains. This struggle is reflected both in her need to destroy the therapist by withdrawing from therapy and making her/it into nothing, and in her anxious statements that the therapist doesn't know anything. At the same time, she also expresses her anger more directly by accusing the rich therapist/aunt of withholding supplies and thoughts from her. It is important to point out that this becomes a bi-logical structure in which the symmetrical fantasy of aunt/ therapist is externalized creating a structure of symmetry wrapped in asymmetry. Because of projective identification the patient experiences her unconscious fantasies as a set of real events in the external world. However, these asymmetrical processes of projection, splitting, and fragmentation seem to increase as she struggles to be a good patient and to understand what is going on in her life. This difficulty is a result of both patient and analyst conceiving of the goal of treatment as a series of progressive moments of increased asymmetrical differentiations of experiences that need to be addressed symmetrically as unconscious experiences that can become symbolized.

If rather than approaching this treatment with an asymmetrical interpretive strategy, attempting to make the unconscious conscious, we might approach it with a symmetrical interpretive strategy, then it would be helpful for the therapist to communicate to the patient that she is two therapists, one good and full and one withholding and selfish. This would facilitate the patient's splitting the world into two symmetrical universes, one all good and one all bad. The therapist could focus her interventions on the patient's unconscious experience and through presenting her interpretations in the symmetrical language of the unconscious facilitate the patient's development of a more cohesive unconscious experience with an increased capacity to use symbols.

I want to present two hypothetical examples of symmetrical interventions. In the early part of the session there seem to be derivatives of a competitive fantasy about who is smarter and the potential negative consequences of being smart and successful. The therapist expresses this in her anxious countertransference statement that after a successful session the patient would leave treatment. The patient expresses this fantasy in her anxious and angry comments about the therapist's not knowing much and with her own persona of not knowing. A symmetrical intervention would involve the therapist's identifying with the projection of "being the dumb one," perhaps responding to the patient's comments about "what does she know" with a comment like "pretty dumb, huh." This would involve a symmetrical strategy of introjective identification, rather than an asymmetrical strategy of differentiating the current therapeutic object from the projection of the historical object. The therapist would efface or dedifferentiate these transference–countertransference experiences involving who is the one who knows and who is the dumb one.

A second possible symmetrical interpretation would involve the patient's association of the therapist with her rich and withholding aunt—a perfect Kleinian image of the greedy, selfish full breast. A symmetrical interpretation of this concrete asymmetrized association would be for the therapist to identify with this image and say that, like the patient's aunt, she keeps all of her riches for herself. Again, rather than differentiating herself from the historical object, the therapist would efface the differences between past and present, allowing her to identify with this unconscious object, and, through processes of reverie or symbolic elaboration, further symbolize this unconscious fantasy. This symmetrical strategy would initiate an enactment of the unconscious fantasy of the ungiving and envied mother, which could lead to a transitional experience that would allow for the symbolic expression and internalization of aggression, greed, and competence.

Introducing symmetrical logic and interpretations involves a volitional shift in the therapist's strategy from asymmetrical interventions that attempt to consciously differentiate objects, that is, make the unconscious conscious, to the use of symmetrical logic and interventions that are directed at the experiential and symbolic elaboration and development of unconscious experience. Perhaps in contrast to the traditional approach of making the unconscious conscious, we might think of this symmetrical therapeutic strategy as making the conscious unconscious (see Rucker and Lombardi 1998 for additional discussions of this concept). Like this patient, many patients are imprisoned in the asymmetrical world of external reality and have not developed the symmetrical symbolic capacities necessary for the integration of unconscious experience; they are unable to make believe, to play, to have pleasure and joy, and to have a creative and passionate commitment to life.

THE PATHOLOGY OF CONSCIOUSNESS: A STUDY OF MASOCHISM AND SUBJECTIVITY

Masochism is the most extreme form of the failure in the development of subjectivity. Masochistic individuals feel as if they have no will or personal power, victims of both other people and of a persecutory fate. They live as an object in an asymmetrical world. The following case of a masochistic man who had previously been in psychoanalytic psychotherapy for approximately twenty years with several different analysts illustrates both the failure in the development of subjectivity and the usefulness of a symmetrical analytic strategy. This patient's excessive use of projective identification and his problems in the development of the capacity for symbolic thought resulted in his experience of the world as a living nightmare where he is the target of imagined and real experiences of hatred and rejection. I will first describe the patient, then suggest an understanding of his masochism as pathology of consciousness, and finally illustrate the neo-Kleinian approach with examples of the clinical process.

The patient is a 50-year-old man who presents a masochistic orientation to life; he feels extremely unhappy, is constantly suffering, dreads each approaching moment, and desperately tries to organize his life in ways that will protect him from the certainties of persecution and impingements from the environment. He has created a world, or in his view he finds himself in a world, in which people, particularly women, treat him cruelly and critically, withholding warmth, affection, sexual contact, respect, and affirmation. Along with his wife and children, he lives in a small, uncomfortable, dirty apartment in a marginal part of the city. This living arrangement is a source of a great deal of conflict, anxiety, and humiliation, because he can readily afford to live in a considerably nicer home. Over time, each spouse has blocked the other's efforts to change their living arrangements. He and his wife are extremely hostile, frequently fighting, withholding positive experience and criticizing each other's actions. Meals are rarely eaten together; each member of the family either "throws something together" or brings in fast food with little thought for the others' meals. There is no routine or family structure; tasks such as shopping, home maintenance, and organizing free time are all done in a chaotic fashion. Most family events become catastrophes; for example, buying a replacement television took a year of procrastination, arguing, reviewing, and re-reviewing *Consumer Reports*, feeling anxious that they will be ripped off, expecting the other to take the responsibility for the purchase, and believing that they could find a better deal at another place or at another time.

The patient's narrative of his unhappy childhood, in a cold, withholding family, lacks affective spontaneity and often sounds like the recycled interpretations of previous analysts. Occasionally a particular memory will momentarily evoke deep sadness in him. He does not remember being held or kissed by his parents either as a child or as an adult. He remembers his father as a cynical man who was critical and doubtful about his capacity to function as an adult or in business. His father's criticism became a constant background noise after the patient joined the family business. He has many memories of being painfully rejected by his mother; perhaps the most profound is when he was about 6 years old and she was chasing him around the family apartment, attempting to hit him with a broom and saying, "I should have let it die." He understands this statement as reflecting both her resentment about being a mother and her wish to have had an abortion. He was toilet trained very early and was told that his mother could not stand the odor of his feces or of having to "touch it" while she changed his diapers.

He first went into therapy in his early 20s because of difficulties in dating and the anxiety that he experienced with women. As a young man he had been occasionally sexually impotent. He continues to be disgusted and frightened by the thought of touching a woman's genitals. The patient and his wife have not had sexual contact in many years and he often sleeps on the floor in a separate room. Over and over again, he describes how his wife treats him badly, haranguing him about how he has failed her and their children and never acknowledging his positive contribu-tions to the family, his relationship with his children, or his business success. Sessions usually begin with the literal question of whether he should divorce his wife or move to a new and more comfortable home. He presents these questions in a highly concrete, repetitive way that suggests he believes that I could, or should, simply tell him what to do and end his unhappiness. The concrete quality of the way he speaks about his life is interesting and one of the things that I focus on in conceptu-alizing our work. He regularly masturbates to sadistic fantasies in which a woman with large breasts is slapped and her breasts are pinched either by a tall black woman or by mechanical devices. The tall, thin black woman is a servant who turns the tables on a domineering, older, short Jewish woman (the patient is Jewish), who is sadistically assaulted and is forced to have sex with the now dominant but previously subservient person. At night, when he is alone or his wife is asleep, he will hug his pillow and talk to it as if it is his "good mommy." He caries on a conver-sation with his pillow/mommy, promising that he will be a good boy, believing that if he could be really good she will come and take care of him, hold him, and kiss him. As he talks about his relationship with his pillow, it sounds like a literal conversation, a child imploring a parent to comfort him or a ritual prayer to a withholding God rather than a per-son contemplating his inner thoughts or wishes.

In sessions, he normally speaks using concrete, asymmetrical, ex-ternalized organizations. There is a striking literalness to his speech, which is an important aspect of the patient's clinical presentation. He presents his concerns about his marriage and his living arrangements as literal, concrete questions that he expects me to answer. He writes down many of my comments and interpretations, which he carries around and re-reads as if these words have a magical or sacred meaning. Sessions are filled with concrete conversational fragments presented as a series of monologues spoken to no one in particular. He may begin a session by saying, "Well, my good man, you seem like a smart fellow. What do you think I should do about so and so. . . ." Or, at other times, he will come into a session filled with rage and in a concrete diatribe tell me about a recent experience with "the bitch."

It is the concrete way that he uses, or should I say organizes, lan-guage that was critical to my understanding his masochistic symptoms and character structure as a pathology of consciousness. I have come to understand this concrete, literal language as reflecting the evacuation of his inner life, an extensive use of projective identification and "symbolic equations." This patient's speech is filled with symbolic equations (Segal 1978), where the word and the act are experienced as identical and action substitutes for thought. The use of symbolic equations precedes the individual's development of the capacity to use symbolic thought in the depressive position. In integrating Matte Blanco's ideas with the Kleinian view of projective identification, I have come to think of patients' use of symbolic equations as asymmetrizations of externalized inner experience, which in a healthier situation would have been reinternalized and organized within the realm of symmetrical logic.

INTERPRETATIONS OF MASOCHISM

From both a traditional and an interpersonal/relational perspective, this patient's masochism would be thought of as an expression of unconscious wishes, fears, hatreds, and identifications or destructive childhood relational patterns. Both Freudian and interpersonal/relational theory conceptualize masochistic pathology as a function of unconscious process, and as a result treatment focuses on making conscious the unconscious. In either orientation, the analyst would organize the treatment around an asymmetrical analytic strategy and attempt to make the unconscious conscious, so that the patient would be able to choose a less self-destructive path. From a classical perspective, the patient's fears of female genitals and his sadistic masturbatory fantasies of a woman torturing another woman would be seen as the expression of unconscious fantasies of the phallic woman, and the underlying wish for and terror of castration, as well as an expression of his own hostility and sadism in a disguised form. From a contemporary interpersonal/relational perspective, the patient's behavior and character structure can be thought of as an expression of his unconscious relational schemas of attachment to a hostile, critical parent and his repetitive choice of the safety and comfort of the known and expected, rather than the anxiety and terror of separation, leaving home both literally and symbolically. Prior therapists have taken both approaches, interpreting his castration anxieties, sadism, and infantile demanding attitudes toward women, his needs for deprivation and to be depriving, and his attachment to bad infantile objects and his fear of separation. Some therapists have been stern and withholding, apparently believing that he needed to "accept reality" and recognize the expression of his unconscious sadistic wishes, while others have been more sympathetic, attempting to provide an experience of a new object, disconfirming his expectations of the rejecting, critical, and withholding parent. This patient's pathology has proved resistant to change, not because of the prior analysts' lack of skill, intention, or commitment, but because of their conception that masochism reflected the expression of unconscious wishes, fears, and relational patterns, which when made conscious would lead to changes in both inner experience and external behavior.

Matte Blanco's theory focuses on the different organizations of thought and experience rather than on the content of repressed mental structures. His idea of bi-logical structures, internal organizations of representations or fantasies, which are made up of variable combinations of symmetrical and asymmetrical thought processes, suggests that both conscious and unconscious processes contribute to psychological organization and that psychopathology reflects an imbalance in either symmetrical, unconscious processes, or asymmetrical, conscious processes. Unconscious thought processes utilize symmetrical logic in which differences between person, place, and time are effaced, similarities emphasized, connections made, and affective experience intensified. Conscious thought processes utilize asymmetrical logic in which differences between past and present, parent and new object, and here and there are developed along with a view of mature thought as independent of affective reactivity. Symmetrical logic, the logic of unconscious processes, seems to be adapted to processing inner experiences, and was first understood as the logic of dreams, but also can be seen as the logic of poetry, art, religious ritual, and intense personal or intimate relationships. Asymmetrical logic, the logic of conscious thought processes, seems adapted to understanding and operating in the external world of rational choice and action. Both forms of logic are necessary; however, the overemphasis of symmetry or asymmetry is related to different forms of psychopathology. I believe that my patient's concrete speech, his focus on external events, his tendency toward lengthy monologues that fragment his relationships with others, and his concrete experience of his pillow as his "good mommy" all reflect an extreme imbalance of asymmetrical logic and define a pathological organization of conscious thought and a failure in the development of subjectivity.

Matte Blanco's (1988) theory operates within the broader context of the Kleinian view of the mind with its emphasis on projective identification, internalization, and the dialectic between the paranoid-schizoid position and the depressive position. From Matte Blanco's perspective, the evacuation of inner, symmetrical experience through projective identification creates an unstable bi-logical structure in which the individual becomes attached to, becomes one with, the unwanted hated object, which is asymmetrically experienced as a persecutory object in the external world that the individual is now unable to flee from.

As a child, the patient's projected hatred, aggression, and sadism had not been contained and transformed through processes of reverie into symmetrical thought, which could have been internalized as vital bi-logical structures. He not only has become an "orphan of the real," but also experiences himself as a prisoner of the real, a victim in a nightmare world of sadists and persecutors, with only his pillow, an external, iconic "good mommy," to free and soothe him if he can only be good enough. I believe that the critical treatment issue with this patient is not understanding the historical roots of his sadomasochistic experience, but rather the transformation of his masochistic asymmetrical organizations of the world (the persecuting beta elements) through the analyst's reverie into symmetrical fantasies (alpha elements) that the patient can internalize as vital, balanced bi-logical structures. The transformation of asymmetrical processes into symmetrical processes is the opposite of making the unconscious conscious, of differentiating the past from the present. I think of this process, making the conscious unconscious, as involving multiple symmetrizations in which the analyst utilizes introjective identification, reverie, enactment, and the development of transitional experiences to facilitate the development of the patient's experience of connectedness rather than alienation, pleasure rather than pain, and the capacity to experience one's inner life in a symbolic and positive way.

A NEO-KLEINIAN INTERPRETIVE APPROACH TO MASOCHISM

Like other patients who present profound masochistic patterns, the work with this patient was quite difficult and involved complex countertransference experiences, including anxiety, boredom, the inability to think, doubts about my value and the value of psychoanalysis and psychotherapy, and devaluing, sadistic, and punitive fantasies about the patient, which occasionally broke through into my behavior. I want to focus on a specific set of interventions, derived from a neo-Kleinian psychoanalytic strategy, and directed at transforming the patient's asymmetrical concrete organization of the world into symmetrical symbolic organization. These interventions represent symbolic enactments of the evolving transference–countertransference situation and were preceded by intense, lengthy periods of reverie, transforming asymmetrical projective identifications into symmetrical experiences that could become the roots of transitional experiences. These interventions may be thought of as a strategy of symmetrizations of the patient's asymmetrical, concrete projective identifications (beta elements), which are elaborated as the analyst's countertransference experience, as contrasted to an asymmetrical strategy, which attempts to differentiate the historical or current events. The interventions that I will describe are directed toward three aspects of the patient's masochism. The first involves his extensive use of projective identification through which he attempts to evacuate all badness that he subsequently experiences asymmetrically as aspects of the external world of conscious experience. This use of projective identification results in a constant focus on the external world as a collection of impinging concrete events and persecutory anxieties, resulting in progressive cycles of asymmetrizations and fragmentations. The second is a pervasive transference paradigm in which the patient is small, weak, and bad and the other is powerful and good. The third is his fixation on the passive paranoid position, which results in his experience of being the passive recipient of the other's actions, unable to act, affect, or make any demands on the other. Each intervention grew out of experiences of frustration and was accompanied by countertransference anxiety as I moved into a more purely symmetrical realm, exposed my own primitive unconscious fantasies, and lost a sense of self–other boundaries, time, and place.

The patient compulsively described each masochistic experience as if it were a new, emotionally devastating event. This lack of connection between his experiences reflects his use of concrete, asymmetrical logic, which fragments and slices reality into smaller segments that he believes should yield an explanation. We can think of this process of segmenting reality as representing a limit of Aristotelian logic, affirming the Gestalt principle that the whole is greater than the sum of the parts. In the clinical situation, the analyst's reverie and symmetrical fantasies consolidate these fragmented experiences into more balanced bi-logical structures in which distinctions between person, place, and time are collapsed, simultaneously introducing the idea of pleasure associated with transitional experience, identification, and merger between self and other.

The first intervention was an attempt to transform his asymmetrical, concrete, and masochistic experience of the world into a symmetrical, sadistic fantasy. This occurred after a long period during which I slowly became aware of a growing sense of annoyance with his alternating monologues about his masochistic relationship with his wife and his sadistic plans for women he barely knew. In the authoritative voice of a knowing therapist, I suggested that I knew a solution to his problem. What he needed to do was to buy a slave who would do everything that he wanted and whom he could freely abuse. I think that my suggestion made him anxious, and he questioned whether I was being serious, asserting the legal and moral prohibitions against slavery. This response reflected his attempt to maintain the asymmetrical conscious logic that defined his life. I acted certain and indifferent to those moral and legal aspects of external reality, continuing to insist that this is what he should do and pointing to recent articles in the newspaper that supported the possibility of purchasing a slave. My fantasy reflected a symmetrization of his sadomasochistic preoccupations with women and simultaneously addressed a central dimension in the transference–countertransference relationship through effacing the difference between the *good object/ analyst* and the *bad object/patient*, which is the subtext in his fantasy of being rescued by his "good mother." Although not operating as a traditional asymmetrical interpretation, in which patient and therapist have a consensual understanding of the patient's dynamics, this series of symmetrical, protosymbolic enactments had several effects on the patient. There are several ways to understand the impact of my fantasy about buying a slave, which I usually repeated in response to his pleas that I tell him what to do about his unhappiness. Over time, this sadistic fantasy seemed to have the effect of shifting the focus of treatment; his extreme asymmetrical monologues became less frequent, and he seemed to develop a somewhat more consolidated sense of self and attempted to initiate some pleasurable activities with his wife. He became more of an agent rather than experiencing himself as primarily acted upon.

A second illustration of the transformation of asymmetrical evacuated experience into a symmetrical fantasy occurred in response to his painful descriptions of his masochistic suffering. After a long period of frustration and difficulty, I began to develop a fantasy that his suffering was part of a religious ritual; it was both prayer and penance for his badness offered to the icon of his good mother/pillow and that when he suffered enough he would be saved. I understood my fantasy of his masochistic suffering as a religious ritual, a symmetrical organization that dedifferentiates historical dimensions of his experience, effacing differences between good and bad, passive and active, object and subject. Again, his initial response was to dismiss my comment as silly. I maintained my viewpoint, staying within my symmetrical enactment, frequently noting how well he practiced his religion, his orthodoxy, and even the possibility that his wife was equally religious in her pursuit of suffering. My religious fantasy became a transitional experience that the patient actively joined in with, a shared symmetrical fantasy that slowly began to reflect a more balanced bi-logical structure joining together the issues of suffering and salvation. As his suffering became experienced symmetrically and symbolically as his active pursuit, he began to raise the question of whether it was worthwhile or whether he should abandon his religion and become a hedonist like me. At this point he became more able to use symbolic processes in elaborating the transitional experience, integrating suffering and salvation within the context of a religious experience. The iconic pillow, which began as a concrete, asymmetrical expression of his longing for salvation, for a good mother, became transformed into his developing capacity to articulate his inner experience, including a sense of being liked, being competent, and being entitled to pleasure. The treatment often focused on a symmetrical transitional experience in which we each articulated the various possibilities involved in staying with or abandoning his religion.

A third illustration focused on his idealization of his current and previous therapists as the source of all knowledge and value, in contrast with his view of himself as the lowly, bad child. This idealization reflected his concrete asymmetrical approach to the world, where all knowledge is outside and in the (m)other as well as viewing his current and past analysts as iconic representations of the "good mommy." One day, in response to a question, I said to him that he had to understand that there were two types of therapists in the world: one type worked for God and tried to get him to be good, and one type worked for the devil and tried to get him to be bad. I then sardonically asked him who he thought I worked for and of course he somewhat jokingly said that it was for the devil. I then said that it was particularly difficult to really know who a therapist worked for because those who worked for God often acted stern and mean in their attempts to get patients to be good, while those who worked for the devil often acted nice and were nurturing so as to fool patients. This countertransference enactment quickly became a shared part of the analytic relationship in which he could think of his previous analysts as having worked for God and me as working for the devil. This transitional experience allowed us to symmetrize the concept of good and bad, so that he could recognize the complexities in human relationships and his own authority and desires. Perhaps because this was the third symmetrical countertransference enactment that I introduced, and in retrospect seemed to consolidate the previous two countertransference fantasies, it facilitated the patient's ability to address our relationship in new ways. He was able to be somewhat aggressive and playful in challenging me, somewhat more thoughtful about his marital and life problems, and somewhat freer in feeling entitled to search for pleasure in the world.

The patient still has a way to go in deciding whether he will continue to live in a fundamentally masochistic lifestyle, but he seems more able to address the issues involved in his masochism as his internal experience rather than as a collection of external events that impinge on his existence. For example, his wife recently asked him whether he was thinking about divorcing her, and he responded that he was not, but that he would just continue to torture her. This comment reflected both his ability to recognize and acknowledge his own aggression and to express it in a more ironic and symbolic form, which represents a new ability to have a symbolic perspective on himself and his life.

In summary, this patient's masochistic pathology is a function of an asymmetrical thought disorder, an overdependence on asymmetrical logic and the evacuation of the contents of his mind. This pathology is a function of the failures in the process in which parents, through reverie, transform the baby's projective identifications, which are experienced as asymmetrical aspects of reality, into symmetrical fantasies that the baby can reinternalize as more balanced bi-logical structures. In my view it is the analyst's capacity to use reverie and to transform the patient's asymmetrical projections into symmetrical fantasies that facilitates the patient's growth and his capacity to be centered in a more integrated subjective world. Matte Blanco's theoretical contributions are particularly useful in illuminating the parallel symmetrical and asymmetrical organizations of experience. They allow us to understand one of the effects of excessive projective identification as involving the patient's failure to develop symmetrical, internal experience and to be orphaned in the world of external asymmetrical experience, which leads to the ability to function as an object, but a failure in the development of the structures of subjectivity.

10

The Subject of the Unconscious

The title of this chapter is ambiguous, evoking the multiple meanings of concepts of subjectivity as it has been used in different psychoanalytic and philosophical contexts and reflecting the multiple meanings of the concept of the unconscious. From a positivist perspective, the title suggests a further discussion of the history and theory of the unconscious. From a postmodern perspective, it suggests an entity, the subject, that resides in the unconscious and functions as a dialectical counterweight to another entity, another subject that resides in consciousness.[1] In conceptualizing subjectivity from a postmodern perspective and as a function of unconscious processes, the reader is left somewhat at sea, lacking the certainty of a single meaning, an objective or consensual truth—this is subjectivity. From a neo-Kleinian and a postmodern perspective, the concepts of the subject, subjectivity, and intersubjectivity are not locatable in the external world of science, of things and of objects, but reside in the generative unconscious, where meanings are created through symmetrical logic and the symbolic processes of the de-

---

1. See David Rapaport (1951) for an early discussion of the dialectic relationship between the id and the ego, or conscious and unconscious thought.

pressive position. This use of the concepts of the subject, subjectivity, and intersubjectivity differs from other uses of these concepts in contemporary psychoanalytic theory.

SUBJECTIVITY IN CONTEMPORARY PSYCHOANALYSIS

Concepts of the subject, subjectivity, and intersubjectivity have increasingly become of interest in psychoanalytic theory (Auerbach and Blatt 2001, Benjamin 1998, Frie and Reiss 2001, Gerhardt and Sweetnam 2000, Ogden 1994, Stolorow and Atwood 1992), as the development of the paradigm shift from the one-person model of psychoanalysis, which defined a scientific certainty of the analyst's authority and the nature of cure, to the two-person relational model, which involves the uncertainty of the constructivist perspective, conceptualizing treatment and cure as a function of the analytic relationship, emphasizing dialogue, mutuality, and a shared experience of authority. In the two-person model of the analytic relationship, both the patient's and analyst's inner experiences contribute to the evolving dialogue; however, in this evolving dialogue each person's speech is suspect, a possible displacement or condensation from other temporal, spatial, or personal relationships. Renik (1998), writing from a contemporary Freudian position, argues that the analyst's experience is irreducibly subjective, and emphasizes the necessity for a technique that allows the analyst and patient to address the analyst's perceptions, experience, and subjectivity. Similarly, Hoffman (1983), writing from a relational perspective, suggests that we consider the patient's comments as a form of "supervision" describing aspects of the therapist's activity outside of his/her awareness. Concepts of subjectivity and intersubjectivity have been adopted by contemporary psychoanalytic theory to describe the phenomenological, uncertain, emergent quality of perceptions, affects, and fantasies that are central to the two person constructivist model. Phenomenological concepts of subjectivity and intersubjectivity have easily filled the void left by discarding the positivist concepts of ego and self in order to represent many of the emergent and uncertain qualities of the contemporary two-person psychoanalytic relationship.

Frie and Reiss (2001) contextualize concepts of subjectivity and intersubjectivity within the broader historical roots of continental philosophy. Rather than presenting a simple phenomenological view of subjectivity, the continental philosophers conceptualized subjectivity as arising out of a dialectical relationship between self and other, which resulted in new organizations of self-consciousness. Frie and Reiss suggest that these philosophical concepts of subjectivity and the historical problems addressed by the continental philosophers provide a parallel to similar problems presented by the development of contemporary relational psychoanalysis:

> Continental philosophers clearly reject the traditional conception of the subject as isolated and closed in on the self. In its place, they seek to formulate a conception of the subject and of subjectivity that is true to our lived experience. Thus they pay particular attention to prereflective and somatic experience, and consider the ways in which we are always and inevitably enmeshed in social contexts. Not by chance, we believe contemporary interpersonal and relational psychoanalysis embrace these same revisions, broadening for inclusion in analysis experiences that were similarly excluded in classical considerations. [p. 299]

Continental philosophers rejected the Cartesian paradigm of the isolated thinker, the basis for the one-person model of psychoanalysis. They conceptualized subjectivity, or self-consciousness, as a function of interaction with other human beings, and awareness of one's subjectivity as a social experience. The continental philosophers held several alternative views of the structure of subjectivity, intersubjectivity, and the development of self-consciousness: a phenomenological perspective in which individual self-consciousness precedes the encounter with the other and is inherent in infantile states of prereflective awareness; a dialectical perspective in which subjectivity is a result of a struggle with the other for recognition; and an existential or generative perspective that conceptualizes subjectivity as an emergent quality of the rootedness of human beings in a cultural matrix. These three philosophical positions can be thought of as parallel to contemporary psychoanalytic concepts of subjectivity and intersubjectivity: the phenomenological subject, subjectivity as a dialectical struggle for recognition, and subjectivity as generative of symbolic meaning. From a broad perspective, subjectivity and intersubjectivity include all three perspectives; however, in actuality, most psychoanalytic theories focus on a single dimension of subjectivity: the phenomenological, the dialectical, or the generative.

THE PHENOMENOLOGICAL SUBJECT

The interpersonal, relational, and intersubjective or self-psychological theories view subjectivity from a phenomenological perspective, one in which each individual in the therapeutic dyad attempts to become aware of and articulate more authentic expression of affects, to more freely disclose personal information, and to negotiate disparities in power. Subjectivity is thought of as inherent in each individual, with intersubjectivity thought of as the intersection of two subjectivities, the articulation of two individuals' experiences of self-awareness, and the progressive development of mutual understanding. In the phenomenological perspective, treatment is focused on each individual's capacity to experience and articulate the affects inherent in the evolving transference–countertransference relationship.

The phenomenological concept of subjectivity is heir to the psychology of the self, which has its roots in the work of Sullivan and Kohut. Stolorow and his colleagues (Atwood and Stolorow 1984, Stolorow and Atwood 1992) conceptualized the *intersubjective theory* as extending self psychology through broadening the concept of the psychological field to include the patient's and analyst's inner experience, and modifying the concept of empathy from a discursive focus on understanding the other to include a performative aspect focusing on the flow of reciprocal influences such as those between infant and mother (Beebe et al. 1997). Intersubjective theory expanded the one-person emphasis of Kohut's theory, which focused primarily on the patient's inner experience with little attention to the therapist's internal experience, other than the inevitable sequences of disruption and repair in the flow of empathic attunement. Stolorow and his colleagues conceptualize treatment as occurring at the intersection of the patient's and therapist's subjectivity, as each participant influences the other, developing an increased capacity to articulate archaic experiences into mature expressions of affect, and becoming progressively more able to articulate and negotiate differences that develop in the transference–countertransference relationship.

The following case (Atwood et al. 1989) illustrates the intersubjective phenomenological approach to subjectivity, focusing on processes of intersubjective influence and understanding the development of disjunctions in the analytic relationship. Atwood and colleagues describe conjunctions and disjunctions as processes of mutual identification and mutual regulation that occur outside of awareness and often lead to impasses in the therapeutic process. Conjunctions and disjunctions involve both constructive and destructive aspects of mutual influences and affective regulation, which results from the patient and therapist identifications or disidentifications that emerge as the transference–countertransference relationship becomes an enactment of earlier relationships. Atwood and colleagues illustrate this process in the psychoanalytic therapy of a 34-year-old woman of Oriental descent whose treatment became progressively mired in an eroticized and romantic transference–countertransference enactment. The patient had a painful history of being rejected by her father because she was female, and she entered therapy because of persistent difficulties in her relationships with men, who she felt were self-involved and not interested in her. The patient had a long-standing self-perception, a belief, that she was deficient as a woman and lacked confidence in her attractiveness to men.

The patient was embarrassed by her romantic interest in the therapist and concerned that talking about it would lead to his withdrawing from her. In response to this expression of the patient's anxiety, and "assimilating the patient's concern into an organizing principle of his own, the therapist reassured her that he would not withdraw from her. He also communicated his understanding that her feelings represented a longing to consolidate and build a sense of herself as a female, as this had never happened in her family" (Atwood et al. 1989, p. 561). As this transference–countertransference enactment evolved, the patient began to ask for more direct responsiveness from the therapist, which culminated in bringing him a present after returning from an eight-week trip in which she fantasized about the two of them being together. The therapist reacted with anxiety, rejecting the gift, which resulted in the patient's feeling crestfallen and angry. The patient felt misled, threatened to leave therapy, and demanded that the therapist directly state that he found her attractive and sexually exciting. This resulted in a therapeutic disjunction in which the therapist became increasingly more intellectualized and distant and the patient more enraged and demanding.

The therapist went for a consultation, which clarified the disjunction that developed between the patient's and the therapist's subjective experience, as their unconscious and unarticulated organizing principles intersected. The patient's organizing principle, her deep subjective belief, was that no man would ever sustain an interest in her as a female.

The therapist's organizing principle, his deep subjective belief that he was required to maintain a woman's sense of her attractiveness in order to avoid her explosive rage, was based on his childhood experience with his mother.

This intersubjective crisis was resolved through the therapist's explanation, perhaps confession, of his failure as an analyst and his confusion about his personal experience, his past, and his current role as a therapist. In his explanation of this analytic disjunction or impasse, the therapist presented an asymmetrical and abstract elaboration of the analytic experience, differentiating his and the patient's experience in terms of conscious intentions, objective roles, and time. The therapist reinstated the objective difference in their roles and the asymmetry of power in their relationship. Atwood and colleagues describe an asymmetrical mode of interpretation in which the therapist conveyed to the patient his understanding of their interaction and how it developed, and his subjective contribution to this intersubjective crisis:

> He communicated to her that he had tried to extend his range of interactions with her in an attempt to be responsive to her needs. She was, however, perceiving and reacting to his oscillation between a responsive mirroring stance and a retreat into a more distant intellectual inquiry, which made her feel like a specimen. He further stated that at this point he wanted to establish a firmer definition of his own boundaries so that he could help restore a therapeutic atmosphere between them. He told her that his ideal as an analyst prevented him from responding directly to her questions about whether he found her sexually attractive and exciting. He further acknowledged that because of a conflict within himself—between a feeling that he must be responsive to her and an equally strong feeling that he must live up to his own analytic ideals—he had sometimes withdrawn from her, as when he had rejected her gift. He said that within the limits of his own view of himself as an analyst, he would like to work with her to reestablish their relationship. The patient responded very favorably. She said that although she thought that his training was somewhat stupid, she understood what had happened and now had an idea of what she could expect. [p. 563]

This approach at resolving the analytic disjunction reflects qualities of personal honesty and the ability to disclose difficult personal experience and actions. However, it is not just the patient's fear of the repulsiveness of desire that Atwood and colleagues suggest is at the root of the problem, but that she has also not been able to experience her desire as a powerful, positive, and creative aspect of her subjectivity. The cognitive and affective confusion involved in this impasse may be thought of as the patient and analyst being enmeshed in a concrete or paranoid symmetrical experience where the patient's gift and the therapist's refusal became symbolic equivalents, an enactment of a metacomplementary, unspoken sexual relationship, one that they each participated in and denied. I believe that the problem in this phenomenological approach to subjectivity is that it obscures the unconscious, imaginative, poetic, symmetrical, and symbolic elements that are lost in the emphasis on articulating conscious, asymmetrical experience. This example of an asymmetrical interpretive strategy can be contrasted with the symmetrical symbolic interpretive strategy suggested by Hanna Segal's (1981) patient who becomes able to express the power and beauty of his sexual desire in the dream image of playing a violin duet with a woman and/or with the therapist (see Chapter 8).

Interpersonal and relational psychoanalysis also presents a phenomenological concept of subjectivity, with each individual the center of his or her own subjective experience and the analytic process occurring at the intersection of the two subjectivities. Ehrenberg's (1992) notion of the analytic relationship as occurring at the "intimate edge" of analytic relatedness illustrates this dynamic. She believes that moments when the analyst and the patient risk disclosing difficult private experiences can lead to a more authentic organization of the analytic relationship and bring the disowned aspects of the patient's self into a broader experience of subjectivity. In the interpersonal and relational view, the psychoanalytic relationship (Aron 1996) can ideally become a "meeting of minds" of two subjects, where each subject comes to deeply understand the other's experience. The interpersonal and relational view conceptualizes intersubjectivity as an intersection of two independent subjects who choose to or become able to disclose their feelings about each other, to each other, disclosing aspects of personal history involving the experience of risk and censure. In interpersonal and relational psychoanalysis the development of the subject involves the development of the capacity to express that which has been known but not articulated (Bollas 1987, Stern 1997) and is thought to reflect a more authentic, core, true, or real aspect of the self. This view of intersubjectivity, like that developed by

Stolorow and his colleagues, can be thought of as involving processes of identification and the modeling of high-risk actions of intersubjective relatedness and disclosure.

The following two cases illustrate how the analyst's discovery and disclosure of unconscious forbidden feelings propel the patient and the analyst into an increased experience of self-consciousness and subjectivity. The articles by Gerson (1996) and Davies (1998) describe analysts' attempts to break out of the constraints of the objective role of therapist into a more personal and subjective form of relatedness through the articulation, or perhaps confession, of feelings and actions that are experienced as shameful, involving a great deal of countertransference anxiety and an imagined censure by the analytic community. These articles present a phenomenological perspective, supporting the idea that it is the act of self-disclosure that leads to the development of subjectivity through the development of more authentic dialogue.

Gerson (1996) finds himself lying to his patient in an attempt to cover up his failure to tell her, in a timely way, that he would be away for several days. On his return he decides to tell the patient about his lie and then asks her to talk about how she understands his actions. Initially, the patient suggested a positive interpretation of his behavior, that he did not tell her that he would be away because he (unconsciously) didn't want to be away from her, or that he forgot because he was too busy listening, or perhaps he liked being with her. However, after a brief silence, the patient changed from ascribing positive motives to the analyst to feeling enraged, stating that the therapist wanted to avoid experiencing her dependency and anger.

Gerson did not report his response to the patient's interpretations, but reports that the patient's comments stimulated his awareness of the possibility that the patient might have to leave the geographic area, and thus terminate the analysis, and that his acting out reflected a reversal of roles in which he could deny his desire for her and his reluctance to lose her. It is as if his inability to tell her about his absence reflected his wish not to know about her possible termination as well as his attraction and desire for her. Gerson's disclosure of his reluctance to miss the patient or to experience desire for her did not have an immediate effect on the treatment; the patient returned to her usual concerns about not being desired and desirable. Gerson came to understand this impasse as reflecting their unconscious "attachment to an image of her as problematic and undesirable [that] came to be understood as an intersubjective resistance to and excitement about her sexuality; this jointly constructed and accepted knowledge began to inform our interactions, and our embeddedness in this transference–countertransference dynamic began to lose its hold" (p. 640).

From this interpersonal/relational perspective, which presents a phenomenological position on the development of subjectivity and intersubjective resistance, like the disjunction in the previous example, comes an opportunity for a deeper understanding of each participant's unarticulated experience and an opportunity to expand self-awareness, self-consciousness, and the experience of subjectivity through the therapist's self-disclosure and risk taking. This illustration of intersubjective relatedness, like the one described by Atwood and colleagues (1989), involves the analyst's inadvertent enactment, which is subsequently articulated as a personal or analytic failure that leads to a historical and asymmetrical understanding that illuminates the patient's difficulties in the experience of being desired and desirable. This sequence can also be thought of as one in which the analyst's experience is initially organized within the concrete symmetrical processes of a frightening acting out of an unknown symbolic equation, which then becomes articulated as an abstract, asymmetrical interpretation linking the analyst's failure to the patient's arrested development. Issues of power are not addressed in Gerson's phenomenological perspective on subjectivity; he maintains a traditional power relationship through a metacomplementary process of asking the patient to interpret his behavior, maintaining the focus on the patient's inner life and her difficulty being desired and not fully exploring his own thoughts, experiences, and history.

Davies (1998) presents a somewhat different perspective on the development of subjectivity in the relational psychoanalytic approach, describing her work with a male patient who has a great deal of anxiety about his sexuality and desire. Here again, the analyst is unaware of her inadvertent or unwitting participation in an enactment of desire and sexuality. The patient initiates a new possibility of intersubjective awareness by asking Davies if she is flirting with him. Davies recognizes that "in this complex communication, my patient asked me to both pardon him for seeing something in me that he believed I did not want him to see, as well as to validate the accuracy of his perceptions so that he might more fully rely on his reality testing skills in what for him had been a dangerous and frightening interpersonal arena" (p. 761). Davies acknowledges her flir-tatiousness, and although the subsequent interactions bring both patient and analyst into a fearful intersubjective space, they manage to negotiate this experience through the development of a transitional experience, a metaphor that Davies initially used to represent and transform their sexual desire from an anxious transference–countertransference experience into a symbolic experience. This transference–countertransference situation is represented by the metaphor of entering a room slowly, where each may lead at different times. This metaphor suggests many sexual associations from that of the primal scene to a scene of seduction. Davies's use of the metaphor of standing on the threshold of a room allowed for an explora-tion of both the anxiety and curiosity of sexuality and desire.

However, Davies moves away from a more symmetrical symbolic approach, developing the transitional experience of sexuality between patient and analyst into an asymmetrical symbolic interpretive strategy through her associations to her husband's beginning awareness of her daughter's sexuality, which transforms the metaphor into a discursive symbol representing the anxieties experienced between parents and chil-dren as sexuality becomes part of family life and each parent becomes aware of the child's budding sexuality. Davies describes the development of subjectivity through an evolving process of symbolization, including becoming aware of her inadvertent enactment of sexual desire, an ac-knowledgment of her subjective and perhaps "inappropriate" feelings, to the development of a symmetrical, transitional experience through which the patient could integrate feelings of sexuality and desire and then to a asymmetrical, contextual, historical interpretation.

In terms of the model of psychic transformation, Davies's initial inadvertent enactment is organized first as a concrete symmetrical ex-perience, and then briefly as a more metaphoric symbolic symmetrical experience that becomes transformed into a symbolic asymmetrical ex-perience as she contextualizes it within a normative, developmental model of adult sexual development. Davies presents a sophisticated phenomenological approach to the development of subjectivity, which involves the transformation of concrete projective identifications through the development of a transitional experience that reorganizes the disso-ciated experience of flirtation into a symbolic symmetrical experience that allows for a deeper integration of desire, sexuality, and fear. How-ever, Davies returns to the traditional power relationship in which she becomes the anxious but understanding parent, the objective and help-ful analyst, presenting a symbolic asymmetrical explanation that returns to the patient's history. It is this last step, the return to the asymmetrical conscious and objective position of the analyst, that I believe differenti-ates the relational approach of the phenomenological subject from ei-ther the dialectical subject or the generative subject.

THE DIALECTICAL SUBJECT

Jessica Benjamin (1988, 1995, 1998) has developed a concept of subjec-tivity and intersubjectivity that integrates the dialectical perspective of Hegel, Lacan, Klein, and Winnicott within a relational treatment con-text. She has been extremely influential in the development of a femi-nist perspective in psychoanalysis and bringing onto the psychoanalytic foreground Hegel's concept of the master–slave dialectic as a formative aspect of the development of self-consciousness and subjectivity. Her work has been strongly influenced by Lacan, a postmodern view of the primacy of language, Winnicott's differentiation of object relating in which the other is the embodiment of projective identifications, and object usage in which the other is recognized as an independent person with his/her own internal world of fantasy, desire, and memory. Benjamin's concept of subjectivity and intersubjectivity differs significantly from the interpersonal and relational concept of the phenomenological subject based on the intersection of two subjectivities. She conceptualizes sub-jectivity as a function of an inevitable, dialectical struggle for power over and recognition by the other. She sees the individual's need for recog-nition as the most vulnerable aspect of the process of differentiation and development, involving the paradoxical need for acknowledgment of independence from those whom the individual is most dependent on. Because of this inherent, human problem of vulnerability, the individual might organize experience around a strategy involving the denial of dependence, rebelliously asserting his/her grandiose[2] self-sufficiency, or alternatively, identify with the all-powerful other, and in a state of ab-

---

2. Benjamin does not differentiate grandiosity from omnipotence, as I have, and describes this problem as the individual's inability to give up omnipotence rather than grandiosity.

solute submission attempt to be the other's imaginary object, the good compliant child.

Benjamin (1988) interprets Hegel's concept of the master–slave dialectic as involving the simultaneous needs for independent action and for recognition, which is at the core of her dialectical concept of subjectivity:

> In Hegel's notion of recognition, the self requires the opportunity to act and to have an effect on the other to affirm his existence. In order to exist for oneself, one has to exist for another. It would seem that there is no way out of this dependency. If I destroy the other, there is no one to recognize me, for if I allow him no independent consciousness, I become enmeshed with a dead, not conscious being. If the other denies me recognition, my acts have no meaning; if he is so far above me that nothing I do can alter his attitude towards me, I can only submit. My desire and agency can find no outlet, except in the form of obedience. [p. 53]

This dialectical struggle between independence and recognition is dramatically portrayed in Sartre's play, *No Exit*, in which he describes the sadomasochistic relationships among individuals consigned to an existential Hell that is constructed through the other's capacity to willfully withhold recognition.

Benjamin (2000) differentiates her work from the interpersonal and relational analysts, who have presented phenomenological concepts of subjectivity. She distinguishes these analysts' use of expressiveness and self-disclosure, which she conceptualizes as a dimension of "personhood," from her view of "subjecthood," which she describes in the following way:

> By this I mean the distinction between the patient's recognizing the analyst's subjectivity (personhood) and recognizing the analyst's independent existence (subjecthood) as outside and different from the patient's mental fantasy. Where I frequently mean the latter (e.g. how we come to accept alterity, otherness), many relational thinkers (e.g., Aron 1996, Hoffman 1998) have meant the former (e.g., how the analyst communicates personal subjectivity). As I pondered this personhood–subjecthood distinction, I began to think that it is imbricated with the developmental differences in recognition. Although my outline of intersubjectivity focused on the crisis of recognition in

which the difference in desire, meaning, and perspective between you and me has to be negotiated, I do include in the idea of inter-subjectivity those early experiences of attunement that are evoked and repaired through the analyst's expressiveness. . . . Much of my writing has been devoted to elaborating the process of mutual unconscious identification (and I would add, often conscious identification on the analyst's part)—identificatory love—which draws on early attunement but uses symbolic rather than procedural-sensory likeness. The evocation of likeness or symmetry—whether in the most primal form of visual and vocal matching or in the developmentally latter forms of shared understanding—is what dissolves complementary power relations. Identificatory fantasies counter the asymmetrical oedipal fantasies of the analytic situation, bridging the generational and gender differences, yielding a symbolic, emotionally charged connection: "Our positions and ages may be different, but we can feel the same." So that most of us agree that the analyst uses her subjectivity, we may differ about whether its purpose is to create attunement and identification, or to establish difference and alterity. [p. 45]

Benjamin's concept of the analyst's identification with her patient can be understood as the analyst's reverie preceding the development of a transitional experience, a new organization within the analytic relationship that she describes as "thirdness." Benjamin (2001) describes thirdness as a mutually generated experience, like Winnicott's concept of object usage, involving an awareness of the analyst's internal experience, that is different from the power struggles of complementary (paranoid-schizoid) relatedness involving the "push-me-pull-you, doer-done to dynamics" (p. 1) of submission or resistance to the other's demands. This concept of intersubjectivity as thirdness, a new organization of experience, utilizing aspects of transitional experience or the development of symmetrical symbolic experience, is similar to Ogden's (1994) concept of the analytic third. Benjamin describes three dimensions of the analytic third: a dimension of rhythmicity or mutual regulation, a symbolic dimension of interpretation, and a moral dimension involving a commitment to the other.

Benjamin (2001) illustrates the development of thirdness in her work with a patient whose self-negating and masochistic difficulties were expressed through the complementarities of her idealization of others, in which the analyst's role was to "join her attacks on herself, to be her critic, at best a stern mentor; her role was to always fail to be a good enough patient or student of analysis" (p. 11). Benjamin describes the development of thirdness, intersubjectivity, in which the complementary relationship of good analyst and hopeless patient is transformed by her inner experience of identification, compassion, and insight, which facilitated a transitional reorganization of the analytic relationship from the complementarities of the paranoid-schizoid position into the symmetry of the intersubjective third. Benjamin's concept of the analytic third extends the Hegelian model of dominance and submission into a new organization of experience in which each person becomes part of a transitional organization of experience, which allows for a joined intersubjective consciousness:

> I could say nothing from a third position, by which I mean this: to be empathic was to be one with her despair, to think she had not ruined herself socially and professionally forever was to be in denial of her dissociated but powerful sense of catastrophe, which was overlaid by such deep shame. There was no insight into this quandary that could not be enlisted in masochistic self-beratement or that did not again leave her alone and humiliated in the deep doom she shared with her mother. This time, my own thoughts were different, crisper somehow. I was aware of her agency in producing her situation, but I couldn't help indignantly thinking, as if she were my own child, that Hannah was at least a match for her friends in integrity, personal insight and intelligence (What's with them, I thought. And why isn't she good enough?). I carried this vision of her other, stronger self, as well as the anger and outrage she couldn't express, and must have conveyed this as I asked her something like why she thought her anxiety and vulnerability were so unacceptable and why she didn't deserve understanding and compassion from her friends. She began the next session saying how surprised and gratified she was by my staunch defense. As if she had suddenly gotten it that I really was on her side. She had thought she was facing reality, trying to take responsibility for her problems by identifying with her friends' judgment of her. I suggested that she indeed did identify with it, in fact she probably elicited their contempt because she shared it. She agreed, "Yes I do Shtick, I make a Shtick out of vulnerability when I'm anxious." I said, "Yes it really is a Stick—you punish yourself with it, and invite people to join you. What you have to be responsible for is

not your vulnerability but your punishing and beating yourself." I now
addressed a familiar form of complementarity between us: I say, "So
it's as if we were arguing, who is responsible, the Nazi or the Jew."
We talk about how she is afraid of being the victor, the aggressor,
the one who triumphs, it is better to be a victim, covered in shame.
[p. 12]

Benjamin describes intersubjective experience as the creation of a
third position in the analytic relationship, which reflects the resolution
of being trapped in a dialectical, metacomplementary, sadomasochistic
relationship in which each person frustrates, persecutes, or controls the
other. Benjamin describes ways of resolving the dilemma of recognition
in the master–slave paradigm. In the above example, if Benjamin would
be the critical analyst, the sadistic master, she would be submitting to
the patient's metacomplementary demand to attack her, and, alternatively, if she would choose to be the compassionate analyst, she would
take on the complementary masochistic position of being minimized and
rejected by the patient. However, Benjamin experiences this dialectical
relationship through a process of reverie, a symmetrical thought process in which Benjamin identifies the patient with her own child and is
able to convey to the patient her transformative, unverbalized fantasy of
the patient's strength and ability through an act of recognition involving a shift from discursive language to presentational language. In this
complicated analytic sequence, Benjamin facilitated a transformation
from the passive paranoid-schizoid position in which the patient experiences herself as a metacomplementary victim to the active paranoid
position where the patient can contemplate a full range of the possibilities of her own aggression, including the ways in which she controls
others in their attacks on her. Benjamin's (2000) concept of intersubjectivity is not a simple ideal of mutual recognition but involves the
repeating experiences of a dialectical breakdown into complementarity
and its repair through mutual recognition. In keeping with Benjamin's
integration of Winnicott's (1971) concepts of transitional experience
and his differentiation of object relating from object usage, the repeating sequences of breakdown and repair can be understood as a process
of transformation from asymmetrical or functionally conscious experiences into a symmetrical or a functionally unconscious organization
of experience.

In agreement with Benjamin's dialectical concept of intersubjectivity, Auerbach and Blatt (2001) describe the constant tension between the need for recognition and the retreat into the safety of narcissism, isolation, and grandiosity.[3] However, these authors also relate the development of subjectivity and intersubjectivity to the child's evolving cognitive capacities, including the ability to play, to enter into situations based on pretending (make believe), and to experience his/her mind as distinct from those of others. Auerbach and Blatt conceptualize subjectivity as dependent on the development of complex cognitive capacities in both normal development and in the therapeutic relationship. They understand the development of these complex cognitive and affective capacities as related to the development of Winnicott's concept of transitional experience:

> For coincident with the emergence of self-reflexivity (subjectivity) is the emergence of pretend play (Piaget 1945)—of transitional object usage (Winnicott 1971); and 2-year-olds are adept at distinguishing between pretense (i.e., make believe) and reality. . . . Transitional object usage, as Winnicott proposed, is the means by which a child negotiates the dilemma of becoming separate and autonomous while remaining attached to caregivers. However, if children at age 2 are quite capable of distinguishing pretense from reality and of using this distinction to cope with emotional dilemmas in their lives, they have much difficulty, prior to age 4 or 5, in grasping the distinction between appearance and reality, between how things look and how they actually are. . . . They also have difficulty before they reach this age that a person's beliefs about the world can be false (Perner, Leekam and Wimmer 1987) and in understanding the subtleties of secrecy and lying (Astington 1993, Meares 1993). In short, although children come to understand the separateness of their bodies sometime in the second year of life, they do not come to understand that their minds are distinct from those of others until sometime in the 5th or 6th year. . . . The discovery of the separateness of one's mind is a crucial step in the development of self-reflexivity because it is then that a child learns that his or her beliefs about the world differ from those of others. It is with a child's discovery of his or her mind's sepa-

3. These authors do not differentiate grandiosity as an isolated individual state and omnipotence as a joined state of transitional phenomena, and therefore use omnipotence in describing this view of isolation and the negation of the other.

rateness, therefore, that transitional object usage comes to be integrated with realistic cognition (Fonagy and Target 1996, Target and Fonagy 1996)—at least under normal circumstances. [p. 434]

Auerbach's and Blatt's emphasis on the individual's evolving cognitive capacities is an important aspect of the development of subjectivity and intersubjectivity that adds an important dimension to the phenomenological perspective through focusing on cognitive processes of creating meaning and on the dialectics of power, aggression, and reparation that are central to the Kleinian model of psychic development. Blatt and his colleagues (1996) have developed an interview procedure for assessing an individual's capacity for self-reflexivity, the Object Relations Inventory, which they use in studying change in the therapeutic process. They see the therapeutic relationship as involving the patient's use of adaptive projective identification and enactments of transitional experiences through which the patient moves beyond the splits of paranoid identifications, in which objects are all good and all bad, to the capacity to experience self and other as both good and bad. This view of the therapeutic process as both a cognitive, intrapsychic developmental process and a dialectical interpersonal process involving projective and introjective identification is quite similar to the neo-Kleinian view that I present. However, they collapse the dimensions of concrete-symbolic thought and realistic-imaginative (asymmetrical-symmetrical) thinking into a single dimension, which results in a linear model of cognitive and emotional development.

THE GENERATIVE SUBJECT

The neo-Kleinian model of thinking describes a two-dimensional dialectical view of psychic structure involving the concrete thought of the paranoid position and the symbolic thought of the depressive position and the bi-logical structures of conscious asymmetrical thought and unconscious symmetrical thought. In separating these two dialectical dimensions, subjectivity, being a subject, becomes located in the unconscious or symmetrical organization of experience, while objectivity, being an object, is located in the conscious or asymmetrical organization of experience. The capacity to create symbolic symmetrical experience, such as transitional experiences, allows for the development of subjectivity, an achievement that is different from that of being an object, and the capacity for reality testing and problem solving. In a fully functioning human being, there is a constant tension, a dynamic instability, between the dialectics of being a subject and being an object, which involves the possibility of organizing any experience as symmetrical or asymmetrical, and concrete or symbolic.

From a neo-Kleinian perspective subjectivity is an organization of experience that utilizes the creative and generative aspects of the unconscious, and is located in the symmetrical symbolic quadrant of the matrix of psychic transformation. The generative unconscious utilizes symmetrical logic to apprehend, perceive, and generate or create meanings, as contrasted with the repressed unconscious and the relational unconscious in which meaning is a function of imposing models of past events onto current experience. The generative unconscious creates meanings through symmetrical symbolic processes of effacing differences and the development of transitional experiences, metaphors, and poetic structures, in which a single instance of an event, one person, represents the entire universe of that experience. This form of creating meaning stands in contrast to the symbolic asymmetrical organization, which uses comparisons of multiple objects to develop differences and in finding abstract or general laws that describe the rules for inclusion in a class.

Ogden's (1997a,b, 1998, 1999, 2001) interest in poetry as a transformative process that is similar to psychoanalytic interpretation speaks to the difference between the asymmetrical organization of experience, which focuses on the development of discursive symbols that convey information through the differentiation of person, place, and time in the external or conscious world, and the development of presentational symbols, the symmetrical organization of experience, which creates similarities of absolute or infinite experience and defines the structure of the unconscious and subjective experience. In his discussions of psychoanalysis and poetry, he focuses on the analyst's capacity to use processes of reverie to create meanings that are developments of the symmetrical symbolic mode of experience. His poetic or symbolic symmetrical interpretation led to the development of an "analytic third," a jointly created metaphoric experience defining the patient's and analyst's relationship, which, like a poetic image or a presentational symbol or a transitional experience, continues to expand meanings through generating a series of deepening and integrating associations and metaphors. Ogden's emphasis on these creative processes as central to psychoanalytic treatment focuses the analyst's efforts on the development of a new subject, a new experience of subjectivity, which is centered in the patient's capacity to transform concrete symmetrical and asymmetrical experiences into symmetrical symbolic processes in organizing, apprehending, and generating experience.

In viewing subjectivity, psychological health, and the goals of psychoanalysis as intertwined with the development of the individual's capacity to use symbolic symmetrical processes, I suggest that each person lives in two parallel universes, one in which he or she is an object in the world of material reality where experience is organized asymmetrically, and the other in which he or she is a subject, the world of psychic reality where experience is organized symmetrically. In focusing on the failures in the development of subjectivity, I have focused on the failures in the development of symbolic symmetrical processes and on the necessity for the analyst to utilize symbolic symmetrical processes such as reverie, enactments, and the development of transitional experiences in facilitating the development of the subject of the unconscious, the subject who can organize experience within the structures of meaning and desire that is represented in the symmetrical symbolic experiences of dreams, poetry, deep friendships, relationships of love, and identifications with ideals. This view of subjectivity as located within the unconscious and as utilizing symbolic symmetrical organizations of experience is similar to the Lacanian speaking subject, who can articulate his own desire through the development and use of metaphor.

The matrix of psychic transformation presents a highly schematized way of understanding the analyst's task of transforming the patient's experience of being an object, organizing experience asymmetrically into being a subject where experience is organized symmetrically. In this matrix, the analyst's activity, his/her enactments and verbal interventions, can be thought of as part of the process of transformation of the patient's experience from that of being a concrete object, a thing in the world, to being a subject, able to elaborate, generate, and integrate the affective power of symbolic symmetrical processes, such as that of metaphors, identifications, poetry, and the absolute affective experience of love and desire. In previous examples I focused on work with patients in which their capacity to utilize symmetrical processes had been truncated, and they were trapped in the asymmetrical world of either concrete or abstract asymmetrical experience. However, psychopathology can also develop as a function of a failure in symbolically integrating concrete symmetrical experience of the paranoid-schizoid position with the depressive position, where the individual remains trapped in symmetrical concrete (paranoid) organizations of experience.

Winnicott's (1971) important distinction between unproductive daydreams or "fantasies" and productive dreams is discussed in his chapter, "Dreaming, Fantasying and Living: A Case History Describing a Primary Dissociation." Winnicott describes a patient who withdraws into a world of fantasy or daydream where she remains dissociated and disconnected from her self and others. He notes that this world of daydreams and fantasy does not allow the presence of another or the creation of meaning, but is only a series of mental activities that take up time. Winnicott describes these mental activities, daydreams, fantasies, and thoughts, which are not directed at creating meaning but rather involve the evacuation of meaning, affective discharge, and the avoidance of displeasure. He compares the patient's repetitive activity of playing solitaire to a possible dream about playing solitaire that would be told to the analyst. He understands daydreams as dissociation, a form of not thinking and maintaining an isolated paranoid position, while he sees the dreams as an attempt to create meaning and to be open to the possibility of interpretation and of the development of transitional experiences involving identifications and symmetrizations of experience in the development of intersubjective meaning.

CLINICAL ILLUSTRATION: LOST IN SPACE

This case example illustrates the experience of a patient who is isolated in the paranoid experience of living in a world of evacuated asymmetrical fantasies that have not been transformed through a parent's reverie, recognition, and the development of transitional experience into a sense of hopefulness, subjectivity, and aliveness. Patients who remain trapped in the concrete symmetrical organization of experience organize the world in paranoid dichotomies of grandiosity and power, deadness and aliveness, master and slave. These patients experience themselves as absolutely powerful or weak, brilliant or stupid, saviors or devils. In the dialectic of the paranoid and depressive position, issues of power and grandiosity are transformed through recognition and reparation into the joined experiences of omnipotence, joy, and the development of personal and cultural transitional experiences.

This patient had a very limited life, and although trained as a computer programmer had not worked in several years. He was in his early 30s and lived with both parents with whom he had a very strained relationship. He felt that people would not accept him and he would often drink in order not to face himself. He felt that he had been a failure in work, in his relationships with women, and in the development of adult sexuality. His affect in sessions and throughout his life was flat, deliberate, hopeless, and depressed. The analyst who had worked with him for several years felt hopeless, often bored, and easily distracted. Treatment was organized using an interpersonal, asymmetrical interpretive strategy that attempted to help the patient differentiate and understand his interpersonal relationships with his parents, co-workers, and the few acquaintances that he occasionally saw. This patient's experience can be located in the concrete asymmetrical quadrant of the matrix of psychic transformation and can be described as deadened, disconnected fragments. He describes himself as an object, always comparing himself to others and feeling that there is little that makes him stand out. The analyst's experience can also be located in this quadrant; she is bored, distracted, and deadened, and has become progressively unable to think as her capacity to link experience, affect, and relationships has become progressively more diminished.

This patient tells the analyst of a very complex, albeit dissociated, set of daydreams or fantasies that occupy much of his waking life and that he thinks of as a set of books that are passively discovered rather than written. In this dissociated narrative there are a series of characters who are in a struggle to rule the universe. The story is much like *Star Wars*, except his themes involve a great deal of violence and sexual abuse. The main character is a frightened young woman, Liberty, who is sold into slavery by her mother, a prostitute, and is bought by an ambivalently perceived character, Satan. Other characters in the story include drug addicts, bisexual and transsexual characters, and various slaves and masters. The narrative involves stories of sexual abuse, heterosexual and homosexual rape, and the struggle against forces that deprive individuals of their freedom.

The analyst responded to these stories in two ways. The first was with a sense of horror and disgust related to the patient's narrative of abuse and humiliation, and the second involved her complex counter-transference anxieties and resistances to an awareness of the patient's dissociated paranoid, persecutory world and his lack of engagement with the external world of relationships and work. The patient described his experience in a passive, paranoid organization in which he was an object both in his life in the external world and in his sadomasochistic daydreams. The analyst's interpretive strategy was based on an interpersonal view of the patient's fantasies as displacements and distortion of real experience, which informed her interpretive strategy in an attempt to help the patient locate the core aspects of these fantasies in more reality-oriented, interpersonal experience. However, this strategy did not work, and the treatment became more deadened, with the therapist becoming despairing, disconnected, and unable to think. In supervision, I suggested that we move in a different direction, understanding the need to develop these autistic, concrete, isolated fantasies into transitional experiences through developing a symmetrical and symbolic approach to the material. First, I helped the analyst recognize her countertransference anxiety and be able to become interested in the patient's narrative through identifying with the characters in the stories rather than only to attempt to link these stories to the historical or current events in the patient's life. In entering these stories, we both became curious, and through identification enjoyed and experienced the pleasures and horrors of this sadomasochistic world. This shift in supervision was from a more objective perspective of being an analytic observer to a subjective perspective simply focused on the patient's internal symmetrical world. Participating in this way first involved a transformation of the therapist's listening experience, which allowed for the development of the symmetrical symbolic processes of reverie, identification, and the development of transitional experiences. These stories became transitional objects that existed first between the analyst and supervisor and then between the patient and analyst, and like a child's imaginary companion, they took on a life of their own.

The analytic work became focused on the evolving story, with minimal attention paid to the patient's life in the external world. This shift in the interpretive strategy from an asymmetrical interpersonal approach to a symmetrical neo-Kleinian approach generated an evolving transitional experience that allowed the patient, perhaps for the first time, to feel that he could bring aspects of his subjectivity into the external world.

In parallel with this shift in analytic experience, the patient began to move toward greater involvement with experience in the external world. He successfully interviewed for and became employed as a computer programmer. He began to date women and began to explore his sexuality. Finally, he was able to move out of his parents' home. Although success is documented by changes in the external world, it is predicated on the patient's development of the capacity to integrate the powerful elements of his unconscious experience into a subjective organization of symmetrical symbolic experience. This transformation from object to subject occurred as a result of the analyst's use of symmetrical strategies, including reverie and transitional experience, which facilitate the transformation of the patient's concrete symmetrical and asymmetrical experience into symbolic and symmetrical experiences. In this way the patient moved from being an object in the world to becoming a subject, able to utilize symmetrical symbolic modes in generating meaning.

CONCLUSION: THE SUBJECT OF THE GENERATIVE UNCONSCIOUS

Grotstein's (2001) development of Kleinian theory, which incorporates Matte Blanco's conceptualization of unconsciousness and consciousness as symmetry and asymmetry, differentiates the ineffable subject of the unconscious from the phenomenal subject of consciousness. He believes that these two different organizations of subjectivity function as "dialectical counterparts constituting a binary opposition" (p. 1) that allows the individual to confront the impossibilities of life, Bion's concept of O, and Lacan's register of the Real. Grotstein conceptualizes psychoanalytic treatment as the analyst's repair of unconscious structures, allowing the patient to develop subjectivity as a function of a generative unconscious, which he differentiates from traditional views of psychoanalytic process:

> Not withstanding the fact that orthodox/classical and especially Kleinian/Bionian analysts emphasize phantasies in their interpretations to analysands, the rationale for this line of approach seems to be to expose the unreality of the phantasy, all the while demonstrating how the unconscious phantasy obtruded into and therefore sabo-

taged the analysand's perception of and relationships to objects in external reality. *I believe the opposite. I believe that the fundamental aim of interpreting unconscious phantasies is to repair the "holes" and "rents" in the phantasmal container. Put another way, unconscious phantasy represents an everflowing mythic stream, an unconscious filter and first defense against "O" (infinity, chaos, the Real), and serves as the most elemental container-processor against it. From this point of view all pathology can be understood as id impairments.* [p. 5, italics in the original text]

Grotstein's view, like the one presented in this book, conceptualizes psychopathology as an insufficiency in the unconscious that is the result of extreme or pathological projective identification through which the contents of the unconscious are evacuated and experienced as aspects of the material world, where they are understood through using conscious, asymmetrical processes as external events. Grotstein emphasizes the importance of not viewing the unconscious as synonymous with a place such as the internal world, but like Bion and Lacan, he conceptualizes the unconscious as symbolic processes that generate meaning, saturating the external world with metaphors and poetic images. Similarly, Ogden's (1997a, 1998, 1999) papers on the similarity between poetry and psychoanalytic interpretation illustrate the analyst's transformation of asymmetrical, concrete, fragmented experience into symbolic symmetrical experience through reverie and the development of metaphors that reorganize the patient's experience from that of being an object, a deadened thing in the world, to a subject able to organize experience as drenched in personal, affective, and alive meaning. This process of transformation involves the analyst's use of concrete symmetrical and symbolic symmetrical strategies of intervention, including the articulation of protosymbolic countertransference fantasies, enactments, identifications, metaphors, transitional experiences, and other symmetrical symbolic processes that collapse the distinctions between person, place, and time. In Ogden's discussion of the similarities between poetry and psychoanalytic interpretation, he emphasizes the powerful effects of symmetrical symbolic organizations of experience such as poetic metaphors and the proto-symbolic experiences such as rhythms of speech, which have the capacity to evoke and generate transitional experiences that involve the mutual development of meaning, a sense of thirdness, which is central to the development of intersubjective experience.

I started this journey with T. S. Eliot's poem "The Hollow Men" in order to evoke the dilemma of the individual's lack of subjectivity, an experience of deadness and of being an object, one among many and not unique, focused on survival through the accumulation of material goods and identifications with external images. I have argued against the analytic injunction to make the unconscious conscious and have rather presented a neo-Kleinian argument for making consciousness unconscious. My paradoxical playing with Freud's famous statement is an attempt to rethink the linked concepts of consciousness and unconsciousness, subjectivity and objectivity, reality and fantasy, and the paranoid-schizoid and depressive modes of experience. Matte Blanco's conceptualization of the conscious and the unconscious mind as different modes of apprehending, organizing, and generating experience moved us from a simple phenomenological and hierarchical view of these processes to a functional view of consciousness, the asymmetrical mode of experience, which organizes experience through observing and generating differences, and a functional view of the unconscious, the symmetrical mode, which organizes experience through observing and generating similarities. This bi-logical approach, in conjunction with the theoretical derivatives of Klein, Winnicott, and Lacan and the clinical perspectives of two-person relational psychoanalysis, has provided the building blocks for a neo-Kleinian approach to psychoanalysis that is centered on the development of the individual's capacity to utilize symmetrical symbolic processes in apprehending, organizing, and generating experience and meaning that results in the experience of subjectivity.

I conceptualize subjectivity as incorporating the phenomenological subject and the dialectical subject into the generative unconscious, a symbolic symmetrical organization, an active approach to the creation of meaning. I also conceptualize the psychoanalytic process as an active process involving the transformation of concrete symmetrical and concrete and symbolic asymmetrical experience into symbolic symmetrical modes of generating meaning involving both analyst and patient as they come together in the creation of transitional experiences. It is the development of this active capacity for the creation of meaning, like Benjamin's (2001) concept of thirdness or Ogden's (1994) concept of the analytic third, that I have thought of as the subject of the unconscious, as each participant in the psychoanalytic dialogue attempts to speak from this unconscious symbolic perspective, the generative unconscious.

References

Adler, A. (1932). *Individual Psychology and Social Problems*. London: C. W. Daniel.

Ahumada, J. L. (1991). Logical types and ostensive insight. *International Journal of Psycho-Analysis* 72:683–692.

Arlow, J. A. (1985). The structural hypothesis. In *Models of the Mind*, ed. A. Rothstein. New York: International Universities Press.

Arlow, J. A., and Brenner, C. (1964). *Psychoanalytic Concepts and the Structural Theory*. New York: International Universities Press.

Aron, L. (1996). *A Meeting of Minds*. Hillsdale, NJ: Analytic Press.

Atwood, G., and Stolorow, R. (1984). *Structures of Subjectivity: Explorations in Psychoanalytic Phenomenology*. Hillsdale, NJ: Analytic Press.

Atwood, G. E., Stolorow, R. D., and Trop, J. L. (1989). Impasses in psychoanalytic therapy. *Contemporary Psychoanalysis* 25:554–573.

Auerbach, J. S., and Blatt, S. J. (2001). Self-reflexivity, intersubjectivity and therapeutic change. *Psychoanalytic Psychology* 18:427–450.

Balint, M. (1968). *The Basic Fault. Therapeutic Aspects of Regression*. London: Tavistock.

Basch, M. F. (1985). Interpretation: toward a developmental model. In *Progress in Self Psychology*, vol. 1, ed. A. Goldberg. New York: Guilford.

Basch-Kahre, E. (1985). Patterns of thinking. *International Journal of Psycho-Analysis* 66:455–470.

Beebe, B., Lachman, F., and Jaffe, J. (1997). Mother–infant structures interaction, presymbolic self and object. *Psychoanalytic Dialogues* 7:133–182.

Benjamin, J. (1988). *The Bonds of Love: Psychoanalysis, Feminism, and the Problem of Domination.* New York: Pantheon.

——— (1990). An outline of intersubjectivity: the development of recognition. *Psychoanalytic Psychology* 7(S):33–46.

——— (1991). Father, daughter: identification, difference, gender heterodoxy. *Psychoanalytic Dialogues* 1:277–300.

——— (1995). *Like Subjects, Love Objects. Essays on Recognition and Sexual Difference.* New Haven, CT: Yale University Press.

——— (1998). *Shadow of the Other: Intersubjectivity and Gender in Psychoanalysis.* New York: Routledge.

——— (2000). Intersubjective distinctions: subjects and persons: commentary. *Psychoanalytic Dialogues* 10:43–56.

——— (2001). *Two-way streets: recognition and intersubjective economy.* Paper presented at the 21st Annual Spring Meeting, Division of Psychoanalysis (39), American Psychological Association.

Beres, D. (1965). Structure and function in psychoanalysis. *International Journal of Psycho-Analysis* 46:53–63.

Bick, E. (1968). The experience of the skin in early object relations. *International Journal of Psycho-Analysis* 49:484–486.

Bion, W. R. (1959). Attacks on linking. *International Journal of Psycho-Analysis* 40:308–315.

——— (1962). A theory of thinking. *International Journal of Psycho-Analysis* 43:306–310. In *Melanie Klein Today. Developments in Theory and Practice*, ed. E. Spillius. London and New York: Routledge, 1988.

Birksted-Breen, D. (1996). Phallus, penis and mental space. *International Journal of Psycho-Analysis* 77:649–658.

Blatt, S. J., and Blass, R. B. (1996). Relatedness and self-definition: a dialectical model of personality development. In *Development and Vulnerabilities in Close Relationships*, ed. G. G. Noam and K. W. Fischer. Hillsdale, NJ: Erlbaum.

Bloom, H., ed. (1985). *Modern Critical Views: Sigmund Freud.* New York: Chelsea House.

Bollas, C. (1987). *The Shadow of the Object: Psychoanalysis of the Unthought Known.* New York: Columbia University Press.

Borgman, A. (1992). *Crossing the Postmodern Divide.* Chicago: University of Chicago Press.

Breuer, J., and Freud, S. (1895). Studies on hysteria (1893–1895). *Standard Edition* 2:1–309.

Britton, R. (1995). Psychic reality and unconscious belief. *International Journal of Psycho-Analysis* 76:19–24.

Buber, M. (1974). *I and Thou*. New York: Touchstone Books.

Burke, W. F. (1992). Countertransference disclosure, the asymmetry/mutuality dilemma. *Psychoanalytic Dialogues* 2:241–271.

Davies, J. M. (1998). Between the disclosure and foreclosure of erotic experience: can psychoanalysis find a place for adult sexuality? *Psychoanalytic Dialogues* 8:747–766.

Davies, J. M., and Frawley, M. G. (1994). *Treating the Adult Survivor of Childhood Sexual Abuse: A Psychoanalytic Perspective*. New York: Basic Books.

Dewald, P. (1972). *The Psychoanalytic Process. A Case Illustration*. New York: Basic Books.

Dimen, M. (1991). Deconstructing difference: gender, splitting, transitional space. *Psychoanalytic Dialogues* 1:335–352.

Dor, J. (1998). *Introduction to the Reading of Lacan: The Unconscious Structured Like a Language*. New York: Other Press.

——— (1999). *The Clinical Lacan*. New York: Other Press.

Ehrenberg, D. (1992). *The Intimate Edge. Extending the Reach of Psychoanalytic Interaction*. New York/London: Norton.

Eigen, M. (1981). The area of faith in Winnicott, Lacan and Bion. *International Journal of Psycho-Analysis* 62:413–433.

Erikson, E. (1950). *Childhood and Society*. New York: Norton.

——— (1959). *Identity and the Life Cycle. Selected Papers*. New York: International Universities Press.

——— (1969). *Gandhi's Truth: On the Origin of Militant Nonviolence*. New York: Norton.

Etchegoyen, R. H., and Ahumada, J. L. (1990). Bateson and Matte Blanco: bio-logic and bi-logic. *International Review of Psychoanalysis* 17:493–502.

Faimberg, H. (1995). Misunderstandings and psychic truths. *International Journal of Psycho-Analysis* 76:9–14.

——— (1996). Listening to listening. *International Journal of Psycho-Analysis* 77:667–678.

Fairbairn, W. R. D. (1954). *An Object Relations Theory of the Personality*. New York: Basic Books.

Feiner, A. H., and Levenson, E. A. (1968). The compassionate sacrifice: an explanation of a metaphor. *Psychoanalytic Review* 55:552–573.

Feldman, M. (2000). Some views on the manifestation of death instinct in clinical. *International Journal of Psycho-Analysis* 81:53–66.

Fenichel, O. (1945). *The Psychoanalytic Theory of Neurosis*. New York: Norton.

Fink, K. (1995). Projection, identification, and bi-logic. *Psychoanalytic Quarterly* 64:136–154.

Fonagy, P. (1995). Psychic reality development and malfunction in borderline personality. *International Journal of Psycho-Analysis* 76:39–44.

Fonagy, P., and Target, M. (1996). Playing with reality I. *International Journal of Psycho-Analysis* 77:217–234.

Freud, A. (1937). *The Ego and the Mechanisms of Defence* (International Psycho-Analytical Library). London: Hogarth.

Freud, S. (1894). The neuro-psychoses of defence. *Standard Edition* 3:45–61.

——— (1898). Sexuality in the aetiology of the neuroses. *Standard Edition* 3:263–285.

——— (1900a). The interpretation of dreams. Part I. *Standard Edition* 4:1–338.

——— (1900b). The interpretation of dreams. Part II. *Standard Edition* 5:339–625.

——— (1905a). Fragment of an analysis of a case of hysteria. *Standard Edition* 7:7–122.

——— (1905b). Three essays on the theory of sexuality. *Standard Edition* 7:130–243.

——— (1905c). On psychotherapy. *Standard Edition* 7:257–268.

——— (1909). Notes upon a case of obsessional neurosis. *Standard Edition* 10:155–318.

——— (1911). Notes on autobiographical account case of paranoia. *Standard Edition* 12:9–82.

——— (1914a). On narcissism: an introduction. *Standard Edition* 14:73–102.

——— (1914b). Remembering, repeating and working through. *Standard Edition* 12:147–156.

——— (1920). Beyond the pleasure principle. *Standard Edition* 18:7–64.

——— (1923). The ego and the id. *Standard Edition* 19:12–66.

——— (1937). Constructions in analysis. *Standard Edition* 23:257–269.

Frie, R., and Reiss, B. (2001). Understanding intersubjectivity: psychoanalytic formulations and their philosophical underpinnings. *Contemporary Psychoanalysis* 37:297–328.

Friedman, L. (1995). Psychic reality in psychoanalytic theory. *International Journal of Psycho-Analysis* 76:25–28.

Fromm, E. (1941). *Escape from Freedom.* New York: Farrar & Rinehart.

——— (1947). *Man for Himself. An Inquiry into the Psychology of Ethics.* New York: Rinehart.

——— (1964). Individual and social character. In *Psychoanalysis and Contemporary American Culture,* ed. H. M. Ruitenbeek. New York: Dell.

———— (1970). *The Crisis of Psychoanalysis*. New York: Holt, Rinehart & Winston.

Gerhardt, J., and Sweetnam, A. (2000). Intersubjective turn in psychoanalysis: theorists, J. Benjamin. *Psychoanalytic Dialogues* 10:5–42.

Gerson, S. (1996). Neutrality, resistance and self disclosure. *Psychoanalytic Dialogues* 6:623–647.

Gill, M. M. (1983). The interpersonal paradigm and the degree of the therapist's involvement. *Contemporary Psychoanalysis* 19:200–237.

———— (1994). *Psychoanalysis in Transition: A Personal View*. Hillsdale, NJ: Analytic Press.

Gill, M. M., and Hoffman, I. Z. (1982). Analysis of transference. Vol. II: Audio-recorded sessions. *Psychological Issues* 54:1–240.

Green, A. (1995). Has sexuality anything to do with psychoanalysis? *International Journal of Psycho-Analysis* 76:871–883.

Greenberg, D. (1990). Instinct, primary narcissism: reform. Beyond the pleasure principle. *International Journal of Psycho-Analysis* 71:271–284.

Greenberg, J., and Mitchell, S. A. (1983). *Object Relations in Psychoanalytic Theory*. Cambridge, MA: Harvard University Press.

Grosskurth, P. (1986). *Melanie Klein. Her World and Her Work*. Cambridge, MA: Harvard University Press.

Grossman, L. (1996). "Psychic reality" and testing in analysis of perverse defence. *International Journal of Psycho-Analysis* 77:509–518.

Grotstein, J. S. (1995). Orphans of the "real": some modern and postmodern perspectives on the neurobiological and psychosocial dimensions of psychosis and other primitive emotional states. *Bulletin of the Menninger Clinic* 59:287–332.

———— (2001). *"Through the unknown remembered gate": revisions of the psychoanalytic concept of the unconscious*. Paper presented at the 21st Annual Meeting, Division of Psychoanalysis (39), American Psychological Association.

Harris, A. (1991). Gender as contradiction. *Psychoanalytic Dialogues* 1:197–224.

Hartmann, H. (1958). *Ego Psychology and the Problem of Adaptation*. New York: International Universities Press.

Hayman, A. (1994). Some remarks about the "controversial discussions." *International Journal of Psycho-Analysis* 75:343–358.

Hirsch, I. (1985). Rediscovery of the participant-observer model. *Psychoanalysis and Contemporary Thought* 8:441–459.

Hirsch, I., and Roth, J. (1995). Changing conceptions of the unconscious. *Contemporary Psychoanalysis* 31(2):263–276.

Hoffman, I. Z. (1983). The patient as interpreter of the analyst's experience. *Contemporary Psychoanalysis* 19:389–422.

———— (1991). Social-constructivist view of the psychoanalytic situation. *Psychoanalytic Dialogues* 1:74–105.

———— (1998). *Ritual and Spontaneity in the Psychoanalytic Process: A Dialectical-Constructivist View.* Hillsdale, NJ: Analytic Press.

Holland, R. (1990). Scientificity and psychoanalysis: the controversial discussions. *International Review of Psychoanalysis* 17:133–158.

Horney, K. (1937). *The Neurotic Personality of Our Time.* New York: Norton.

Isaacs, S. (1948). The nature and function of phantasy. *International Journal of Psycho-Analysis* 29:73–97.

Jacobs, T. J. (1993). Inner experiences of analyst: contribution to analytic process. *International Journal of Psycho-Analysis* 74:7–14.

Jacobson, E. (1964). *The Self and the Object World.* New York: International Universities Press.

Jacobus, M. (1999). The origin of signs. *Journal of Melanie Klein and Object Relations* 17:23–94.

Joseph, B. (1975). The patient who is difficult to reach. In *Countertransference and Technique in Psychoanalytic Psychotherapy,* ed. P. L. Giovacchini.

———— (1982). Addiction to near-death. In *Melanie Klein Today,* ed. E. B. Spillius. New York: Routledge.

———— (1988).Projective identification—some clinical aspects. In *Melanie Klein Today,* ed. E. B. Spillius. New York: Routledge.

Kennedy, R. (1997). On subjective organizations: toward a theory of subject relations. *Psychoanalytic Dialogues* 7:553–582.

Kernberg, O. (1975). *Borderline Conditions and Pathological Narcissism.* New York: Jason Aronson.

———— (1976). *Object Relations Theory and Clinical Psychoanalysis.* New York: Jason Aronson.

———— (1993). Convergences and divergences in contemporary psychoanalytic technique. *International Journal of Psycho-Analysis* 74:659–673.

Khan, M. (1963). The concept of cumulative trauma. *Psychoanalytic Study of the Child* 18:286–306.

———— (1964). Ego distortion, cumulative trauma, the role of reconstruction. *International Journal of Psycho-Analysis* 45:272–279.

———— (1974). *The Privacy of the Self.* New York: International Universities Press.

———— (1986). Outrageousness, compliance and authenticity. *Contemporary Psychoanalysis* 22:629–650.

Klein, M. (1921). The development of a child. In *Love, Guilt, and Reparation and Other Works 1921–1945,* ed. M. Klein. New York: Delacorte Press/ Seymour Lawrence, 1975.

———— (1922). Inhibitions and difficulties at puberty. In *Love Guilt, and Repa-*

ration and Other Works 1921–1945, ed. M. Klein. New York: Delacorte Press/Seymour Lawrence, 1975.

—— (1928). Early stages of the Oedipus conflict. In *Love, Guilt, and Reparation and Other Works 1921–1945*, ed. M. Klein. New York: Delacorte Press/Seymour Lawrence, 1975.

—— (1946a). Notes on some schizoid mechanisms. In *Envy and Gratitude and Other Works 1946–1963*, ed. M. Klein. New York: Delacorte Press/Seymour Lawrence, 1975.

—— (1946b). Notes on some schizoid mechanisms. *International Journal of Psycho-Analysis* 27:99–110.

—— (1955). On identification. In *Envy and Gratitude and Other Works 1946–1963*, ed. M. Klein. New York: Delacorte Press/Seymour Lawrence, 1975.

—— (1957). *Envy and Gratitude: A Study of Unconscious Forces*. New York: Basic Books.

—— (1975). *Love, Guilt, and Reparation and Other Works 1921–1945*. New York: Delacorte Press/Seymour Lawrence.

Kluzer-Usuelli, A. (1992). Significance of illusion in Freud and Winnicott: controversial. *International Review of Psychoanalysis* 19:179–188.

Kohut, H. (1977). *The Restoration of the Self.* New York: International Universities Press.

—— (1979). The two analyses of Mr. Z. *International Journal of Psycho-Analysis* 60:3–27.

—— (1984). *How Does Analysis Cure?* Chicago: University of Chicago Press.

Kristeva, J. (2000). From symbols to flesh: the polymorphous destiny of narration. *International Journal of Psycho-Analysis* 81:771–788.

Lacan, J. (1977). *Ecrits: A Selection.* New York: Norton.

—— (1978). *The Four Fundamental Concepts of Psychoanalysis.* New York: Norton.

Lachmann, F. M., and Lichtenberg, J. (1992). Model scenes: implications for psychoanalytic treatment. *Journal of the American Psychoanalytic Association* 40:117–138.

Langer, S. (1942). *Philosophy in a New Key.* Cambridge, MA: Harvard University Press.

Lasch, C. (1978). *The Culture of Narcissism.* New York: Norton.

Leary, K. (1994). Psychoanalytic "problems" and postmodern "solutions." *Psychoanalytic Quarterly* 63:433–465.

Levenson, E. (1983). *The Ambiguity of Change.* New York: Basic Books.

—— (1985). The interpersonal (Sullivanian) model. In *Models of the Mind*, ed. A. Rothstein. New York: International Universities Press.

—— (2001). The enigma of the unconscious. *Contemporary Psychoanalysis* 37:239–252.

Lewin, S. (2001). *Telling time: illusions of linear temporal process in psychotherapy.* Unpublished doctoral dissertation, Adelphi University.

Lindon, J. (1994). Gratification and provision in psychoanalysis: should we get rid of the rule of abstinence? *Psychoanalytic Dialogues* 4:549–583.

Lorenz, K. (1966). *On Aggression.* New York: Harcourt, Brace & World.

Mahler, M., Pine, F., and Bergman, A. (1975). *The Psychological Birth of the Human Infant: Symbiosis and Individuation.* New York: Basic Books.

Matte Blanco, I. (1975). *The Unconscious as Infinite Sets: An Essay in Bi-Logic.* London: Duckworth.

——— (1988). *Thinking, Feeling and Being.* London and New York: Routledge.

Marcuse, H. (1955). *Eros and Civilization.* London: Routledge.

May, R. (1972). *Power and Innocence. A Search for the Sources of Violence.* New York: Norton.

McDougall, J. (1989). The dead father. *International Journal of Psycho-Analysis* 70:205–220.

Meissner, W. (1978). *The Paranoid Process.* New York: Jason Aronson.

Meltzer, D. (1966). The relationship between anal masturbation and projective identification. *International Journal of Psycho-Analysis* 47:335–342. In *Melanie Klein Today: Developments in Theory and Practice. Vol. 1: Mainly Theory,* ed. E. B. Spillius. London and New York: Routledge, 1988.

Miller, J. P. (1985). How Kohut actually worked. In *Progress in Self Psychology I,* ed. A. Goldberg. New York: Guilford.

Mitchell, S. A. (1988). *Relational Concepts in Psychoanalysis: An Integration.* Cambridge, MA: Harvard University Press.

Mitchell, S. A., and Aron, L. (1999). *Relational Psychoanalysis: The Emergence of a Tradition.* Hillsdale, NJ: Analytic Press.

Munroe, R. (1955). *Schools of Psychoanalytic Thought.* New York: Dryden.

Newirth, J. (1989). *Psychological structure, regression and clinical psychoanalysis.* Paper presented at the annual meeting of the Division of Psychoanalysis, American Psychological Association, Boston, April 6.

——— (1990). The mastery of countertransferential anxiety: an object relations view of the supervisory process. In *Psychoanalytic Approaches to Supervision,* ed. R. C. Lane. New York: Brunner/Mazel.

——— (1994). Object relations perspective: Alexander Portnoy in search of self. In *Comparing Schools of Psychoanalytic Therapy,* ed. B. Buirski. Northvale, NJ: Jason Aronson.

——— (1996). On not interpreting: the metaphor of the baby, enactment and transitional experience. *American Journal of Psychoanalysis* 56:415–430.

——— (1999). Power in the psychoanalytic relationship: symmetrical, complementary, metacomplementary. *Journal of Melanie Klein and Object Relations* 17:135–144.

Niederland, W. (1974). *The Schreber Case: Psychoanalytic Profile of a Paranoid Personality.* New York: Quadrangle/New York Times Books.

Ogden, T. (1982). *Projective Identification and Psychotherapeutic Technique.* New York: Jason Aronson.

―――― (1986). *The Matrix of the Mind. Object Relations in the Psychoanalytic Dialogue.* Northvale, NJ/London: Jason Aronson.

―――― (1992). The dialectically constituted/decentered subject of psychoanalysis. II. The contributions of Klein and Winnicott. *International Journal of Psycho-Analysis* 73:613–626.

―――― (1994). The analytic third: working with intersubjective clinical facts. *International Journal of Psycho-Analysis* 75:3–20.

―――― (1995). Analyzing forms of aliveness and deadness of the transference-countertransference. *International Journal of Psycho-Analysis* 76: 695–710.

―――― (1997a). Listening: three Frost poems., *Psychoanalytic Dialogues* 7:619–640.

―――― (1997b). Reverie and metaphor: thoughts on how I work as a psychoanalyst. *International Journal of Psycho-Analysis* 78:719–732.

―――― (1998). A question of voice in poetry and psychoanalysis. *Psychoanalytic Quarterly* 67:426–448.

―――― (1999). The music of what happens in poetry and psychoanalysis. *International Journal of Psycho-Analysis* 80:979–994.

―――― (2001). An elegy, a love song, and a lullaby. *Psychoanalytic Dialogues* 11:293–311.

Perry, H. S. (1999). Sullivan's search for a rational psychotherapy. *Contemporary Psychoanalysis* 35:373–395.

Phillips, A. (1988). *Winnicott.* Cambridge, MA: Harvard University Press.

Piaget, J. (1945). *Play, Dreams and Imitation in Childhood.* New York: Norton, 1962.

Racker, H. (1968). *Transference and Countertransference.* New York: International Universities Press.

Rangell, L. (1996). The "analytic" attitude in psychoanalytic treatment: how analysis works. *Psychoanalytic Inquiry* 16:140–166.

Rapaport, D. (1951). *Organization and Pathology of Thought.* New York: Columbia University Press.

―――― (1967). *The Collected Papers of David Rapaport,* ed. M. Gill. New York: Basic Books.

Rayner, E. (1981). Infinite experiences, affects, characteristics of unconscious. *International Journal of Psycho-Analysis* 62:403–412.

―――― (1995). *Unconscious Logic: An Introduction to Matte Blanco's Bi-Logic and Its Uses.* New York and London: Routledge.

Renik, O. (1995). Ideal of anonymous analyst and the problem of self-disclo-sure. *Psychoanalytic Quarterly* 64:466–495.

——— (1996). The perils of neutrality. *Psychoanalytic Quarterly* 65:495–517.

——— (1998). The analyst's subjectivity and the analyst's objectivity. *International Journal of Psycho-Analysis* 79:487–498.

Richards, A. D., and Lynch, A. A. (1998). From ego psychology to contemporary conflict theory: an historical overview. In *The Modern Freudians*, ed. C. S. Ellman et al. Northvale, NJ: Jason Aronson.

Rodman, F. R. (1987). *The Spontaneous Gesture: Selected Letters of D. W. Winnicott.* Cambridge, MA: Harvard University Press.

Rose, J. (2000). Symbols and their function in managing the anxiety of change. *International Journal of Psycho-Analysis* 81:453–470.

Rosenfeld, H. (1971). Theory of life and death instincts: aggressive aspects of narcissism. In: *Melanie Klein Today. Vol. 1: Mainly Theory*, ed. E. B. Spillius. London and New York: Routledge, 1988.

Roth, P. (1969). *Portnoy's Complaint.* New York: Random House.

Rucker, N. G., and Lombardi, K. L. (1998). *Subject Relations: Unconscious Experience and Relational Psychoanalysis.* New York and London: Routledge.

Sampson, H. (1992). The role of "real" experience in psycho pathology and treatment. *Psychoanalytic Dialogues* 3:509–528.

Sartre, J. P. (1956). *Being and Nothingness.* New York: Philosophical Library.

——— (1989). *No Exit and Three Other Plays.* New York: Vintage.

Sayers, J. (1989). Melanie Klein and mothering—a feminist perspective. *International Review of Psychoanalysis* 16:363–376.

Schafer, R. (1976). *A New Language for Psychoanalysis.* New Haven, CT: Yale University Press.

——— (1978). *Language and Insight.* New Haven, CT and London: Yale University Press.

——— (1983). *The Analytic Attitude.* New York: Basic Books.

——— (1992). *Retelling a Life: Narration and Dialogue in Psychoanalysis.* New York: Basic Books/HarperCollins.

——— (1994). Commentary: traditional Freudian and Kleinian Freudian analysis. *Psychoanalytic Inquiry* 14:462–475.

Schatzman, M. (1972). *Soul Murder: Persecution in the Family.* New York: Random House.

Searles, H. F. (1979). *Countertransference and Related Subjects.* New York: International Universities Press.

Segal, H. (1957). Notes on symbol formation. *International Journal of Psycho-Analysis* 38:391–397. In *Melanie Klein Today: Developments in Theory and Practice*, ed. E. B. Spillius. London and New York: Routledge, 1988.

—— (1978). On symbolism. *International Journal of Psycho-Analysis* 59:315–320.

—— (1979). Notes on symbol formation. In *Melanie Klein Today: Developments in Theory and Practice*, ed. E. B. Spillius. London and New York: Routledge, 1988.

—— (1981). *The Work of Hanna Segal*. New York: Jason Aronson.

—— (1994). Salman Rushdie and the sea of stories. *International Journal of Psycho-Analysis* 75:611–618.

Singer, I. (1971). The patient aids the analyst. In *In the Name of Life*, ed. B. Landis and E. Tauber. New York: Holt, Rinehart & Winston.

Spence, D. (1982). *Narrative Truth and Historical Truth: Meaning and Interpretation in Psychoanalysis*. New York: Norton.

Spillius, E. B., ed. (1988). *Melanie Klein Today: Developments in Theory and Practice. Vol. 1: Mainly Theory*. London and New York: Routledge.

Spillius, E. B. (1996). Concept of psychic reality in the theoretical currents today. *International Journal of Psycho-Analysis* 77:85–88.

Steiner, J. (1987). Pathological organization, paranoid-schizoid, depressive positions. *International Journal of Psycho-Analysis* 68:69–86.

—— (1994). Patient-centered, analyst-centered interpretations: countertransference. *Psychoanalytic Inquiry* 14:406–422.

—— (1997). Review of "What Do Psychoanalysts Want? The Problem of Aims in Psychoanalytic Therapy." *International Journal of Psycho-Analysis* 78:163–166.

Steiner, R. (1985). British Psychoanalytical Society's controversial discussions. *International Review of Psychoanalysis* 12:27–72.

Stern, D. B. (1996). The social construction of therapeutic action. *Psychoanalytic Inquiry* 16:265–293.

—— (1997). *Unformulated Experience. From Dissociation to Imagination in Psychoanalysis*. New York: Analytic Press.

Stolorow, R. D., and Atwood, G. E. (1992). *Contexts of Being: The Intersubjective Foundations of Psychological Life*. Hillsdale, NJ: Analytic Press.

Stolorow, R. D., and Brandschaft, B. (1987). Developmental failure and psychic conflict. *Psychoanalytic Psychology* 4:241–254.

Stolorow, R., Brandschaft, B., and Atwood, G. (1987). *Psychoanalytic Treatment: An Intersubjective Approach*. Hillsdale, NJ: Analytic Press.

Sullivan, H. S. (1953). *The Interpersonal Theory of Psychiatry*. New York: Norton.

Symington, J. (1985). The survival function of primitive omnipotence. *International Journal of Psycho-Analysis* 66:481–488.

Symington, N. (1990). Possibility of human freedom, its transmission: Bion's thought. *International Journal of Psycho-Analysis* 71:95–106.

Target, M., and Fonagy, P. (1996). Playing with reality II. *International Journal of Psycho-Analysis* 77:459–480.

Trop, J. L., and Stolorow, R. D. (1992). Defense analysis in self psychology: a developmental view. *Psychoanalytic Dialogues* 2:427–442.

Watzlawick, P., Beavin, J., and Jackson, D. (1967). *Pragmatics of Human Communication. A Study of Interactional Patterns, Pathologies, and Paradoxes.* New York: Norton.

Weiss, J., Sampson, H., et al. (1986). *The Psychoanalytic Process: Theory, Clinical Observation and Empirical Research.* New York: Guilford.

Winnicott, C., Shepard, R., and Davis, M. (1989). *Psychoanalytic Explorations.* Cambridge, MA: Harvard University Press.

Winnicott, D. W. (1945). Primitive emotional development. *International Journal of Psycho-Analysis* 26:137–143.

——— (1949). Hate in the counter-transference. *International Journal of Psycho-Analysis* 30:69–74.

——— (1958). *Collected Papers. Through Paediatrics to Psychoanalysis.* New York: Basic Books.

——— (1960). Ego distortion in terms of true and false self. In *The Maturational Process and the Facilitating Environment.* New York: International Universities Press, 1965.

——— (1963). The development of the capacity for concern. *Bulletin of the Menninger Clinic* 27:167–176.

——— (1969). The use of an object. *International Journal of Psycho-Analysis* 50:711–716.

——— (1971). *Playing and Reality.* London: Tavistock.

——— (1977). *The Piggie: An Account of the Psychoanalytic Treatment of a Little Girl.* New York: International Universities Press.

——— (1987). Letter to Melanie Klein. In *The Spontaneous Gesture. Selected Letters of D. W. Winnicott,* ed. F. Rodman. Cambridge, MA: Harvard University Press.

——— (1989). The squiggle game. In *Psychoanalytic Explorations.* ed. C. Winnicott et al. Cambridge, MA: Harvard University Press.

Wolstein, B. (1975). Countertransference: psychoanalysts' shared experience and inquiry with patient. *Journal of the American Academy of Psychoanalysis* 3: 77–90.

Index